Public Procurement Policy

T0298611

Appropriate laws and regulations are an essential tool to direct the action of procurers toward the public good and avoid corruption and misallocation of resources. Common laws and regulations across regions, nations and continents potentially allow for the further opening of markets and ventures to newcomers and new ideas to satisfy public demand. This book collects original contributions, from both economists and lawyers, related to the new European Union Directives just approved in 2014 by the EU Parliament.

Uniquely, this book combines juridical and technical expertise so as to find a common terrain and language to debate the specific issues that a Public Administration in need of advancing and modernizing has to face. This format features, for each section, an introductory exchange between two experts of different disciplines, made of a series of sequential interactions between an economist and a lawyer that write and follow up on one another. This is to enrich the liveliness of the debate and improve the mutual understanding between the two professions.

There are four sections characterized in this book: supporting social considerations via public procurement; green public procurement; innovation through innovative partnerships; and Lots – the Economic and Legal Challenges of Centralized Procurement.

This book will be of interest to policy-makers, practitioners working in the field of EU public procurement as well as academics.

Gustavo Piga is Professor of Economics at the University of Rome Tor Vergata, Italy.

Tünde Tátrai is Associate Professor at the Corvinus University of Budapest, Hungary.

The professional partners of the 2nd Interdisciplinary Public Procurement Symposium were the Faculty of Business Administration of the Corvinus University of Budapest, the Faculty of Economics of the University of Rome Tor Vergata, the Hungarian Association of Logistics, Purchasing and Inventory Management and the Prime Minister's Office of Hungary.

The economics of legal relationships

Sponsored by Michigan State University College of Law
Series Editors:
Nicholas Mercuro
Michigan State University College of Law
Michael D. Kaplowitz
Michigan State University

*The first three volumes listed above are published by and available from Elsevier

Public Procurement Policy

Edited by Gustavo Piga and Tünde Tatrai

Routledge
Taylor & Francis Group

LONDON AND NEW YORK

First published 2016
by Routledge

2 Park Square, Milton Park, Abingdon, Oxfordshire OX14 4RN
52 Vanderbilt Avenue, New York, NY 10017

Routledge is an imprint of the Taylor & Francis Group, an informa business

First issued in paperback 2020

British Library Cataloguing in Publication Data
A catalogue record for this book is available from the British Library

Library of Congress Cataloging in Publication Data
Public procurement policy / edited by Gustavo Piga and Tünde Tatrai.
    pages cm
    1. Government purchasing–European Union countries. 2. Government
    purchasing–Law and legislation–European Union countries. I. Piga,
    Gustavo, 1964– II. Tatrai, Tünde.
    JN30.P9325 2015
    352.5′3094–dc23   2015004495

ISBN: 978-1-138-92150-4 (hbk)
ISBN: 978-0-367-59873-0 (pbk)

Typeset in Times New Roman
by Wearset Ltd, Boldon, Tyne and Wear

Contents

Illustrations

Figures

Tables

Contributors

Marta Andrecka is Postdoctoral Fellow in the Department of Law, Business and Social Sciences, Aarhus University, Denmark.

Eleanor Aspey is Lecturer in Law at the School of Law, University of Manchester, UK.

Christopher H. Bovis is Professor of Business Law at University of Hull, UK.

Richard Craven is Senior Lecturer in Law at Northumbria Law School, Northumbria University, UK.

Elisabetta Iossa is Professor of Economics at the University of Rome Tor Vergata, CEPR and IEFE-Bocconi, Italy.

Shirley Justice is Senior Project Manager at CSR Netherlands, The Netherlands.

Wouter Lohmann is Consultant and Researcher at STIPPT, University of Twente, The Netherlands.

Elisabetta Manunza is chaired Professor of Public Procurement Law at the University of Utrecht, The Netherlands.

Joaquim Nunes de Almeida is Director of Public Procurement at the DG Internal Market and Services, European Commission, Belgium.

Gustavo Piga is Professor of Economics at the Department of Business, Government and Philosophy Studies at the University of Rome Tor Vergata, Italy.

Veljko Sikirica is Senior Procurement Specialist at Procurement Department – Policy unit, European Bank for Reconstruction and Development, UK.

Giancarlo Spagnolo is Professor of Economics at Rome Tor Vergata University, and also a Senior Research Fellow at SITE-Stockholm School, Sweden.

Carine Staropoli is Associate Professor at the Paris School of Economics, Université Paris 1, France.

Marc Steiner is Judge for Swiss Federal Administrative Court, Switzerland.

Tünde Tátrai is Associate Professor at Corvinus University of Budapest, Hungary.

Jan Telgen is Professor of Public Procurement at University of Twente, The Netherlands.

Martin Trybus is Professor of European Law and Policy and is the Director at the Institute of European Law, Birmingham Law School, University of Birmingham, UK.

Niels Uenk is Consultant and Researcher at STIPPT, University of Twente, The Netherlands.

Sandeep Verma is a Member of Senate at J.N.V. University, India.

Tomaž Vesel is President at the Court of Audit, Slovenia.

Oana Pantilimon Voda is Senior Legal Advisor at Corvers Procurement Services BV, The Netherlands.

Christopher R. Yukins is Lynn David Research Professor in Government Procurement Law and Co-Director of the Government Procurement Law Program at The George Washington University Law School, USA.

Introduction

Joaquim Nunes de Almeida

Public procurement is a key economic activity of governments, accounting for a large proportion of Gross Domestic Product (GDP) of the EU Member States. The governance of public procurement is complex because of multiple, mixed and conflicting objectives. On the one hand, the design of public procurement rules plays a key role in determining the efficiency of the system to provide taxpayers value for money, in ensuring competitive conditions for market players, in contributing to European market integration, in fostering buyers' accountability. On the other hand, public procurement is of great economic importance: it can stimulate growth and investment, steer innovation; it is also seen as a strategic tool to stimulate 'green' technologies and social inclusion, or to foster the modernisation of the public administration and of the services the State delivers to citizens and business.

Opening up a dialogue between involved parties and disciplines seems therefore a necessity to address today's challenges with a sufficiently wide perspective, bringing together amongst others lawyers and economists. Practitioners and academics tend to see public procurement in different ways; they tend to give priority to different aspects. I believe that every effort to put together mind sets and intellectual culture is particularly welcome and is fully in line with our own new policy approach based on multidisciplinarity.

Two important developments have occurred in 2014 at EU level:

- EU public procurement legislation underwent a major reform, including, for the first time, a balanced and flexible legislation for the award of concessions.
- The European Parliament and the Council have also adopted the Directive on e-invoicing in public procurement. This initiative will contribute to reducing barriers to e-invoicing across borders in the EU by providing a European standard.

1 Country approach

The application of public procurement rules is very diverse across the different EU Member States. In particular, some countries face a number of systemic problems that hinder their capacity to use public procurement in an effective and efficient way. Those problems can include: incompliant law, complex and constantly changing legislation, weak institutional framework, low rate of absorption of EU funds, red tape, low professionalisation of staff, corruption, low level of cross-border procurement, etc.

In these next two years, Member States will have to transpose the new Public Procurement Directives. This represents a unique opportunity for them to undertake, in parallel with the transposition of the legal texts, a strategic review of their overall public procurement systems to address those systemic problems. This could imply an in-depth reform not only of their public procurement systems, but of their public administration in general.

The European Commission's (later referred as 'EC') role is to steer this process by supporting Member States in their reform efforts. This goes beyond facilitating the transposition of the Directives; it aims at supporting a reform of the institutional set-up and modernising public administration, with a view to increase the overall efficiency and effectiveness of public procurement. Therefore, the EC will engage Member States in a policy dialogue to address their specific needs and problem areas. A pilot phase has been launched, which involves the EC working in partnership with some Member States facing different kinds of challenges, and it will be gradually extended to others. These countries have engaged to develop national public procurement strategies that will steer the process of modernising their public procurement systems.

In addition to this structured policy dialogue with some Member States, other tools will be used with the same aim: the European Semester's Country Specific Recommendations, the elaboration of action plans related to the use of European Structural and Investment (ESI) Funds, as well as a more pro-active and targeted infringement policy.

2 Sectoral approach

Another source of wide divergence as regards public procurement are the sectors of the economy. Thus, the EC has adopted a sectoral policy approach to complement the country approach referred to in above.

To put these new considerations into practice, the EC has started to collect more systemic knowledge on how public procurement systems work in the various sectors of the economy. The first domains we concentrated on were procurement in health, IT, waste management, and urban planning. The main challenge for the teams in charge of this task was to bridge the legal and economic expertise. This allows better understanding the market structures and practices in each of the sector concerned and identifying patterns or anomalies in the application of the rules.

With this approach in mind, we collected information on publication levels, competition intensity, cross-border penetration or to identify asymmetric pricing strategies, differences in time-efficiency of procedures, use of procedures to which access is limited, and so forth. This allowed us to define with more precision the problems that are sector specific (e.g. vendor lock-in for IT, improperly implemented public–public or public–private cooperation in waste management, market access restrictions in health). The identification of sector-specific weaknesses or malfunctioning in public procurement will help us to target them in a more efficient way.

Common themes also appeared across the three sectors. They were mainly linked to professionalism of public buyers (e.g. lack of technological expertise, inappropriate use of selection criteria, collusion, corruption), as well as the potential of purchase aggregation. It is planned to take contacts with Member States where the problems persist.

3 The Single Market

Beyond country and sector approaches another important leg of our work is the consolidation of the Single Market. Cross-border competition and transparency are the two key principles of a genuine Single Market in public procurement. The implementation of these principles is expected to create a level playing field and establish competitive market conditions for carrying out purchases by public authorities. This is turn shall result in better procurement outcomes.

Compared to the business-to-consumers and business-to-business markets, the public procurement market (B2G) is by far less integrated at the European level: cross-border public procurement is 2.5 times smaller than import penetration on the private sector. Significant differences in prices for presumably homogeneous products, for example in some segments of the medical sector (e.g. medical devices such as scanners), may also indicate malfunctioning of the Single Market. This could reveal either poor public procurement practices in some Member States or deliberate market segmentation by private operators (or both).

Other symptoms of an ill functioning of the Internal Market include striking inequalities among Member States in the participation of non-national operators in the national public procurement markets. The differences between Member States in the value of indirect cross-border awards vary from nearly 0 per cent to 44 per cent, with the EU average estimated at around 13.4 per cent. Although this gap can be partially explained by different structures of demand between the private and public buyers, it indicates insufficient market openness of the public sector across the EU.

This of course also means that it is necessary to find means to incentivise Member States to look beyond their borders. Today, all authorities are obliged to publish their intentions to contract at European level in portal TED.[1] Clearly, this is not enough for them to actually look beyond their local markets. We need to think creatively about what could make them buy abroad, such as stimulating joint cross border procurement, incentivising the use of tendering documents in languages easily understood by a wider European market, and highlighting best practice so as to demonstrate that those that look for solutions in the wider European market get better and cheaper solutions. Indeed, speaking different languages is an issue, but a wise use of IT tools can at least partially help to overcome the problems in accessing markets at distance (electronic access to tender documentation, e-submission, etc.).

Moreover, two work streams fall in the activities to simplify cross-border participation in public procurement:

- the European Single Procurement Document, a European self-declaration providing preliminary evidence in replacement of certificates issued by public authorities, and
- the revised standard forms.

Both aim at making easier for business to access information on public procurement procedures taking place in another Member State. The question of transparent information leads me to introduce the next item, corruption.

4 Corruption

Public procurement is a hot spot for corruption. Corruption in public procurement means public funds including EU funds are wasted on an enormous scale. Taxpayers' money to pay for hospital equipment, books for schools or safer roads ends up sitting in the pockets of the corrupt. Calculations are that in the EU Member States around €120 billion is lost each year to corruption, an amount comparable to the European Union's total annual budget. Corruption distorts competition in the Internal Market and can reduce the quality, sustainability and safety of public projects and purchases. When procurement is corrupted by private interests and not directed by the public good, citizens' and companies' trust in governments is eroded. Business representatives therefore echo the call of NGOs like Transparency International for a comprehensive EU anti-corruption strategy.

The Council of the European Union recently affirmed that it is a common endeavour of the EU and its Member States to fight corruption in a coherent manner and to promote high anticorruption standards across the EU. The Council, the European Ombudsman, and the Court of Auditors of the European Union welcomed the first EU Anti-corruption report with its special chapter on public procurement as a first step in this direction. The new public procurement and concessions Directives which are currently being transposed by the Member States contain various elements for the prevention and detection of corruption in public procurement, like enhanced transparency, an extension of the scope of the Directives to the vulnerable post-award phase and monitoring and reporting obligations.

The EC is currently looking into introducing an even more effective and proactive policy to tackle corruption in public purchasing. Initiatives may include setting clear rules for the protection of whistle-blowers, awareness raising for a culture of integrity in a clean public sector and for businesses and making use of indicators and IT tools for better monitoring the procurement process.

5 Professionalisation

Beyond corruption, the other enemy of efficient buying from public administration is incompetence. Member States have not yet seized the potential for savings of a greater professionalisation of their purchasing public sector. Public procurement is perceived not as a business function, but as an administrative exercise, focused mainly on legal compliance. It is estimated that the costs of bureaucratic waste and inefficiency are much higher than the cost of corruption (Bandiera *et al.*, 2009).

Having transposed correctly a legal framework is certainly a necessary, but certainly not a sufficient, step to achieve a desirable functioning of a public procurement system. The work is unfortunately much more complicated than simply to transpose European legislation in a formally correct way.

For these reasons the EC is developing a policy to promote professionalisation of public buyers. The policy aims at contributing to a more efficient spending of 19 per cent of the EU GDP. The policy will include *inter alia* professionalisation plans, promotion of defined training schemes, capacity building and exchange of best practice. Market intelligence, business skills and a focus on skills must become the heart of public purchasing. In short, public procurement needs to become a business skill – rather than an inefficient (at best) or corrupt (at worse) administrative endeavour.

6 Central Purchasing Bodies (CPBs)

The Public Procurement landscape is characterised by a high dispersion of players: 300 000 contracting authorities in EU, and many more economic operators. Ensuring wide implementation of EU policy is a significant challenge in such a context.

Closely involving CPBs – in view of their size and the central role played – is fundamental to ensure the implementation of public procurement policy. In some Member States, CPBs manage an increasing share of public procurement value. This method of purchasing offers visible benefits: for example, by consolidating purchases across a number of purchasing bodies, significant efficiencies and simplification can be introduced into the system. Nevertheless, the increasing role of CPBs also carries with it a number of risks (e.g. reduced access for SMEs due to a larger size of contracts, reduced decentralisation, impact on the supply market, etc.). For these reasons, CPBs should be at the heart of the implementation of our policy.

Points referred to earlier – such as professionalisation of public buyers, improved functioning of the Member States procurement systems, or digitisation as well as the sectoral approach – cannot be adequately addressed without taking CPBs properly into account. This calls for the development of a policy to maximise benefits generated by CPBs and address some concerns. Such policy could include issues such as increasing CPBs transparency, raise their role in the development of public procurement policy, or leverage CPBs to foster cross-border procurement.

6 Conclusions

The EU has now a new legal framework and we need to make it work by establishing the right priorities where it is dysfunctional, and deal with them in cooperation with the Member States. This is about reforming the administrative culture in many of our Member States. This is very much linked with looking at things from a wider perspective.

Legislation is important to ensure equal treatment of tenderers, and transparency with regard to tender procedures covered by the regime. Public procurement is too frequently and wrongly perceived as a purely legal domain. This (mis)perception is present at all levels: from public authorities and firms to policymakers. Such approach is not efficient leading to sub-optimal implementation of the rules and/or wrong policy choices.

However, this is not the full story. Public procurement is changing. It requires many skills: legal, economic, managerial, knowledge of IT, markets and technology, just to refer to the key ones. It includes many players – contracting authorities, suppliers, budgetary authorities, IT providers, and several other public bodies like courts, or bodies issuing attestations. To capture all these dimensions, the only way to embrace the much needed reforms is to be holistic in our policy approach and hence be multidisciplinary in our analysis and initiatives.

Note

1 Tenders Electronic daily, available at http://ted.europa.eu/TED/main/HomePage.do.

Reference

Bandiera, O., Prat, A., and Valletti, T. (2009): Active and Passive Waste in Government Spending: Evidence from a Policy Experiment. *American Economic Review*, vol. 99, n.4, 1278–1308, 2009.

Part I

Supporting social considerations via public procurement

1 Colloquium

Martin Trybus
Gustavo Piga and Tünde Tátrai

1 Martin Trybus – Supporting social considerations through public procurement: a legal perspective

1.1 Introduction

The primary objective of public procurement is to provide the contracting authority and entity with the supplies, services, or works it needs to operate – unless it wishes to provide them itself, in-house. Connected to this function are the objectives of value for money, competition transparency, and the opening of procurement markets (non-discrimination). Public procurement laws need to serve these primary objectives and should also be simple and user-friendly for the contracting officers or committees. However, governments and legislators have always been aiming to promote other objectives such as social, environmental, and industrial policy objectives through public procurement. These are called "secondary", "horizontal" (Arrowsmith and Kunzlik, 2009), "strategic" (EU Commission, 2010), or "sustainable" objectives, or just "green and social procurement" (Caranta and Trybus, 2010). Secondary objectives can be taken into account inter alia in the technical specifications, in the qualification and selection process, at the award stage, in the contract conditions, and other stages of a procurement procedure. Procurement laws will require, accommodate, or prohibit such practices. Technical specifications and contract conditions may inter alia specify environmental standards, require the employment of young people or the long-term unemployed, require adherence to labour laws for example on the basis of the ILO standards, or prohibit certain sources for materials, for example if their production involved child or slave labour or if these goods originate in politically problematic areas. Rules on qualification and selection may either limit the procurement procedure to certain favoured groups (for example to disabled workshops as in the 2004 and 2014 EU procurement Directives) or disqualify or de-select bidders who do not meet certain minimum social or environmental requirements. At the award stage bidders from a favoured group may inter alia be given a margin of preference (as for example black-owned businesses in post-Apartheid South Africa), additional points in their overall score in comparison with non-favoured bidders (as for example in some contracts in the US), or require the life-cycle costing of goods (inter alia the 2014 EU procurement Directives). Other measures include the compulsory splitting of larger contracts to make them more accessible to (employment creating) SMEs (as for example in France) or the requirements of direct payments from the contracting entity to (SME) subcontractors (as for example in Italy) for similar reasons.

1.2 Primary v. secondary objectives

The better but not unanimous view is that secondary objectives compromise the primary objective(s). A German expression for secondary objectives – *vergabe-fremde Aspekte* (English: "aspects alien to procurement") – linguistically captures this problem and leaves no doubt as to the opinion on these "alien" aspects. This opinion advocates that contracting authorities and entities should only aim to achieve value for money and ensure the timely and efficient procurement of goods and services. The concern of those opponents of secondary objectives is that their promotion in public procurement laws and procedures will compromise these primary objectives disproportionately. It is after all the taxpayer's money that is spent in times of tight budgets. The disqualification or de-selection of bidders because they do not meet certain social or environmental requirements will reduce competition through the exclusion of these bidders. Social and environmental specification and contract conditions might discourage certain economic operators from bidding and thus reduce competition and create an unnecessarily complex and burdensome procurement process which will increase the costs of the procedure and the risk of litigation when this complexity leads to mistakes. Similarly, the splitting of contracts may add complexity, discourage participation (of larger companies), and might be abused to keep a contract under the value thresholds of some procurement laws (such as those in the EU). Limitations and margins of preference compromise competition and value for money, for example driving companies of non-favoured groups into costly alliances with companies owned by favoured groups, the costs of which are ultimately shifted to the contracting authority or entity. Overall, contracting officers are overburdened with a complex procurement process and a difficult set of contract conditions which they often do not have the expertise and resources to enforce anyway. Advocates of the promotion of secondary objectives through public procurement argue that especially the State and bodies governed by public law cannot simply conduct their considerable purchasing activities like any private individual or company. The taxpayer's money has to be spent efficiently but the State also has important social and environmental policies to promote. Public procurement is one instrument at the disposal of the State, in addition to inter alia criminal law, labour law, environmental law, planning law, State aids, and tax law, by which the State can pursue these policies. To a certain extent the State is buying social justice (McCrudden, 2007) or a clean environment. Purging procurement law from any social and green objectives would deprive the State of an important policy instrument. This divide between opponents and advocates of secondary objectives is often a political one amongst law makers, with (post-)communists, socialists, social democrats (labour, democrats) and greens normally in favour and conservatives (republicans), Christian democrats and liberals against (for example Germany).

1.3 Social considerations

The controversy over secondary objectives outlined above is most pronounced with regards to social considerations. For example, in EU public procurement law, there has been a move towards accommodating environmental objectives, most clearly progressed in the landmark decisions of the European Court of Justice in Case C-513/99, Concordia Bus Finland and Case C-448/01, EVN Wienstrom and in the innovations regarding inter alia environmental standards and Life-cycle costing in the new Public Sector Directive 2014/24/EU and the new Utilities Directive 2014/25/EU. The promotion of SMEs is also accommodated in the new EU instruments but is generally seen as a separate issue anyway, due to the positive impacts of increased SME participation on competition. In contrast, social objectives, addressed by the European Court of Justice in the seminal judgments of Case C-31/87, Gebroeders Beentjes and Case C-225/98, Nord Pas de Calais and also accommodated more than before in the new Directives 2014/24/EU and 2014/25/EU, are subject to an inconsistent and overall much more reserved regime. While it could almost be argued that environmental considerations and the promotion of SMEs are (no longer) secondary objectives, social considerations clearly still are. With the benefit of being able to look at a long tradition of US federal procurement regulations since the nineteenth century, Joshua Schwartz has described the role of social objectives as a pendulum: swinging from periods during which the emphasis is clearly on value for money and social considerations are almost not taken into account, to periods were issues such as the promotion of gender and race equality, support for under-developed regions or employment programmes are more important. The EU pendulum has recently swung slightly towards secondary considerations, but it is too early to say whether it will swing further in that direction or swing back towards value for money.

1.4 Conclusions and thesis

The promotion of social considerations through public procurement and its regulation remain one of the most controversial issues in public procurement regulation. To facilitate discussion, the following conclusions are deliberately provocative. The author himself is not as sure about his overall position on the topic as these conclusions might suggest.

1   Public procurement law at national, European or international level should generally not aim to promote social considerations because this compromises the primary objective of effective procurement and the related objectives of value for money, competition, non-discrimination, and transparency.

2   Public procurement should not aim to accommodate social objectives since it makes public procurement procedures excessively complex and difficult to conduct without mistakes and violations of such a convoluted procurement law, often resulting in costly litigation. A public procurement law accommodating social considerations is not a user-friendly law. Excessive complexity and litigation also compromise the primary objective of efficient procurement through added costs and delays.

3   Social objectives are nevertheless important considerations which governments and legislators must not neglect. However, there are many alternative and better suited instruments to promote social considerations – inter alia criminal law, labour law, tax law, or State aids (subsidies) – normally with their own control and enforcement system to ensure the legal obligations regarding these objectives are complied with in practice. Procurement officers or committees normally lack the staff, powers and/or resources to effectively control and enforce social objectives enshrined in procurement law. Thus public procurement law is not the most effective instrument to promote social considerations.

4   There can be and should be exceptions to the "no social considerations in public procurement rule" advocated in points 1–3 above. Examples include labels guaranteeing that the production of a certain good did not involve slave or child labour, since these labels can easily be integrated into the qualifications stage of competitive procurement procedures and the additional costs are limited. Disabled workshops are another example for a desirable exception, also because most of the relevant contracts will be of low value (and thus for example below the value thresholds of the EU procurement Directives). However, single-source direct awards should be possible in such a case – the competitions between disabled workshops under the EU Directives, for example, are only justified for higher value contracts. Finally, in extreme political situations such as post-Apartheid South Africa, a temporarily and substantially limited regime promoting previously disadvantaged groups can be justified. In such a situation certain social considerations can be more important than value for money.

2   Gustavo Piga, Tünde Tátrai – Supporting social considerations through public procurement: economic perspective

There is no consensus in the scientific literature regarding the enforcement of social considerations in public procurement. The original meaning of social aspect in public procurements included the following: labor standards, unemployment, equal employment opportunities for disabled workers, racial equality and human rights. This approach has been recently broadened in the official EU position.

Taking the European Guide (Buying Social – A Guide to Taking Account of Social Considerations in Public Procurement, 2010) as a starting point, the following priorities should be considered as relevant in public procurement:

- promoting 'employment opportunities'
- promoting 'decent work'
- promoting compliance with 'social and labor rights'
- supporting 'social inclusion' and promoting social economy organizations
- promoting 'accessibility and design for all'
- taking into account 'ethical trade'
- seeking to achieve wider voluntary commitment to 'corporate social responsibility' (CSR)
- protecting against human rights abuse and encouraging respect for human rights
- promoting 'SMEs'.

It is a question of both theoretical and practical importance how to divide various public procurement policy purposes into groups. However one has to acknowledge that it is problematic to define the content of 'social aspects', especially when 'partly social' aspects are also involved in public procurement. Furthermore, it is also a valid assumption to state that such purposes are inseparable from each other. For example, according to McCrudden's (2004) view, it is – by nature – difficult to divide the social and the environmental considerations from each other since both of them are to be included into the broader notion of sustainability:

> There remain tantalising issues concerning how similar 'green' procurement is to social procurement, including the extent to which these two sets of initiatives complement or cut across each other. This will clearly affect the extent to which acceptance of international or regional standards in the area of social procurement will be possible in the context of sustainable procurement.
>
> (McCrudden, 2004)

According to the latter opinion: Are green procurement aspects similar, and can they be merged into social procurement aspects? In order to make the necessary distinction between the competing categories, we would have to identify which social procurement raises certain specific legal and policy issues regarding their compatibility with international and regional legal frameworks.

One of the most typical examples is given by Medina-Arnáiz (2010) when assuming that a gender equality aspect exists in public procurement. Based on a Spanish case, she clarifies that even the legal argumentation should be based on the primacy of the social aspect:

> the principle of equal treatment between women and men, as well as the express prohibition of any type of discrimination on the grounds of gender can be seen as a guiding principle for legal systems and as such, should be integrated and observed in all public action (gender mainstreaming).

While one needs different legal frameworks to promote specific policy preferences, from our point of view it is necessary to handle the different preference aspects uniformly in order to promote systemic sustainability in public procurement. Ideally, one would want to find an existing model which classifies and positions the development of public procurement systems with regard to sustainability so as to enable progress for contracting authorities and legislators in the course of implementation in the way that they should apply the value for money approach. In this way the stakeholders would operate in an accountable and transparent manner and would gradually develop public procurement for socially beneficial purposes.

Telgen, Harland and Knight (2007) established a seven-stage model that can be connected to our topic to find the best way of making public procurement more sustainable.

The development levels indicated above enable the realization of sustainable purposes in a different way. The highest (5–6–7) levels appear to have higher probability to implement sustainable public procurement – according to our interpretation.

Further examination is needed concerning the green and social standpoints as to whether the 'value for money' logic should be considered as a main condition for supporting certain broader government policy objectives. If the answer is yes, than there is a real opportunity to deliver broader government objectives and shape the public procurement system based on sustainable characteristics.

It is not possible to create sustainable procedures simply by applying a social criterion because the evaluation criteria, the technical content and the contractual obligations should serve more than just demonstrative purposes. The goal is to render the entire procurement process sustainable at the level of contracting authorities and to raise public procurement to the level of policy and its inclusion in sustainability strategies. 'The cited 7-stage model pointed out that through the poor management of sustainability at regulatory level, ab ovo substantially less can be achieved because it is not clear what the legislator intends to achieve' (Tátrai, 2014).

We believe that social preferences should be separated from other aspects but the main problem is a false assumption that sustainable public procurement can be feasible using a legislative tool also in a relatively less developed public procurement environment and culture. In reality, a certain relevant level of

Table 1.1 The seven-stages model

Stage	Level of development
1	Sourcing and delivery of goods and services
2	Compliance with legislation/regulation
3	Efficient use of public funds
4	Accountability
5	Value for money
6	Supporting of broader government policy objectives
7	Delivery of broader government objectives

development, a certain ethical attitude, clear legal background and explicit policies are needed to effectively implement social aspects in public procurement.

If the foundation is strong, the next step is to be done by the regulator and the policy maker, by identifying the main characteristics of prioritizing social needs from the legal point of view. But social aspects are different from green aspects: it is far less settled what contracting authorities should think about prioritizing social aspects. If the policy maker views SME support as a social aspect because of the potential impact on employment, then the expected additional advantages should be defined before setting the legal framework. If the policy goal is to promote women- or veteran-owned businesses or to prefer manufacturers who are compliant to the minimum standards of the ILO then such priorities should be clearly defined in the legislation and at the policy level. This is the only way to deliver government objectives such as social aspects with respect to the opinions of the relevant stakeholders. In such a top-bottom approach, it is also possible to consider efficiency and ethical aspect – depending on the creativity of contracting authorities.

One last point. Many times social considerations in procurement are challenged or opposed because they lead to fraud and distortions and an amount of discretionality on the part of the procurer that can be abused. Fake unemployment conditions, large firms that have artificially created smaller entities to compete in set-asides contracts for small firms, working conditions that are hard to check once the contract is awarded are all simple examples that make the point. This has be traded off with the well-known effect that introducing social considerations in the public sector often has significant and positive implications in terms of the adoption of those standards in the private sector as well, with potentially large final effects. Which one of the two effects to give more weight to possibly depends on the quality and professionalism of the public procurer team in spotting abuses and in monitoring contract conditions and performance, therefore, on the culture, ethics and law performance of the specific country.

3 Martin Trybus – Response to Paper 2

3.1 Different secondary considerations: different approaches?

The question of whether secondary or horizontal objectives should be accommodated in public procurement regulations and award decisions might require different answers depending on the type or category of secondary consideration. Thus the different categories of secondary or horizontal objectives need to be differentiated.

First, environmental considerations or objectives are increasingly developing into a separate category. For example, in EU public procurement law, there has been a move towards accommodating environmental objectives, most clearly progressed in the landmark decisions of the European Court of Justice in Case C-513/99, Concordia Bus Finland and Case C-448/01, EVN Wienstrom and in the innovations regarding inter alia environmental standards and Life-cycle costing in the new Public Sector Directive 2014/24/EU and the new Utilities Directive 2014/25/EU. It is argued that especially through the use of technical specifications and the closely related contract performance conditions, environmental considerations can be taken into account in the pre-procurement and the post-procurement phases without affecting the procurement phase proper. Moreover, Life-cycle costing, which does affect the procurement phase proper, can be conducted in a manner which does not undermine the objectives of non-discrimination, equal treatment, transparency, and value for money. It implies a different understanding of value for money. Thus environmental considerations can be accommodated in public procurement regulation and decisions without compromising the primary objective(s). It could therefore even be argued that they are not really secondary considerations. Moreover, the transparency of technical specifications, contract performance conditions, and Life-cycle costing might make it easier to police and enforce environmental objectives though public procurement.

Second, the promotion of SMEs is often generally seen as a separate issue due to the positive impacts of increased SME participation on competition. Moreover, for example with regards to the EU Directives it needs to be taken into account that the economies of all Member States are dominated by SMEs. While the French economy, for example could be seen as dominated by large companies, the country also boasts 2.5 million SMEs. Similarly, in Germany the likes of Volkswagen, Siemens, and Bosch are complemented by hundreds of thousands of companies of the Mittelstand. In Italy 99.9 per cent of all enterprises are SME, with a particularly large proportion of very small or "micro" companies and the small and medium-sized EU Member States have SME-based economies to match. For example, almost all of the 547,440 Hungarian companies are SMEs. The situation in countries outside the EU will be similar. Public procurement regulation in the EU or elsewhere cannot be written for large companies only – SMEs have to be able to bid for contracts as prime contractors and perhaps more importantly as subcontractors. Whether the promotion of SMEs is to be considered a secondary or horizontal objective depends on how this is accommodated in the procurement law. The new Public Sector Directive 2014/24/EU, for example, contains four main "new" regimes for the promotion of SMEs: the division of contracts into lots, the European Single Procurement Document, the limitation of participation requirements, and direct payments to subcontractors. The European Single Procurement Document, for example, merely aims to reduce red tape and equally benefits larger companies, the division into lots may compromise efficiency and value for money.

In contrast, social objectives, which are the subject of this contribution, addressed by the European Court of Justice in the seminal judgments of Case C-31/87, Gebroeders Beentjes and Case C-225/98, Nord Pas de Calais and also accommodated more than before in the new Directives 2014/24/EU and 2014/25/EU, are subject to an inconsistent and overall much more reserved regime. While it could almost be argued that environmental considerations and the promotion of SMEs are (no longer) secondary objectives, social considerations clearly still are. A scheme to integrate the long term unemployed in the execution of a public procurement contract, for example, will have to be paid for by the contracting authority and therefore make the contract more expensive than it would be without such a scheme. A margin of preference for a disadvantaged group will normally affect competition and undermine value for money. In other words the contracting authority will have to pay for this margin. Following labour laws and standards needs to be enforced and the contracting authority has to provide the staff and resources to police compliance with these standards. It is not a useful exercise when bidders guarantee compliance with all sorts of laws and standards in the tender documents when this is not followed up and controlled.

3.2 What is needed from economists?

What is needed from economists, are mechanisms that measure the effect of the accommodation of social considerations in public procurement regulations and decisions. In other words what is needed as a crucial contribution of the "other" discipline is reliable data on the costs of promoting social objectives through public procurement. What does the taxpayer have to pay for a scheme for the long term unemployed in a works contract or a margin of preference for a disadvantaged group in comparison to awarding the contract to the lowest bid or the economically most advantageous tender? The figure also needs to take the costs of a control and enforcement mechanism into account. Ideally an informed debate also needs data on the costs of running such a policing mechanism through contracting officers or committees compared to running through other agencies such as the revenue service, offices for labour security, or social authorities. If the costs are small then a strong argument for accommodating social objectives in public procurement contracts and awards is made. If the costs are considerable then an argument against such an accommodation is made. To what extent is reliable data of this kind available?

4 Gustavo Piga, Tünde Tátrai – Response to Paper 1

The reflexions of Martin Trybus are challenging and open up many venues for debate. Beside his four final conclusions, other considerations from his main train of thought have awakened our interest.

First, we acknowledge the intuition of Prof. Trybus that attention to social considerations might vary over time due to budget tightness and to political majorities. A pendulum is indeed moving. In what direction?

Let us start first with the conditions of public finances. Budgets are usually tight during recessions. One should thus expect social considerations to become more relevant in downturns, an empirically testable implication. Martin Trybus argues, to the contrary, that the promotion of social considerations

> in public procurement laws and procedures will compromise these primary objectives disproportionately. It is after all the taxpayer's money that is

spent in times of *tight budgets* (our emphasis added). The disqualification or de-selection of bidders because they do not meet certain social or environmental requirements will reduce competition through the exclusion of these bidders.

In this case social considerations should be pro-cyclical, disappearing when times are bad, not to overburden the public budget already stressed by low revenues and higher expenditures for unemployment support. Is this the case? Obviously there cannot be full and final proof but we would venture to argue 'no'. One example will suffice to generate the debate. Recessions are periods of high unemployment. Inserting in procurement tenders a social qualification that exclusively unemployed personnel is to be hired (or that this will be a factor for better points in a MEAT tender) might end up reducing total costs for government and thus lower the burden of taxpayers and improve welfare by reducing unemployment subsidies and spending related to stressful conditions. This is maybe why the new EU directives, coming out in a tough economic moment for Europe, are socially-intensive as Trybus points out. All in all it would seem that our point is that, in evaluating the relevance of social considerations, one is to consider its 'total' impact on society and the economy.

As for political swings that generate changes in the relevance of social considerations in public procurement (left-wing governments supposedly using more of those), we simply annotate it as another interesting testable implication that should drive new studies by researchers, not being sure that a regularity on that front might emerge so obviously.

Prof. Trybus' interesting final considerations deserve some comments on our part:

1   'Public procurement law … should generally not aim to promote social considerations because this compromises the primary objective of effective procurement and the related objectives of value for money, competition, non-discrimination, and transparency'.

   This point begs the question: who decides what the primary objective of procurement is since the concept of 'effectiveness' is related to the capacity to reach the goal, which thus remains to be defined? As for value for money, competition, non-discrimination and transparency, shouldn't these be considered instruments rather than goals per se?

   Trybus, however, goes beyond this points and argues that social considerations necessarily 'reduce competition and create an unnecessarily complex and burdensome procurement processes which will increase the costs of the procedure and the risk of litigation when this complexity leads to mistakes'.

   We have already argued that lower competition might in this case come with lower overall social costs. But there are other reasons to believe that costs for society might at least in principle decline. As for SMEs preferences, where the advantage is one of having permitted to potentially vibrant small firms to survive and succeed, thanks to set-aside contracts or price preference against large firms, one should consider that the total net costs of inserting in the procedure social considerations favoring SMEs should be calculated over a long span of time, allowing for the benefits of future greater participation and competitiveness to be internalized:. The same goes for giving greater weight, for example, to unemployment which has typically permanent costly effects for society, leading to the abandonment of the labor force because of discouragement. Finally, the presence of criteria that favour firms that would face an uphill battle otherwise (imagine giving more points to a firm that hires unemployed less productive individuals) forces other firms to bid more aggressively than they would have otherwise, making the procurement process possibly less costly.

This is not to say that Trybus' concern – 'procurement officers … normally lack the staff, powers and/or resources to effectively control and enforce social objectives enshrined in procurement law' – is a warning that should be left unheard. Facing it would call for a greater level of professionalism that often also normal procurement procedures require.

2   'However, there are many alternative and better suited instruments to promote social considerations – inter alia criminal law, labour law, tax law, or State aids (subsidies)', says Prof. Trybus. While this one too is a relevant empirical issue that researchers should study and deepen, we remain optimists on the role of public procurement in achieving social goals. First, taxes and subsidies are also costly. Second, public procurement while large, 16 percent of GDP on average in the world, is not pervasive. Setting work practices or standards for firms that participate in those public tenders has the feature of a social experiment that might initially be of little dimension but might subsequently extend itself to the daily routine of the firms even in their non-public sales, if deemed useful. For example an unemployed worker might remain hired in the firm that used him/her initially in the public contract, having been considered productive and effective for the establishment. New standards of organization of work in the supplier environment, forced by the public sector might generate new practices that would have been too costly to implement in the absence of a specific (and large) demand by the public buyer. All this to say that social considerations, well thought-out and monitored in their implementation, might represent a source of innovation and change that benefit society as a whole, the private sector and governments.

5 Martin Trybus – Conclusions

Gustavo Piga and Tünde Tátrai have made a number of highly relevant points that are well taken. It is conceited that a political divide between an "anti-social considerations political right" and a "pro-social considerations political left" might oversimplify things, especially when political parties are often not that clearly right or left any more. Most importantly, their point of an increased importance of social considerations in times of economic crisis and that the overall long-term costs have to be taken into account is a strong one. However, four concluding reiterating points are made. First, social considerations to be promoted in public procurement often have a distinctly national flavour. It is after all, for example, unemployment amongst the nationals of the procuring national or local government that is to be reduced through public procurement, not unemployment in other Member States. There is therefore often a danger of protectionism undermining the objectives of the EU and its procurement legislation. Second, a convoluted and overcomplicated procurement law – and the most recent EU procurement Directives are more convoluted and complicated than their predecessors, not least because of the accommodation of social objectives – increases the danger of procurement officers making genuine mistakes, leading to litigation and thus increased costs through delays, recommenced procurement proceedings, and damages. These costs, admittedly not yet sufficiently quantified by reliable data, are also a factor. Third, all three authors of this contribution agree on the importance of social considerations, from the fight against unemployment to the promotion of ILO standards. However, a crucial question already discussed above is whether public procurement is the right instrument to promote social considerations. As Piga and Tátrai rightly point out, the alterative instruments, such as labour law, taxation, or State aids are also costly. Costs are and unavoidable by-product of all available instruments. What many of the alternative instruments have is specific enforcement mechanisms, ranging from State aid simply not being paid unless certain standards are met, to national revenue services collecting taxes or allowing deductions, to labour security offices raiding construction sites to check compliance with labour standards. Procurement officers often simply lack the capacity to enforce all social requirement promised to be met in the tender. Finally, the best way to promote social considerations in public procurement remains in the pre-procurement phase (when deciding what to buy) and in the post-procurement contract-management phase; through technical specifications and contract performance conditions rather than through qualification, shortlisting and award criteria. This is where the secondary objectives can be reconciled with the primary objectives of procurement.

6 Gustavo Piga, Tünde Tátrai – Conclusions

Prof. Trybus makes a critical point: what is needed from economists is data, reliable data on the costs of promoting social objectives through public procurement. There is no doubt that promoting social objectives is at the heart, for an economist, an empirical question: are the benefits (calculated over time and internalizing all effects) of moving away from a traditional best value for money approach to adopt social considerations greater than the costs?

While empirical studies are on the rise and often show that social considerations do pay off (see for example Hubbard and Paarsch and also Marion), one should keep in mind that, as we argued in our first statement, the effectiveness of social considerations in a given country is strictly related to the quality of its institutions, legal systems, culture and should therefore not be taken as a pure benchmarking exercise applicable independently of those variables.

But for Prof. Trybus's question 'what is needed from economists' is a good reminder that each discipline must play a role in the debate of whether push for social clauses or not in public procurement. Other disciplines might have a say too. Prof. Trybus argues that: 'There can be and should be exceptions to the "no social considerations in public procurement rule".... Examples include labels guaranteeing that the production of a certain good did not involve slave or child labour,... disabled workshops are another example for a desirable exception ... in extreme political situations such as post-Apartheid South Africa, a temporarily and substantially limited regime promoting previously disadvantaged groups can be justified. In such a situation certain social considerations can be more important than value for money.'

What connects these three examples of acceptable social procurement mentioned by Prof. Trybus is not so much their low cost but their (high) moral value. What is 'moral' enough to justify the adoption of a social criterion in public tenders is not the domain of economists or lawyers alone: political scientists, philosophers, sociologists and citizens at large must be included. Keeping also clearly in mind that what might be dubbed not enough 'morally relevant' today might become so tomorrow. The debate must remain open.

References

Arrowsmith, S. and Kunzlik, P. (2009): *Social and Environmental Policies in EC Public Procurement Law* (Cambridge University Press).

Caranta, R. and Trybus, M. (2010) (eds.): *The Law of Green and Social Procurement in Europe* (Djøf: Copenhagen, 2010).

European Commission (2010): Buying Social – A Guide to Taking Account of Social Considerations in Public Procurement.

Hubbard, T. P. and Paarsch, H. J. (2009): Investigating Bid Preferences at Low-Price, Sealed-Bid Auctions with Endogenous Participation, *International Journal of Industrial Organization*, 27(1), 1–14.

Jones, D. S. (2011): Recent Reforms to Promote Social Responsibility Procurement in East-Asian States: A Comparative Analysis. *Journal of Public Procurement* 11(1), 61–94 Spring.

Marion, J. (2007): Are bid preferences benign? The effect of small business subsidies in highway procurement auctions, *Journal of Public Economics* 91(7–8), 1591–1624.

McCrudden, C. (2007): *Buying Social Justice* (Oxford University Press).

McCrudden, C. (2004). Using Public Procurement to Achieve Social Outcomes, *Natural Resources Forum*, 28: 257–267.

Medina-Arnáiz, R. (2010): Integrating Gender Equality in Public Procurement: The Spanish Case, *Journal of Public Procurement*, 10(4), 540–563.

Tátrai, T. (2014): Stages of development towards sustainable public procurement. International Public Procurement Conference, Dublin.

Telgen, J., Harland, C., and Knight, L. (2007): Public Procurement in Perspective. In L. Knight, C. Harland, J. Telgen, K. V. Thai, G. Callender, and K. McKen (eds.), *Public Procurement: International Cases and Commentary* (pp. 20–22). London and New York: Routledge.

2 The role of public procurement in the fight to eradicate modern slavery in the UK construction industry

Richard Craven

1 Introduction

The chapter discusses the potential role of public procurement, i.e. the process by which government acquires goods, works and services from third parties, as an element in global attempts to counter forms of "modern slavery", such as forced labour.

There are certain industries, including manufacturing, construction, agriculture and hospitality, which present a high risk of modern slavery. For the purposes of the chapter, the UK construction industry is adopted as a case study. Here, the construction industry's "special characteristics", e.g. the nature of the work and flexibility of the labour market, give rise to important concerns regarding the protection of workers, especially in relation to migrant and vulnerable workers: "[t]he construction industry is notorious for its short term contracts, complex [subcontracting] chains and informal employment practices, all of which leave workers open to exploitation". (UCATT, 2011. p. 12). Thus, for some, the industry is a breeding ground for "social dumping" and violations of workers' human rights (see section 3.2 below). The way in which the industry was hit by the recent economic downturn has exacerbated these worries, i.e. as contractors look to their workforces for cost savings, and so specific attention is warranted.

The chapter begins with an introductory consideration of public procurement as a tool to pursue social policy. In section 3 the chapter outlines the problem of "modern slavery", along with a consideration of the UK construction industry, and concerns over transparency and accountability often linked to complex subcontracting chains, which make the industry quite susceptible to labour violations. Section 3 will also detail and assess global efforts to combat modern slavery, looking at specific efforts in the US, the EU and recent attempts in the UK where the Modern Slavery Bill is currently before Parliament. The next section, section 4, reviews the extent to which member states and "contracting authorities" may, under EU public procurement law, seek to uphold respect for human rights in the performance of public contracts. The chapter concludes with a targeted commentary on the scope under the Public Sector Directive 2004/18/EC and the new Public Procurement Directive 2014/24/EU for human rights policies in public procurement, focusing, in particular, on a specific way in which EU reforms appear to facilitate the effectiveness of such policies: new, more detailed rules on subcontracting chains (article 71 Directive 2004/18).

2 Socially responsible public procurement

The public spending of EU member states is potentially very powerful. These domestic markets represent a large proportion of EU GDP, between 15 and 18 per cent according to estimates. From an internal market perspective, the way in which these contracts are awarded may present significant barriers to trade (for example, from discriminatory treatment in award). The EU therefore regulates public procurement to promote an internal market in public contracts (Arrowsmith, 2012). Thus, in line with this, a regulatory system has been developed, based, inter alia, on principles of transparency, non-discrimination and equal treatment, in order to limit the extent to which member state public procurement may operate to inhibit intra-EU trade. In particular, specific procedural legislation has been put in place for high value procurement, providing detailed rules, backed up a system of review and remedies for cases of non-compliance.

There are other reasons for governments to regulate or use public procurement, and these do not always sit easily alongside free trade agreements, or, indeed, efficiency and value for money objectives (themselves grounds for regulating the procurement process): so called, "horizontal" objectives, objectives in addition to the acquisition of goods, works or services, such as industrial, social, environmental or political objectives (McCrudden, 2007; Arrowsmith and Kunzlik, 2009; Caranta and Trybus, 2010). Because of the propensity for the pursuit of horizontal policies through public procurement to operate in a way that restricts trade (e.g. to mask discriminatory treatment), the EU tends to regard such use of procurement with distrust, and it is tightly controlled under EU law. Nevertheless, across the EU, there is a long history of public procurement being looked to as a key policy tool. Indeed, Daintith (1979) discussed how, in addition to legislation ("imperium"), government may use its wealth to achieve policy, "dominium" (Daintith, 1979, p. 68 discussed in Davies, 2008). Also, with respect to labour standards, the focus of the chapter, Arrowsmith details how for many years in the UK formally commencing under the 1891 House of Commons Fair Wages Resolution, government sought to use public contracts to instil raised levels of pay and labour conditions in the private sector (Arrowsmith, 1995). These policies, at the outset mainly limited to pay, expanded in breadth considerably over the years for example covering hours of work and, from 1946, recognising the right to join a union and providing for reference to collective agreements in setting conditions. According to Arrowsmith, the policy was only withdrawn in 1983 following a change in policy under the Thatcher government; however, the impact of the policy is perceived to have been minimal; some of the perceived reasons for this lack of effectiveness are highlighted by Arrowsmith (some of which are pertinent to the present discussion):

[e]nforcement normally depended on complaints by individuals who were generally unaware of their rights, and even where the will to enforce existed within departments, it was hampered by a lack of sanctions. Compliance was a term of the contracts, often with a right to terminate for breach, but this was not done in practice because of the inconvenience, and also possible legal difficulties arising from the vagueness of the policy's requirements. There were some instances of debarment, but these were rare, and their effectiveness hampered by disagreements between departments whether to debar. Further, the provisions could not be enforced by employees; but the government often did not compel back payments to underpaid workers.

(Arrowsmith, 1995)

A number of legitimate rationales may be viewed to lie behind the use of public procurement in such a strategic manner as that set out above. For example, government may wish to associate itself with high standards (Arrowsmith and Kunzlik, 2009), e.g. to set an example to the private sector and avoid criticism; this appears evident in the UK policy above and is also an element in recent US legislation in relation protections against the risk of human trafficking on public contracts (see section 3 below). Also, public procurement may, for example in the way that it taps into private contractors' profit motivations, be perceived as more effective than other policy instruments (or at least complementary); for instance, in the UK, debate over the Modern Slavery Bill[1] suggests that, in relation to certain aspects, general measures to counter modern slavery may be too blunt an instrument; thus, public procurement could present a suitable alternative.

In the build up to new public procurement directives, and in the wake of financial turmoil in Europe in which living standards suffered considerably, there has appeared a renewed appreciation of the potential power and effectiveness of public procurement as a social policy instrument,[2] with an important role to play as the EU strives towards the 2020 objectives it has set for itself.

3 Modern slavery

3.1 Background

"Modern slavery" is a phrase used by prospective legislation in the UK, the Modern Slavery Bill, which refers to a range of abhorrent side effects flowing from (or at least exacerbated by) globalisation, including human/people trafficking, and forced and child labour. The chapter is predominantly concerned with forced labour, the primary definition for which is proffered by article 2 of ILO Convention No. 29 (1930):

all work or service that is exacted from any person under the menace of any penalty and for which the said person has not offered himself voluntarily.[3]

However, there exist numerous definitions and some confusion over precise distinctions between the different crimes, e.g. due to considerable overlap, particularly in relation to forced labour and human trafficking (these two terms are often used in an interchangeable manner). In view of these difficulties, in reviewing definitions for forced labour, Skrinankova (2010) notes that the "reality of forced labour is not a static one, but a continuum of experiences and situations ... [and] a continuum should therefore be used to describe the complexity of the exploitative environments and concrete individual situations of workers". (Skrinankova, 2010, p. 6). The lack of clarity, coupled with the covert nature of the crime and difficulties over detection, means the scale of forced labour is hard to gauge. The ILO, for instance, (conservatively) estimate that, at any given time between 2002 and 2010, 20.9 million people were victims of forced labour globally, with 880,000 of these in forced labour in the EU,[4] and there is a general consensus that these levels are rising.[5]

In addition to standing in breach of core labour standards, as set out in the eight fundamental ILO Conventions to which all EU member states have ratified and must respect, the crime of forced labour represents a breach of fundamental human rights. In accordance with the UN Universal Declaration of Human Rights "[n]o one shall be held in slavery or servitude; slavery and the slave trade shall be prohibited in all their forms" (article 4). Article 4 European Convention on European Human Rights sets forth a corresponding prohibition of slavery and forced labour, and the European Court of Human Rights has held article 4 ECHR to extend to place positive obligations on governments to ensure an effective system is in place to maintain the prohibition.[6]

Also, the Charter of Fundamental Rights of the European Union (binding from 2009) proffers rights, freedoms and principles, which are directly relevant to working conditions, and conform to the UN Charter and core ILO conventions to which all member states are signatories. Article 5 of the Charter prohibits slavery: "[n]o one shall be held in slavery or servitude. No one shall be required to perform forced or compulsory labour. Trafficking in human beings is prohibited".

3.2 The UK construction industry and modern slavery

In Europe, forced labour is prevalent throughout a range of workplaces, including agriculture, construction, domestic work and hospitality (Portugal *et al.*, 2006). The chapter's focus is the UK construction industry. In targeting the construction sector, the chapter avoids discussion of the issue of "extraterritoriality" and "legal imperialist" or "universalist" allegations, which would be a necessary element for an analysis of the use of EU public procurement practices to tackle forced labour outside Europe, e.g. supplies manufactured in "sweatshops" in developing and least developed countries (Hanley, 2002).

The construction industry, because it predominately involves manual labour, work is generally temporary and often performed by low-skilled, migrant workers (predominantly from accession states) (workers are "generally employed on a temporary basis according to the vicissitudes of the market") (Balch and Scott, 2011), warrants specific attention, as not only may local labour laws be undermined, but the situation gives rise to abuse of human rights (Allain et al., 2013).

The construction industry represents a substantial part of the UK economy; according to government statistics, construction contributes approximately £90 billion in economic output (6.7 per cent of value added), and provides 2.93 million jobs, equivalent to roughly 10 per cent of total UK employment.[7] For the EU as a whole, the sector employs some 11 million workers. The industry has "special characteristics" which present a high risk of labour exploitation: For instance, as identified by Cremers (2006), the "location of production is mobile", so for example employees cannot be located at a fixed workplace; the "production is of temporary duration", with labour contracts, if any, often of a fixed term nature, related to completing one project, building or constructing an item; and the "building process is characterised by a unique production chain, with principal contractors, suppliers, specialised subcontractors and all sorts of subcontractors and self-employed", including "bogus self-employed". In relation to this latter point, there exist deep concerns over the effectiveness of regulatory efforts designed to protect workers flowing from the reliance in building construction on contingent forms of labour through subcontracting, particularly labour only subcontracting where workers are recruited via labour market intermediaries (such as employment agencies). In particular, with evidence suggesting subcontracting chains to be increasingly long and complex, there are mounting issues with accountability and transparency.

In the UK, the structure of the construction industry, "[o]ver 50[%] of the … industry's 250,000 firms have just one employee, 80[%] have 1–3 employees, and more than 90[%] are micro firms employing fewer than 10 workers", (Allain et al., 2013, p. 21) makes the widespread use of subcontracting logical, for example subcontractors may be brought in as and when needed to carry out specific tasks (e.g. when specialist skills are required). In addition, the volatility of the industry, which is especially susceptible to market conditions, presents the need for a highly flexible workforce. Thus, "labour market intermediaries" (employment agencies) can play an important role, "finding, selecting, hiring, deploying, training, firing, or administering workers for [main contractors] more efficiently or effectively than they could achieve themselves" (Allain et al., 2013, p. 17). Indeed, in addition to this role, the use of agencies gives rise to potential cost savings, e.g. through hourly rates of pay, and avoidance of pension costs, national insurance and tax (plus other add-on costs associated with direct employment). Also, in avoiding the status of direct "employer", i.e. where intermediaries act as a substitute employer or where the worker is classified as "self-employed", responsibility and risk can be minimised. Due to the above commercial attractions, it is no surprise that the UK agency market, which has been left very much free from regulation, is the biggest in the EU.

The cost-cut pressures felt by contractors and sub-contractors, often operating on narrow margins, e.g. in bidding for work, particularly in the austere times we have experienced in recent years, can mean labour is looked upon for savings, e.g. there is evidence of labour priced at or just above the UK minimum wage. The corollary of this is that, in extreme cases, intermediaries, themselves under pressure to save on costs and make a profit, may be forced to "cut corners" (Allain *et al.*, 2013). For example, they may respond by extending the supply chain further, outsourcing the requirement to other intermediaries with lower labour costs who may in turn outsource the work. The risk of exploitation escalates as the supply chain grows in complexity, particularly if it extends beyond the knowledge of the main contractor. (Allain *et al.*, 2013.) Thus, exploitation in the form of "the use of employment finder fees, zero hours contracts, excessive productivity targets, compulsory overtime, work on demand, payment of less than minimum wages, and bogus deductions" is, unfortunately, not unfamiliar to the industry (Allain *et al.*, 2013, p. 17).

The issues highlighted in this section are as problematic for government buyers as they are for the private sector. For example, in 2008, the Union of Construction, Allied Trades and Technicians (UCATT) reported on its finding of "appalling systematic abuse of vulnerable migrant workers" on the redevelopment site of a PFI hospital (a public contract worth £600 million).[8] Here, a small sub-subcontractor proving dry lining services employed several Lithuanian workers, some of whom received as little as £8.80 for working a 40 hour week (approximately £0.22 per hour):

> [t]he workers were paid below agreed minimum rates for the site operated by [the] main contractor..., they did not receive overtime (some workers worked in excess of 70 hours and took home less than £100) and were charged excessive deductions for rent, tools and utility bills.[9]

3.3 The fight against modern slavery

The EU is adopting a wide-ranging strategy to address modern slavery, "human trafficking".[10] However, in terms of legislation, as the EU has already legislated quite extensively to promote worker protection, effectiveness and compliance is, in view of the existence and scale of the modern slavery problem, in some areas, clearly an issue. Here, the debate over the deficiencies of the Posted Workers Directive 96/71/EC is enlightening and pertinent when it comes to the construction industry.

The Posted Workers Directive arises out of the competitive advantage enjoyed by certain member states, typically new Eastern European members states, arising from disparities across the EU in labour standards. For some, the competitive advantage is "unfair", and can undermine local labour standards and risks resulting in a "race to the bottom" in labour protection; this is a problem, characterised as "social dumping", which, according to Commission rhetoric, must be tackled (EU Commission, 2014). In addressing "social dumping", a term which has not been properly defined, the risks of detrimental protectionism are patent, for example where, in accordance with trade theory, member states enjoy a comparative advantage from a low-cost workforce. In seeking to strike the adequate balance between market integration and worker protection, the Posted Workers Directive was eventually put in place. Interestingly, for some, EU social partners at least, the Directive can be seen to have some of its origins in attempts in the late 1980s to introduce into the public procurement rules an obligatory social clause, corresponding with ILO Convention No. 94, "Labour Clauses in Public Contracts", for public works contracts (several EU member states are signatories). It may be recalled that, although the UK ratified ILO Convention 94 in 1950, it was later, in 1982, denounced by the UK under the Thatcher Government, pursuing an agenda of trade liberalisation and deregulation.

The Posted Workers Directive 96/71/EC seeks to ensure a minimum level of protection for "a person who … [temporarily] … carries out his or her work in the territory of an EU Member State other than the state in which he or she normally works". A "posted worker" is to receive the basic employment rights, i.e. in relation to work and rest periods, holidays, rates of pay, the conditions for hiring out workers, health and safety, protection for pregnant women, equal treatment and non-discrimination, that apply in the "host" member state (the member state where the work is performed).

Recently, shortcomings of the Posted Workers Directive, in terms of implementation and effectiveness, have become clear, and, to remedy the situation, a supplementary directive on enforcement has been proposed by the Commission and negotiations on this are ongoing. The Directive's lack of impact, for which there are multiple explanations, is in part put down to enforcement difficulties which, in the context of construction, in many ways results from its "special characteristics" (elaborated above) where non-compliance with contractual and legal labour obligations can be difficult and costly to detect and punish.

A key battleground in the negotiations towards an enforcement directive for the Posted Workers Directive has been the issue of liability in subcontracting chains, e.g. joint and several liability (or indeed chain liability). For some, this would be an effective and dissuasive measure, necessary for the protection of workers and to ensure compliance of subcontractors with legal and contractual obligations. For the Commission, "[j]oint and several liability is a mechanism of self-regulation between private actors and a far less restrictive and more proportionate system than possible alternative systems such as pure state intervention by inspections and sanctions" (Proposal, 2012). The matter is, however, controversial, particularly due to the way in which, if mandated by the EU, this would impinge on national contract laws and freedom of contract. At present, research suggests that only eight member states (plus Norway) have systems of "joint and/or several liability for parties other than the direct employer with regard to social security contributions, taxes, and/or (minimum) wages" (EU Study, 2011). These appear distinct in both substantive and procedural terms, and the operation of such restrictions, albeit potentially justifiable and proportionate, is fraught with difficulty in view of the conflict with the freedom to provide services (Art. 56 TFEU).

The UK is currently legislating on modern slavery: the Modern Slavery Bill. There were hopes for the introduction of transparency measures for subcontracting and supply chains akin to those in California's Transparency in Supply Chains Act 2010. Here, since 2012, under this State measure, retailers and manufacturers with annual worldwide gross receipts of more than $100 million and which do business in California are required to disclose their efforts to eradicate slavery and human trafficking from their direct supply chains for tangible goods offered for sale. In general reports on the law are positive and there are prospects of similar regulation at US federal level; however, at the time of writing, the placing of similar proactive responsibilities on private businesses, will unlikely form part of the UK's modern slavery legislation (an excuse for the failure was impending EU activity on the matter) (Government response, 2013). Also, extension of the Gangmasters Licensing Authority, which is perceived to have been successful in its role operating a licensing scheme for businesses who provide workers to agriculture, horticulture, forestry, shellfish gathering and food and drink processing and packaging was, for cost reasons, not practicable in present conditions (Government response, 2013).

The role of public procurement as a means to tackle modern slavery has not been a prominent feature of discussions in either the EU or UK. This can be contrasted with the US. The US, reflecting the government's zero-tolerance policy regarding federal employees and contractor personnel engaging in any form of modern slavery (see the 2000 Trafficking in Persons Protection Act), has seen a series of attempts to use federal contracting as a key instrument in the fight against trafficking in persons, and bolster existing rules, which did not ignore the subject (e.g. the 2003 amendment of Trafficking Victims Protection Act). This began mainly with mandated training for contracting officers with responsibilities for oversight of federal contracts, and progressed under the Executive Order 13627, "Strengthening Protections Against Trafficking in Persons in Federal Contracts". According to the Executive Order, "[a]s the largest single purchaser of goods and services in the world, the United States Government bears a responsibility to ensure that taxpayer dollars do not contribute to trafficking in persons" (Executive Order, 2012). In September 2013, the Federal Acquisition Regulatory Council published proposals which put in place quite extensive requirements for contractors and subcontractors to act affirmatively to prevent human trafficking and forced labour. These rules are nearing implementation; however a review of the specific proposals is beyond the scope of this chapter.

It is too early to judge the impact of the US measures described above; however, provided enforcement is "consistently vigorous and incisive", in accordance with research, i.e. that in relation to US equal treatment policies, there is little reason to doubt the potential for tangible results (Morris, 1990).

4 EU public procurement law and modern slavery

EU public procurement law, the TFEU, Public Sector Directive 2004/18/EC and now Public Procurement Directive 2014/24/EU, provides scope for horizontal objectives, such those relating to labour standards; the primary mechanisms for the government to use public procurement to combat modern slavery will be considered here.

Importantly, the new Public Procurement Directive 2014/24/EU on the face of it, to an extent, elevates member state obligations in the fields of environmental, social and labour law to principles of procurement (Art.18(2)). The consequences of this are not yet clear. Other than this, the extent to which the new directive makes serious advancement to better enable social procurement is debatable.

The Public Procurement Directive 2014/24/EU introduces a new mandatory exclusion ground (article 57(1)(f)) for contractors convicted of people trafficking (as defined in Directive 2011/36/EU); however, because under article 45 Public Sector Directive 2004 a contractor with past of labour law violations, a "grave professional misconduct" (recital 34), could be excluded from a procurement process the above introduction may only be of limited practical importance (Priess, 2014). Indeed, as these provisions are primarily intended for the assessment of main contractors, and, as has been discussed, the risk of modern slavery mainly derives from subcontracting and supply chains the strengthened provisions, although an important symbol, lack relevance.

In the award of a contract, breach of labour law may allow for a tender which is "abnormally low". Because of this, article 55 Public Sector Directive enables a contracting authority to reject such tenders; however, before it may do so, a contracting authority must seek details of aspects of the tender to verify any rejection decision. Showing better appreciation of the reality of the situation, article 69 Public Procurement Directive 2014/24/EU explicitly recognises subcontracting chains as a source for contractors to make cost savings and provide cheaper bids. If the low price of a tender (i.e. in comparison to other tenders) cannot be sufficiently explained, an authority may assume it to be based on technically, economically or legally unsound assumptions or practices, and it may be rejected (see also recital 103). The rejection is mandatory for cases where an authority establishes that the low price results from non-compliance with applicable social, labour or environmental law (article 69(3)).

In relation to contract performance conditions, which are recognised as a common method for the pursuit of worker protection objectives in procurement, article 26 Public Sector Directive 2004/18/EC states that conditions governing the performance of a contract may, in particular, concern social and environmental considerations. As explained in recital 33, contract performance conditions are permitted provided they are not directly or indirectly discriminatory, for which obligations on core labour standards would not be problematic, and are indicated in the contract notice/contract documents (see also recital 104 Public Procurement Directive). The Public Procurement Directive leaves article 26 (now article 70) very much untouched. However, although overlooked in the past, the significance of contract administration and enforcement, for which the success of contract compliance practices appears to hinge, does appear to be moving more into the foreground at EU and member state level.

5 The subcontracting chain: transparency and accountability

5.1 Background

The Public Sector Directive 2004 very much steered clear of regulation post-award, and there were minimal rules on subcontracting. The directive simply clarifies that authorities are able to request, or may be required by member states to request, for tenders to indicate any share of the contract which was intended to be subcontracted and proposed contractors (article 25). The Commission's own research (EU Commission, 2011), the accuracy of which is seriously doubted, indicated subcontracting to be minimal (7–9 per cent of all contracts awarded between 2006 and 2009 where subcontracting was recorded); so, understandably, early proposals to reform the directive proffered no major changes in this respect. The legislative process, and in particular input from the social partners and the EU parliament, however, resulted in the provision on subcontracting, article 71 of the Public Procurement Directive 2014/24/EU, burgeoning in detail.

The negotiations towards the modernisation of EU public procurement, which resulted in Public Procurement Directive 2014/24/EU, overlapped with continued efforts to introduce an enforcement directive to accompany the Posted Workers Directive (see section 3 above). Here, not surprisingly in view of the discussion in section 3 above, subcontracting has been a prominent feature of the talks, and, similar arguments, e.g. over subcontractor liability, have been deployed in both sets of negotiations.

The Public Procurement Directive 2014/24/EU explicitly recognises that the primary purpose behind the new rules relates to the importance of subcontractor observance of environmental, social and labour obligations (recital 105). Thus, complementing the clarification over and enhanced scope for the pursuit of such obligations under Public Procurement Directive 2014/24/EU, the focus may be shifting towards the effectiveness of authority attempts to pursue environment, social and labour obligations. Article 71 Public Procurement Directive 2014/24/EU commences by obliging member states to ensure subcontractor compliance with environmental, social and labour obligations through appropriate action (e.g. monitoring and enforcement) by competent national authorities (e.g. labour inspection agencies (see article 71(1) and recital 105). This provision, on its own, clearly will not have an appraisable impact on practice; however, it is just the starting point, and article 71, in addition to maintaining the wording previously found in article 25 Public Sector Directive 2004 (now article 71(2)), goes on to provide further stipulations in relation to subcontractor transparency.

5.2 Transparency

Article 71 Public Procurement Directive 2014/24/EU seeks to engender main contractor and subcontractor compliance with environmental, social and labour obligations through information requirements. According to recital 105, "it is ...

necessary to ensure some transparency in the subcontracting chain" in order to give:

> authorities information on who is present at building sites on which works are being performed for them, or on which undertakings are providing services in or at buildings, infrastructures or areas, such as town halls, municipal schools, sports facilities, ports or motorways, for which the contracting authorities are responsible or over which they have a direct oversight.

Thus, under article 71(5) Public Procurement Directive 2014/24/EU, apparently targeting construction works and services, the following transparency requirement is put in place:

> [i]n the case of works contracts and in respect of services to be provided at a facility under the direct oversight of the contracting authority, after the award of the contract and at the latest when the performance of the contract commences, the contracting authority shall require the main contractor to indicate to the contracting authority the name, contact details and legal representatives of its subcontractors, involved in such works or services, in so far as known at this point in time.

It is presumably hoped that greater transparency will encourage greater care in subcontractor selection, and facilitate more effective contract management; in some ways, the provision imposes what in most cases would seem to correspond with good practice on the part of authorities and main contractors in administering construction projects.

Commission statistics, which reveal that subcontracting was recorded in only 7–9 per cent of all contracts awarded between 2006 and 2009, do not appear reliable, raising doubts over the importance attached to subcontracting issues by contracting authorities across Europe. If properly recorded henceforth, which article 71 should better encourage, the data on subcontractors flowing from article 71(5), and which must be reported to the Commission under article 84 (e.g. where possible, authorities should identify the main contractor's subcontractor/s), could itself be enlightening in terms of the nationality of subcontractors and differences in practice across member states.

For practical purposes, the article 71 information requirements do not kick in pre-award; at this stage, based on modern practice, the main contractor cannot be expected to have subcontracting arrangements in place. The provisions should be adhered to post award, prior to performance of the contract, and are then ongoing (relevant if an authority seeks to apply exclusion grounds to subcontractors, see below). Article 71(5) places a continuing notification obligation on the main contractor with respect to any changes to subcontractor information during the course of the contract as well as information of any new subcontractors which are subsequently involved in the works or services. The recitals stress that the obligation to deliver the required information rests with the main supplier (recital 105), and the second paragraph of Art.71(5) clarifies that member states, in transposing the rules, can choose to make the main contractor responsible for delivery of the information – although quite how this might work effectively in practice remains to be seen.

A particular feature potentially negating any meaningful impact, i.e. in view of the discussion in section 3 above, is that article 71(5) applies only to subcontractors to the main contractor, not for example sub-subcontractors. The extension of the requirements to subcontractors of the main contractor's subcontractors or further down the subcontracting chain is however expressed as optional for member states and individual contracting authorities (article 71(5)(b)). Thus, whether or not the worker protection concerns identified in section 3 are addressed completely depends on member states' individual transposing laws and policies and individual authorities.

5.3 Supply chains

Despite the new transparency provisions, article 71 shies away from more contentious obligations. For example, the article 71(5) requirements are mandatory for "works contracts and in respect of services to be provided at a facility under the direct oversight of the contracting authority", but only optional for other contracts, e.g. supply contracts (article 71(5)(a)). Again, member state transposition and the practical application of article 71 will be insightful, as there are signs of increasing desire for enhanced transparency of domestic and global supply chains across the EU (Arrowsmith and Maund, 2009, p. 436).

5.4 Exclusion

Article 71(6)(b) sets out the way in which exclusion grounds (article 57) are to be applied to subcontractors. The provision confirms "authorities may … verify or may be required by member states to verify whether there are grounds for exclusion of subcontractors". In accordance with article 71(5), if excluding subcontractors, this occurs post award of the contract, so not at the same time as the assessment for the main contractor. The fact the assessment necessarily occurs later on, perhaps when works and services are underway, is a limitation, as the complications and delays associated with exclusion at this stage make the option unattractive.

If the exclusion grounds are applied to subcontractors, and a subcontractor falls foul of a compulsory ground (see above), the main contractor will be required to replace the subcontractor. Thus, although regarded by some as lacking practical importance and being potentially quite onerous for authorities, the impact of new mandatory exclusion grounds, such as article 57(1)(f) Public Procurement Directive 2014/24/EU for contractors convicted of people trafficking, has the potential to be felt through the application of exclusion grounds to subcontractors (and sub-subcontractors). If the non-compulsory grounds for exclusion apply, according to article 71(6)(b), the authority has a discretion over whether or not to replace the subcontractor (unless otherwise required by a member state). The application of the exclusion grounds to subcontractors should necessitate that, other than timing of the assessment, the rules are applied in the same way as they would be to the main contractor; thus, for instance, the rules must be applied in a proportionate manner (article 57(6)); so there is scope for sub-contractor "self-cleaning".

5.5 *Joint and several liability, and chain liability*

Interestingly, the issue of joint and several liability over the protection of workers, which has been an important battleground in the debate over an enforcement directive to the Posted Workers Directive, infiltrated the negotiations towards the Public Procurement Directive 2014/24/EU. On numerous occasions, the European Parliament has called for the Commission to introduce legislation on joint and several liability, in particular for long subcontracting chains, and, arguably, public contracts could be a starting point for the introduction of such an EU-wide concept (legislation on the procurement process for public contracts is, however, probably not a suitable place for such rules). In the end, as with the posted workers enforcement directive, joint and several liability was not taken forward; article 71 simply confirms that:

> [w]here the national law of a Member State provides for a mechanism of joint liability between subcontractors and the main contractor, the Member State concerned shall ensure that the relevant rules are applied in compliance with the conditions set out in Article 18(2) (i.e. to ensure that in the performance of public contracts economic operators comply with applicable obligations in the fields of environmental, social and labour law).

Likewise, other aggressive suggestions, e.g. limitations on the size of subcontract chains, were not taken forward. Nevertheless, depending upon the way in which joint subcontractor liability develops in practice in public procurement, the foundations could be put in place for expanded regulation.

6 Concluding remarks

The public procurement directives have paid little attention to subcontractor issues before; seemingly, with the regulatory focus being on market integration, this is because subcontracts are, in line with the terms and conditions of the public contract, negotiated and awarded on a commercial basis generally between profit-maximising undertakings; as such, from a procurement law perspective, these agreements do not pose a threat to the internal market. These contracts do however, as is increasingly recognised, in some circumstances, give rise to concerns when horizontal objectives are legitimately sought using public procurement. The Public Procurement Directive 2014/24/EU, in confronting the issue of transparency in subcontracting chains, a problem area with which member states (and the EU) may be reluctant to intervene in a more head on way, seeks to bolster the effectiveness of labour protection regulation via public procurement through better contract administration and enforcement. In particular, depending upon member state transposition, article 71 may extend the application of exclusion grounds, giving them much greater practical relevance.

Public Procurement Directive 2014/24/EU, in addressing subcontractor issues, does not do so in a way that would be harmful to the internal market; for example, the imposition of limits on the length of subcontracting chains (a maximum chain of three subcontracts was proposed at one point), was flatly rejected in negotiations over the text of article 71. There may be some dissatisfaction, e.g. amongst the Social Partners (EUTC) over the diluted strength of much of article 71, i.e. its predominately non-mandatory, clarificatory (rather than prescriptive) nature. However, limits on the burden for the private sector and flexibility may be necessary; individual procurement officers, provided they are equipped with the necessary skills, judgment and resources, may be best placed to identify high risk procurements where tight control of subcontracting/ supply chains is appropriate. In this respect, however, the new rules operate as merely guidance, and thus, the necessity of the addition of these provisions to already lengthy and complex public procurement legislation can be questioned.

In the EU, with governments keen to take and wanting to be seen to take action, and not be associated with, abhorrent crimes such as modern slavery, the public procurement process will increasingly come under focus. An appreciation of the crime, in the construction sector, suggests problems mainly flow from limited transparency and accountability linked to labour-only subcontracting, which inhibit effective contract administration and enforcement. For contracting authorities, in high risk situations, which must be assessed on a case by case practice, contractual means to require enhanced transparency (e.g. open book accounting) and even accountability (e.g. joint liability) may be necessary (e.g. where general legislative action is not feasible) and, for many, represent good practice, e.g. facilitating value for money (e.g. there may be reduced risk of corruption). Article 71, a fairly innocuous provision because of the cautious manner with which it is mostly phrased, in which member states in transposing the directive, and contracting authorities procuring under the directive, are given the choice over how rigorous transparency rules for subcontractors are to be, may be taken to represent endorsement and, if article 71 is read together with recital 105 and article 18(2), encouragement of such practices, and it is now for member states and individual authorities, where appropriate, to push for subcontracting and supply chains transparency (equipping individual procurement officers with specific knowledge, skills and resources to act will be an important element).

Notes

1 See www.parliament.uk/business/committees/committees-a-z/joint-select/draft-modern-slavery-bill/.

2 See for example A new strategy for the Single Market: At the service of Europe's economy and society, Report to the President of the European Commission, José Manuel Barroso by Mario Monti (9 May 2010).
3 See also *Siliadin* v. *France* (73316/01) (2006) 43 E.H.R.R. 16 (ECHR) (2005); and *CN and V* v. *France* (App. No. 67724/09), judgment of 11 October 2012.
4 See *ILO Global Estimate of Forced Labour*, (ILO, 2012).
5 See for example Ruwanpura and Rai (2004). Forced labour: Definition, indicators and measurement. *Forced Labor*, 1. The Work Free Foundation estimate 29.8 million people to be in slavery.
6 See *Siliadin* v. *France* (73316/01) (2006) 43 E.H.R.R. 16 (ECHR) (2005); *Rantsev* v. *Cyprus and Russia* (2010) 51 E.H.R.R. 1); *O* v. *Commissioner of Police of the Metropolis* [2011] U.K.H.R.R. 767. See also *Key case-law issues: prohibition of slavery and forced labour – article 4 of the Convention* (Council or Europe/European Court of Human Rights, 2012) and *Forced labour in the UK* (JRF, 2013).
7 See   www.statistics.gov.uk/hub/business-energy/production-industries/building-and-construction/index.html.
8 See   www.ucatt.org.uk/ucatt-uncovers-appalling-systematic-abuse-vulnerable-workers-pfi-hospital.
9 www.ucatt.org.uk/ucatt-uncovers-appalling-systematic-abuse-vulnerable-workers-pfi-hospital.
10 Commission, Human trafficking in the EU. See also http://ec.europa.eu/dgs/home-affairs/what-we-do/policies/organized-crime-and-human-trafficking/trafficking-in-human-beings/index_en.htm.

References

Allain, J., Crane, A., LeBaron, G. and Behbahani, L. (2013): *Forced labour's business models and supply chains.* (JRF, 2013) www.jrf.org.uk/publications/forced-labour-business-models-supply.
Arrowsmith, S. (1995): Public Procurement as an Instrument of Policy and the Impact of Market Liberalisation. *Law Quarterly Review.* 235, 242.
Arrowsmith, S. (2012): "The Purpose of the EU Procurement Directives: Ends, Means and the Implications for National Regulatory Space for Commercial and Horizontal Policies", Chapter 1 in Barnard, Gehring and Solanke (eds), *The Cambridge Yearbook of European Legal Studies: Volume 14, 2011–2012* (Oxford: Hart, 2012).
Arrowsmith, S., and Kunzlik, P. (eds). (2009): *Social and environmental policies in EC procurement law: new directives and new directions.* Cambridge University Press.
Arrowsmith S., and Maund C. (2009): "CSR in the utilities sector and the implications of EC procurement policy: a framework for debate" in Arrowsmith, S. and Kunzlik, P. (eds). (2009). *Social and environmental policies in EC procurement law: new directives and new directions.* Cambridge University Press.
Balch, A., and Scott, S. (2011): "Labour Market Flexibility and Worker Security in an Age of Migration" in Sciortino, G. and Bommes, M. (eds) *Foggy Social Structures: Irregular Migration, European Labour Markets and the Welfare State.* Amsterdam University Press, 143–168.
Cremers, J. (2006): Free movement of services and equal treatment of workers: the case of construction. *Transfer: European Review of Labour and Research*, 12(2), 167–181.
Caranta, R., and Trybus, M. (eds). (2010): *The law of green and social procurement in Europe.* DJØF Publishing.

Daintith, T. Regulation by Contract: The New Prerogative' (1979). *Current Legal Problems*, *32*, 41. discussed in Davies, A. C. (2008). *The public law of government contracts*. Oxford University Press.

EU Commission (2011): *EU public procurement legislation: delivering results: summary of evaluation report.* http://ec.europa.eu/internal_market/publicprocurement/docs/modernising_rules/executive-summary_en.pdf.

EU Commission (2014): Labour law and working conditions – Social Europe guide – Volume 6 (04/03/2014) Catalog N.: KE-BC-13–002-EN-C.

EU Study (2011): *Study on the protection of workers' rights in subcontracting processes in the European Union* (Project DG EMPL/B2 – VC/2011/0015) file:///C:/Users/ttatrai/Downloads/Subcontracting_Final%20Study_FINAL.pdf.

EUTC: EU public procurement framework – ETUC position (March 2012) www.etuc.org/documents/eu-public-procurement-framework-%E2%80%93-etuc-position.

Executive Order – Strengthening Protections Against Trafficking In Persons In Federal Contracts (September 25, 2012) www.whitehouse.gov/the-press-office/2012/09/25/executive-order-strengthening-protections-against-trafficking-persons-fe.

Government response (2013): The government response to the report from the joint committee on the4 draft modern slavery bill session 2013–14 HL PAPER 166/HC 1019: Draft Modern Slavery Bill. www.gov.uk/government/uploads/system/uploads/attachment_data/file/318771/CM8889DraftModernSlaveryBill.pdf.

Hanley, C. (2002): Avoiding the issue: the Commission and human rights conditionality in public procurement. *European Law Review*, 6, 714–735.

McCrudden, C. (2007): *Buying social justice: Equality, government procurement, and legal change*. Oxford University Press.

Morris, P. E. (1990): Legal Regulation of Contract Complience: An Anglo-American Comparison. *Anglo-American Law Review*, 19, 87.

Portugal, A. P. A. V., Guichon, A., and Van den Anker, C. (2006): Trafficking for Forced Labour in Europe.

Priess H. J. (2014): The rules on exclusion and self-cleaning under the 2014 Public Procurement Directive. *Public Procurement Law Review* 112.

Proposal (2012): Proposal for a Directive of the European Parliament and of the Council on the enforcement of Directive 96/71/EC concerning the posting of workers in the framework of the provision of services /*COM/2012/0131 final – 2012/0061 (COD)*/ http://eur-lex.europa.eu/legal-content/EN/TXT/?uri=CELEX:52012PC0131.

Ruwanpura, K. N., and Rai, P. (2004): Forced labour: Definition, indicators and measurement. *Forced Labor*, 1.

Skrivankova, K. (2010): Between decent work and forced labour: examining the continuum of exploitation. *York: Joseph Rowntree Foundation*.

UCATT (2011): *The hidden workforce building Britain* (University of Manchester, UCATT and Community Links, 2011), www.community-links.org/linksuk/wp-content/PDF/UCATT.pdf.

3 Addressing social considerations in PP

Best practices for fighting social dumping in Slovenia

Tomaž Vesel

1 Introduction

Economic crisis has a significant impact on Slovenia. Like many European countries, Slovenia has also found itself at a turning point, when it is required, aiming at achieving balanced public finances, to provide for the reduction of public debt while at the same time creating favourable conditions for the recovery of the economy. However, focusing exclusively on the reduction of public debt in turn means less investment, i.e. less new public investments, which are essential for economic growth. At any given time, responsible public spending and the related efficient conduct of public procurement procedures are therefore crucial for public finances. This means that the state in its consumption should act with prudence and provide that it will purchase in the market goods, services and works at the best price, whereby the best value should not mean the lowest price, but the most economically advantageous tender. Notwithstanding the selected criterion, the price should cover all the actual costs (both material costs and labour costs), because otherwise the state in the short term may be recording positive effects since it will spend less than planned due to low prices of services and goods and will therefore be able to use the saved funds for the purchase of new goods, services and works, yet in the long term, such financial policy does not lead in the direction of the objectives set, i.e. the reduction of public debt and the recovery of the economy.

With the policy of reducing prices in the public sector, major suppliers who are doing well in the private sector may namely supersede small and medium-sized enterprises, as they can substitute the difference in the basic tender price, which does not necessarily cover all the material costs and labour costs, by raising prices elsewhere, for example, in the private at the expense of their reputation. Should this be permitted, there may be situations where in a particular branch, due to the collapse of small and medium-sized enterprises, there may be no adequate competition left, and the tenderer who initially offered a low price significantly increases the price in the renewed public procurement procedure after the expiry of the contract. On the other hand, we have been facing in practice the situations where the successful tenderer is not able to substitute the difference in price respectively the excess of actual costs in time, which presents a problem especially in cases of concluded long-term contracts. Thus, the success-ful tenderer goes bankrupt already during the execution of the contract.[1] In such instances, the state not only loses the contractor who would have carried out services or works at a low price and completed the agreed project, but also incurs incidental expenses as it is forced to restart the public procurement procedure in order to complete the project as planned (EU Commission, 2011).[2]

If such conduct is allowed in the market, a state cannot reduce in the long term assets used for the provision of certain goods and thus to some extent also public debt, because on the one hand due to the collapse of companies there are increasing costs for social transfers and, on the other hand, due to the increased number of unemployed there comes a reduction in consumption and hence in the demand for goods, which is essential for creating an appropriate environment for the recovery of the economy. Therefore, the awareness has been recently intensi-fied in the field of public procurement that in the use of public funds a positive impact on the development of the society is no longer based solely on the price but it is necessary to take into account other aspects, which provide the basis for the Government to implement appropriate policies. It may be difficult for the state to influence the way companies operate in their territories, yet it may apply deliberate policies and appropriate measures to ensure that companies that are involved in certain territorial and social environment will not only pursue profit maximisation, but will operate at a higher level of awareness of the impact they have on the environment by establishing socially responsible management. The constitutional principle of free economic initiative may provide for tenderers their entrepreneurial freedom, but at the same time requires from the state to monitor market games and ensure a balance between entrepreneurial freedom and social principles.[3]

2 Social dumping

Abnormally low price of services is often the result of social dumping. In service industries such as cleaning, public transport, security services, labour costs are the most important cost factor and they play a major role in determining the price for the offer in the tender process. However, the criterion of the lowest price is normally applied, which is why tenderers when formulating the tender price try to create savings based on low labour costs – forms of employment, wages and working conditions. It is necessary to point out that this is not only the matter of complying with the rules on the minimum wage, prescribed by law in the Republic of Slovenia,[4] but rather of the actual working conditions such as working time, the amount of leave and the possibility of using it. Workers are not ensured such rights within the legal framework and the tenderers as entre-preneurs try to achieve in this way the lowest costs possible and consequently employ the minimum number of workers for the provision of services. It is diffi-cult to predict such conduct of tenderers beforehand or prevent it by excluding their tenders from the public procurement procedure, since an average contract-ing authority normally does not have adequate expertise to be able to evaluate when an abnormally low tender may be related to social dumping. This is particularly true in cases where the prices of received tenders are of the similar amount, even though in the private sector market companies offer the same services at significantly higher prices. On the other hand, the contracting authority in identifying such practices of tenderers is dealing with their entrepreneurial right of free pricing. It should be noted that a low price by itself does not necessarily mean that a tenderer does not intend to comply with labour and social legislation, since it may be able to substitute the difference in the price with another transaction carried out at a significantly higher price.

Even greater difficulties in detecting such practices are observed in instances where tenderers try to cover the misuse of rights of workers by including subcontractors. They do this, for example, by transferring the implementation of transactions to their subsidiaries, which are established under the legal order providing less rights for workers, or pointing to their capacities, or by entrusting their work to workers as subcontractors or sole proprietors, who are forced into their self-employment. As regards the latter, in reviewing and evaluating tenders, the most advantageous tenderer may in no case be accused of violation of labour legislation, as there are no longer workers as natural persons involved but rather entrepreneurs who operate in the market as independent economic operators, who are not obliged to comply with the rules on minimum wage and the labour legislation in relation to tenderers they cooperate with (Jorens *et al.*, 2011).[5] According to Slovenian legislation, it is not necessary for subcontractors to demonstrate their compliance with the conditions for the determination of basic, technical and human skills, whereby the exceptions are only a statutory requirement that they must have settled their outstanding obligations relating to the payment of social security contributions or payment of taxes and an explicit requirement by the contracting authority that tenderers are obliged to indicate their technical or professional staff.[6] In this second instance namely, the contracting authority by concluding a contract with the most advantageous tenderer does not enter into a contractual relationship with a subcontractor, since according to the Slovenian legislation[7] it is the main contractor who is responsible to the contracting authority for the work of its subcontractors, i.e. the most advantageous tenderer who is normally required to submit to the contracting authority a performance bank guarantee before the execution of works.

3 How to prevent social dumping?

In the continuation, there are options considered of how to prevent or disable social dumping in public procurement procedures, as well as several cases from the Slovenian practice indicated.

3.1 Legislation in general

In the Slovenian legislation, the violation of labour and social legislation is not considered an immediate reason for the exclusion of a particular tender in the evaluation and pre-selection phase of the public procurement procedure. This is not provided for in Directives 2004/18/EC[8] and 2004/17/EC[9] either. Both Directives only include the provision on the compliance with labour legislation, i.e. Article 27 of 2004/18/EC[10] (and Article 39 of 2004/17/EC), which has been transposed in Article 40 of ZJN-2. As regards the exclusion, there exists an exhaustive list of cases in which the personal situation of the supplier may lead to its exclusion. According to Article 45 (2 f) of the Directive 2004/18/EC, it is possible to exclude suppliers but only when they have not fulfilled obligations relating to the payment of taxes in accordance with the legal provisions of the country in which he is established or with those of the country of the contracting authority. Another exhaustive list of criteria is related to the economic, financial or technical capacity of tenderers, which is used for selection purposes. In assessing economic and financial standing, social considerations regarding labour law provisions cannot be included, while the assessment of technical capacity leaves some room for social considerations by using specific know-how in the social field as a criterion (Article 48(5) of the Directive 2004/18/EC).

3.2 Institute of abnormally low tender

According to the Slovenian and European legislation, the possibility of the exclusion due to the violation of labour and social legislation is represented by the institute of abnormally low tender, under which a contracting authority, in the event that it establishes an abnormally low tender and wants to exclude it based on Article 49 of ZJN-2,[11] should request in writing from the relevant tenderer a detailed information and justification of those elements of the tender which it considers essential for the fulfilment of the contract respectively which affect the ranking of tenders. These elements may also relate to the compliance with the regulations relating to employment protection and working conditions in force at the place where the work, service or supply is to be performed. The contracting authority must verify those constituent elements by consulting the tenderer, taking account of the evidence supplied. Where the contracting authority establishes that a tender is abnormally low, the tender can be rejected. The a forementioned institute is deemed only an indirect solution to the problem of social dumping, since a contracting authority must detect an abnormally low price, which in practice, however, as explained above, is difficult and there are very few instances where the most advantageous tender was actually excluded due to the violation of labour legislation. Moreover, there exists a high probability that the excluded tenderer will appeal against the decision of the contracting authority. It is not in the interest of the contracting authority that the procedure to award a public contract be delayed due to the lodged review claim or even repealed due to the abnormally low price of the sole complete most advantageous tender on account of the violation of the labour legislation. The contracting authority is namely incurred unnecessary costs, not just because of the renewal of the procedure but also because of the fact that in the event of the expiry of the contract it must temporarily award a public contract for an interim period (EU Evaluation Report, 2011).[12]

On the other hand, an abnormally low offer in itself does not indicate the violation of labour legislation. In its case No 018–29/2010 Higher Court in Ljubljana, District Court in Ljubljana and Health Insurance Institute of Slovenia, where the contracting authority excluded from the public procurement procedure the applicant's tender because the tender price failed to include all the costs related to the female workers performing the cleaning service, the National Review Commission decided that it could not identify any violation of labour regulations. Since the contracting authority in its contract notice did not require from the provider of the service to shift to the contracting authority all the labour costs incurred during the execution of the public contract, the National Review Commission assessed that the contracting authority did not have an adequate basis to verify whether the applicant with its tender price would comply with the minimum legal requirements regarding wages and holiday pay for the work performed by female workers. From the perspective of the contracting authority, the contracting authority namely pays for the ordered service and not necessarily for all the work of workers required to carry out the service. Therefore, the decision of tenderers about what share of the cost of workers who will be carrying out the cleaning service at the contracting authority will be shifted to the contracting authority is entirely dependent on their business policy and is exclusively within their jurisdiction. Based on the foregoing, the National Review Commission concluded that the contracting authority solely on the basis of the calculation of the tender price envisaged by the applicant for the execution of the contract was not entitled to identify the potential violation of the labour legislation and thereby the irregularity of the applicant's tender (point 19 of paragraph 1 of Article 2 of ZJN-2). It should therefore not have excluded this tender from the procedure to award a public contract. Owing to this decision, the institute of abnormally low tender as the reason for excluding the tender on account of any violation of the labour legislation and thereby social dumping has lost its relevance.

3.3 Contract performance clauses

The European Commission has in "A Guide to Taking Account of Social Considerations in Public Procurement"[13] published an opinion that many social considerations, depending on their nature, can be included only at certain stages of the procurement procedure. For example, social considerations regarding labour conditions are generally more appropriate to be included in the contract performance clauses, as in general they do not qualify as technical specifications or selection criteria, within the meaning of the Procurement Directives. On the other hand, it is generally more appropriate to include accessibility considerations in the technical specifications. Regarding the rules governing contract performance clauses, the European Commission determines that contract performance clauses are obligations which must be accepted by the successful tenderer and which relate to the performance of the contract. It is therefore sufficient, in principle, for tenderers to undertake, when submitting their tenders, to meet such conditions if the contract is awarded to them. Tenders from tenderers who have not accepted any such conditions would not comply with the contract documents and could not therefore be accepted. However, the conditions of contract need not be met at the time of submitting the tender but at the time of concluding the contract with the successful tenderer.

Included under contract performance clauses are also pay clauses, governed by Convention No 94 and Recommendation No 84 ILO.[14] The rationale behind the adoption of Convention No 94 and Recommendation No 84 lies in the desire to prevent public authorities from entering into contracts involving the employment of workers at conditions below an acceptable level of social protection, and moreover, to encourage public authorities to raise the bar and act as model employers. So the aim of the Convention is to remove wages and working conditions from the price competition necessarily involved in public tendering. Therefore, the Convention requires tenderers to be informed in advance, by means of standard labour clauses included in tender documents, that, if selected, they would have to observe in the performance of the contract wages and other labour conditions not less favourable than the highest minimum standards established locally by law, arbitration or collective bargaining. Tenderers should prepare their offers accordingly. The core requirement of the Convention is the insertion of labour clauses covering wages, hours of work and other working conditions in all public contracts to which it applies (Labour Clauses Guide, 2008). The merit of this Convention also lies in the fact that it applies to subcontractors, yet it has not yet been ratified in the Republic of Slovenia and it is therefore not binding on the contracting authorities to include such clauses in public contracts.

In practice, however, only the inclusion of labour clauses in the contract does not guarantee the prevention of social dumping in public procurement procedures, since according to the judgment of the European Court of Justice contract performance clauses should neither play a role in determining which tenderer gets the contract nor be disguised technical specifications, award criteria or selection criteria, [however] it is permissible to set additional conditions of contract, which are separate from the specifications, selection criteria and award criteria.[15]

Given that the clauses apply only to the implementation phase, the contracting authority may take action only in the implementation phase, while it will not be possible to preliminary exclude the tender which is the most advantageous on account of non-compliance with the social and labour legislation. In practice, tenderers normally demonstrate that they meet the relevant tender conditions and requirements regarding the compliance with the social and labour legislation by signing a declaration that they accept all the terms and conditions of the contracting authority. The contracting authority does not verify prior to the awarding of a contract whether the selected tenderer actually ensures its workers legitimate working conditions. As laid down in Convention No 94, national authorities must provide for adequate sanctions, such as the withholding of contracts when contractors fail to comply with the terms of the labour clauses.

Second, they must take measures, such as the withholding of payments due under the contract, so that the workers concerned can receive the wages to which they are entitled.

However, despite these potential sanctions, the contracting authorities in practice are not willing to terminate or annul the contract, particularly in cases where they are satisfied with its execution, because otherwise they are faced with examining and proving violations of the labour legislation in the provision of services, where their role is only that of a buyer or purchaser of services. Due to the early termination of the contract, they are incurred additional unforeseen costs resulting from the implementation of a new procurement procedure, while in the meantime, pending the re-awarding of the contract, they have to ensure alternative services for their regular operation. All these circumstances certainly discourage contracting authorities from taking serious action based on such contractual clauses. In addition, public contracting authorities compared to other buyers or purchasers of services in the private sector are undoubtedly at a disadvantage, because they are entrusted also the responsibility and burden of legitimate operations of tenderers as other contractual parties, thereby opening up the controversy of the efficiency of public procurement. It would therefore be sensible to move the verification of possible violations of the labour legislation to the evaluation phase, i.e. prior to the selection of a tenderer and awarding of the contract, which has been considered also in the new Directive 2014/24/EU.[16]

3.4 De Lege Ferenda legislation

It is provided for in point 40 of preamble of the new Directive 2014/24/EU:

> Control of the observance of the environmental, social and labour law provisions should be performed at the relevant stages of the procurement procedure, when applying the general principles governing the choice of participants and the award of contracts, when applying the exclusion criteria and when applying the provisions concerning abnormally low tenders.

As regards the abnormally low tender, it is laid down in point 103 of the preamble:

> Rejection should be mandatory in cases where the contracting authority has established that the abnormally low price or costs proposed results from non-compliance with mandatory Union law or national law compatible with it in the fields of social, labour or environmental law or international labour law provisions.

Based on the above, there exists a possibility of excluding a tender in the event of the established violation of the labour and social legislation, as governed by point a) of paragraph 4 of Article 57 of Directive 2014/24/EU, which lays down that contracting authorities may exclude or may be required by Member States to exclude from participation in a procurement procedure any economic operator in any of the following situations: (a) where the contracting authority can demonstrate by any appropriate means a violation of applicable obligations referred to in Article 18(2).[17] The same applies to subcontractors who must now also comply with the labour legislation.[18]

Such an arrangement should certainly be favoured yet the question remains how contracting authorities are to verify respectively identify any violation of the social and labour legislation to provide the basis for the exclusion of a particular tender from a public procurement procedure. If the verification will be done based only on the submission of a statement in which tenderers declare their compliance with the social and labour legislation, it will not be possible to prevent social dumping in public procurement procedures respectively exclude tenders from the procedure. The continuation therefore sees the presentation of an example of good practice of detecting such practices of tenderers in setting prices, without prejudice to their right to entrepreneurial freedom.

3.5 Example of good practice – University Medical Centre Maribor

An example of good practice on how to avoid cases of potential social dumping in advance is the University Medical Centre Maribor, where the contracting authority in its procedure to award a contract for the "cleaning of rooms" initially verified the minimum compliance with the labour legislation based on the system of structural prices. The system of structural prices means that tenderers are to specify in their tenders in advance all the types of costs covered by the total tender price.

In the procedure to award a contract for the "cleaning of rooms", the tenderers had to first indicate in the table which was an obligatory pro-forma annex (Table 3.1), data on the total number of employed workers they intended to include in the performance of the cleaning service. To this end, the contracting authority in the contract notice included the requirement that there had to be at least 121 workers present daily in the performance of work (80 workers in the morning shift, 40 workers in the afternoon shift and one worker in the night shift), whereby each shift lasted eight hours. The contractor was left to decide the number of hours an individual worker was present in each shift (for example, one worker performs his/her eight-hour duty in a single shift, two workers four hours per shift, etc.), but had to ensure the total presence of workers of 29,524 hours per month (121 employees $\times$ 8 hours $\times$ 30.5 days per month = 29,524 hours per month). Considering the fact that the tenderers were able to apply different methods for allocating

Table 3.1 Required number of workers present on the day

MON.	TUE.	WED.	THU.	FRI.	SAT.	SUN.	TOTAL NUMBER OF EMPLOYED WORKERS FOR THE PROVISION OF 29,524 H/MONTH

working hours between their workers, there came to differences in the number of workers indicated in their tenders.

It is necessary to emphasise that the contract notice included the requirement that all the workers be employed respectively in the employment relationship, which, however, does not necessarily seem disputable or illegal, even though the National Review Commission decided otherwise.[19] The contracting authority did not specify where or to what extent (full time or part time) the workers had to be employed. Moreover, it did not require from tenderers to employ workers in advance for the performance of the service. The workers could be employed with the tenderer as the main contractor, with the subcontractor, or could be secondees. It was only required that the workers due to the sensitive nature of the work be employed, tidy, vaccinated against hepatitis B, equipped with the means for personal protection, as provided for in the environmental protection regulations, underwent their medical examination and passed their safety at work and fire safety examinations, whereby the contracting authority had to be informed about potential new employments.

In this way, the contracting authority avoided in advance the issue of self-employed workers and the related abuses of the labour legislation, as well as the issue of employment of workers at subsidiaries established in another state due to lower labour costs and the related reference to the capacity of other operators.[20] Due to this requirement of the contracting authority, no tenderer was in a privileged position, which makes the decision of the Commission all the more interesting. It seems that with the requirement, the contracting authority did not interfere with the entrepreneurial freedom of tenderers but rather ensured that in the preparation of their tender prices all the tenderers derived from the same starting points. Based on the total number of employed workers, the contracting authority verified whether a certain tenderer complied with the labour legislation and would be able to carry out the cleaning service. In the event that the number of envisaged workers was not sufficient to carry out the planned hours of cleaning, the contracting authority had the possibility to exclude such tender preliminarily. The contracting authority naturally published in advance its calculation of the minimum quota of required employed workers to ensure their minimum presence required for the desired level of service.[21]

It should be noted that the determination of the total number of workers required by the contracting authority is deemed essential for the contracting authority to be able to easily verify whether a particular tenderer considered in the total tender price minimum statutory labour costs per worker, which, on the other hand, prevents the possibility of manipulation in explaining the abnormally low tender price[22] and the reference to the right to entrepreneurial freedom of the most advantageous tenderer.

As part of their tenders, the tenderers were required to indicate in Table 3.2 the structure of monthly costs, where they were asked to enter basic data per unit of one worker, such as gross monthly salary, employer's contributions, the cost of meals and transport, holiday pay, the number of days of leave, the cost of replacing absent employees, the cost of detergents, small tools, PE bags, etc.

Table 3.2 Structure of monthly costs

SeqNo.	Type of cost	Cost/month excluding VAT
1	Gross 1/worker/month	
2	Employer's contributions (16.1%)	
3	Meals/worker/month	
4	Transport/worker/month	
5	Holiday pay/worker/month (= annual holiday pay, 12 months)	
A.1	**Total labour cost/worker/month (=1+2+3+4+5)**	
A.2	**Total labour cost (=A1 × number of employed workers from Table 3.1)**	
6	Number of days of leave/worker/year	
B	Cost of replacing absent employees from Table 3.1	
C	**Cost of detergents, small tools, PE bags/month**	
D	**Cost of depreciation of fixed assets/month**	

In this way, the contracting authority was able to verify already during evaluation and pre-selection phase whether the tender prices covered statutory labour costs and material costs. Since the contracting authority required that the workers be employees, no problems were encountered in the calculation of costs due to potential self-employees, since the contractors tendering under the present contract notice had to operate only as workers and not as entrepreneurs. Subcontractors as a consortium of tenderers had the opportunity to participate as well, but they had to submit to the contracting authority data on their employed workers, and the tenderer respectively main contractor had to include them in its specification of costs.

The contracting authority could also in this way verify whether the tenderers when formulating their tenders complied with the labour legislation in terms of working time, annual leave, absence from work, etc. If the customer established that the minimum statutory requirements were not complied with, such a tender could be excluded already in the evaluation and pre-selection phase. The contracting authority, for example, excluded the tenderer who in the table under the heading "Number of days of leave" indicated 17 days, which is lower than prescribed by law.[23] The tenderer filed an appeal against the contracting authority's decision, but the National Review Commission[24] rejected the review claim and confirmed that the envisaged 17 days of leave were not in accordance with the labour legislation. Since the tenderer failed to demonstrate that the indicated average number of days of leave per worker was the consequence of the fact that workers were not or would not be employed for the full-year period but only for a short term, the Commission rejected the tenderer's review claim as unfounded.

Due to the violation of the labour legislation, the Commission repealed also the contracting authority's decision on the selection of the most advantageous tenderer, who met the requirement of obligatory presence of contractor of 29,524 hours per month by indicating the formula 158 workers × 187 hours (174 regular hours + 13 hours of overtime) = 29,546 hours per month. It was namely evident from the indicated formula that the selected tenderer was considered the most advantageous tenderer on account of the fact that the tenderer anticipated for each worker 13 hours of overtime per month. In this way, it lowered the labour costs and required less workers to comply with the contracting authority's requirements compared to other tenderers. Owing to the system of structural prices, also other tenderers were able to immediately notice based on the information about the total tender price that the most advantageous tenderer when formulating the tender price failed to comply with the labour legislation. Consequently, the second most advantageous tenderer lodged a claim for review against the contracting authority's decision. The National Review Commission upheld the claim and repealed the contracting authority's decision to award the contract. In its explanatory note, the National Review Commission stated:

> The National Review Commission agrees with the applicant that the pre-determination of overtime work for a five-year period in the absence of any exceptional circumstances (indicated in Article 143 of ZDR) is not admissible. Provision of paragraph 1 of Article 145 of ZDR namely provides that overtime work according to Article 143 of this Act may not be imposed if the work can be performed within full working hours by means of the appropriate organisation and distribution of work, distribution of working time, introduction of new shifts, or employment of new workers. According to the assessment of the National Review Commission this means that overtime work should be considered an exception to full working hours and may be imposed only in exceptional circumstances, i.e. only in cases exhaustively indicated in Article 143 of ZDR: "Upon the employer's request, the worker shall be obliged to perform work exceeding full working hours – overtime work: in cases of an exceptionally increased amount of work; if continuation of work and production process is required in order to prevent material damage or threat to the life and health of people; if this is necessary to avert damage to work equipment that would otherwise result in suspension of work; if this is necessary in order to ensure the safety of people and property and the safety of traffic; and in other exceptional, urgent and unforeseen cases provided by the law or by the branch collective agreement." Only exceptional, urgent and unforeseen cases apply from the indicated provision, which, however, according to the National Review Commission have not yet occurred and are questionable also for the future. The amount of work which must be considered by tenderers in planning the organisation of work is indicated in point C of the specifications of requirements in the contract notice and is thus already known and the mere contracting authority's warning that in case of emergency situations there would be additional cleaning required, does not provide a legal basis for the successful tenderer to predict in advance for the period of five years 13 hours of overtime a month. The National Review Commission assesses that the overtime work for a five-year period cannot be planned in advance and it is also

not possible to predict its quantity since it is dependable upon exceptional, urgent and unforeseen circumstances, which in the present case are not certain to occur. The structure of workers is questionable as well and so is the possibility to impose such amount of overtime work to everyone, since based on the paragraph 2 of Article 145 of ZDR an employer may not impose work beyond full working hours.

(Articles 143 and 144 of ZDR)

Already by establishing a structural price in the contract notice, the contracting authority prevented the possibility of social dumping. In this way, the tenderers in formulating their tenders derived from the same starting points and were competing with each other only at the expense of the amount of earnings calculated in the total tender price. It was thus assured that the tenderers complied with the social and labour legislation, which is essential for responsible and efficient public procurement and the creation of a competitive environment, especially in the procurement of labour-intensive services. On the other hand, the system of structural prices enables a transparent detection of violations of the applicable social and labour legislation without providing any further evidence or referring to entrepreneurial freedom. Such a system allows the contracting authority to preliminarily exclude a tender, even the most advantageous, prior to the awarding of the contract, and thus protect the market against its impact on the distortion of competition.

4 Examples of redundancies

Focusing solely on the reduction of costs of public spending, on the other hand, results in a tendency to delegate the performance of tasks to the private sector, aiming to ensure a rapid reduction of the public sector, i.e. outsourcing. In this context, the contracting authority is inadvertently faced with the issue of redundancies and it is thus necessary to consider carefully whether the delegation of tasks is reasonable from the perspective of the overall economic situation. Namely, if in the private sector lower costs of services are a mere consequence of dismissals of workers, wage cuts and material costs but not also of the modernisation of the system of operation and management, the state by reducing the size of the public sector to balance the public finances will not achieve positive effects either. In the short term, the state will reduce its costs yet due to the dismissals of workers and wage cuts it will not increase the demand for goods and will thus not create favourable conditions for economic growth. It is therefore important in the case of outsourcing that government organisations are clear about objectives and then test their realism. These may include cost reductions, improved service, investment in IT, technical expertise, boosting a local economy and full accountability and transparency of costs and performance.[25] Only if the private sector provides some added value for the transferred respectively offered services, aside from the reduction of costs, which with good governance could be done by the state itself, the outsourcing would be reasonable and the state committed to integrate social and environmental considerations into the procurement process.

In the case of outsourcing, the question of redundancies remains though. Some contracting authorities try to protect their workers against their dismissal by determining in their contract notices that the tenderers will have to use and employ their workers, however, such conduct raises the question of legality.

4.1 Employment of workers as a qualification assessment criterion and additional criterion in the evaluation of tenders

The contract notice requirement to employ the contracting authority's workers cannot be set as a condition for the recognition of tenderer's ability to execute the public contract. The selection process namely enables the contracting authorities to assess candidates' ability to deliver the requirements specified in the contract. The Procurement Directives contain an exhaustive list of technical capacity selection criteria, which can be applied to justify the choice of candidates. Selection criteria differing from those set out in the Procurement Directives would therefore not comply with the Directives. In order to establish such a link, social considerations may be included in the technical selection criteria only if the achievement of the contract requires specific "know-how" in the social field (Buying Social, 2010).[26] According to Beentjes case[27]:

> Specific experience relating to the work to be carried out was a criterion for determining the technical knowledge and ability of the tenderers. It is therefore a legitimate criterion for checking contractors' suitability under Articles 20 and 26 of the directive,

but the Court found that a condition calling for employing long-term unemployed[28] bore no relation to checking tenderers' suitability on the basis of their economic and financial standing and their technical knowledge and ability. However, a criterion regarding combating unemployment (and other criteria which are not linked to the subject matter of the contract) can be taken into account at the award stage only as "an additional criterion" in order to choose between two equivalent tenders.[29]

4.2 Employment with contract performance clauses

As has already been mentioned, according to the Commission the contract performance clauses are generally the most appropriate stage of the procedure to include social considerations relating to employment and labour conditions of the workers involved in performance of the contract.[30] By way of contract performance clauses, the recruitment of workers of the contracting authority becomes the obligation of the tenderer, yet such a requirement should be consistent with the fundamental principles of public procurement and should not discriminate directly or indirectly against non-national tenderers.

The National Review Commission in case 018–293/2012, the Valdoltra Orthopedic Specialty Hospital, thus decided that the contracting authority's requirement for the contractor to permanently accept the contracting authority's workers, based on the Treaty on the acceptance of workers (Form No 18), by concluding employment contracts with them, was disproportionate. The National Review Commission assessed that the contracting authority could not on the basis of Article 4 of ZJN-2 require from tenderers a pre-defined organisational form for the execution of the contract. This applies especially in cases of company transfers, whereby the contracting authorities may not by way of public contracts require from tenderers the assumption of their part of activities and thus the employment of their workers for an indefinite period. In accordance with point nine of the first paragraph of Article 2 of ZJN-2, a public service contract shall be a contract having as its subject the provision of services or the execution of one or more services and not a permanent transfer of activities including workers. The contracting authority may not make the conclusion of a contract conditional on specific ways of personnel management.

The indicated position of the National Review Commission can be agreed with, since tenderers cannot be forced into concluding employment contracts for an indefinite period with workers who they do not know and who are bound to a specific territory. Otherwise, local tenderers are preferred to other tenderers, especially those from other Member States.[31] And considering the fact that the workers concerned remain in their employment relationships with tenderers even after the termination of the contract, the contracting authority in this way transfers the problem of its redundancies to the tenderers. It is highly probable, that after the termination of the contract the tenderers will find the way to dismiss the contracting authority's workers if no longer needed, which means that the contracting authority and the state do not achieve the desired objective of reducing the public sector while maintaining the employment of workers. Also questionable is the contracting authority's requirement for tenderers to recruit workers only for the duration of the contract, whereby after the termination of the contract the workers would be taken over by the newly selected tenderer.[32] In such cases, the existing tenderers as the existing contractual parties have advantage over new tenderers, who are required to make an internal reorganisation of the company. However, in doing so, they have to face the problems of their employees, which negatively affects the interest in obtaining such a contract. Due to the lack of competition, the existing tenderer as the contractual partner may significantly increase the price, which again may raise a question about the rationality of outsourcing. One of the solutions to the above problem could be that the contracting authority's workers remain employed with the contracting authority while the contracting authority by way of contract notice requirements includes them in the work process, as was done in the case of the General Hospital Celje in the procedure to award a contract for the "cleaning of rooms".[33] In this way it is ensured that the workers of the contracting authority maintain their current jobs while the tenderers may at the expense of the additional contracting authority's workforce and thus lower labour costs reduce the total tender price.

The contracting authority will thus not burden the tenderers with the issue of redeployment of its workers, all the tenders will be treated equally, the contracting authority will be able to control and prevent cases of social dumping and the workers will maintain their jobs despite the outsourcing of services.

5 Conclusion

The current economic crisis has demonstrated that the market alone, without the involvement of the state, will not be able to maintain its own legitimacy. Focusing merely on the objective of reducing public spending and concluding contracts with the tenderers whose prices are abnormally low and do not even cover the actual costs does not contribute to the balancing of public finances. Also other objectives can be pursued with public procurement. Tenderers who at the expense of social dumping cause distortion of the market discourage other tenderers from participating in public procurement procedures. Therefore, there exists the need for new regulations which enable the elimination of such tenders in the phase prior to the conclusion of the contract while the burden of verifying the compliance with the labour and social legislation remains with contracting authorities. The system of structural prices is a good example of a simple preliminary verification of tenders. Tenderers will no longer be able to refer to their entrepreneurial freedom and the possibility of substituting the excess of costs in the final tender price elsewhere. It seems appropriate that the issue of compliance with social rules should be addressed in the phase prior to the conclusion of the contract, where the contracting authority has a wide range of options to verify the conditions of the execution of the contract, compared to the implementation phase, where the verification is extremely difficult since the contracting authority is merely a contracting party. It may in principle be expected from contracting authorities that they do not always equate the most advantageous tender with the cheapest one, yet it is at the same time necessary to provide them appropriate support in the preparation of tender documentation. At the time of completely different fiscal situation compared to previous years, also public contracting authorities started to be drawn attention to the increasing problem of abuse of social achievements of modern society, the exploitation of foreign and often ignorant work force, avoidance of responsibility by means of subcontractors, poor working conditions, irregular payments and avoidance of social security contributions, ignoring the employment protection provisions and other practices. The problem of social issues and public procurement is no longer tied solely to the issue of the inclusion of people with disabilities or other protected groups. The practice shows that social dumping has become a substantial problem in labour-intensive industries and consequently in awarding service and works contracts. Should such practice be allowed, this will fundamentally change also the labour market, which, however, the state due to numerous indirect negative effects cannot and should not afford. Public procurement can be an appropriate instrument for the regulation of the labour market, yet the contracting authorities, aside from adequate legislative framework, need the support of supervisory institutions and notably an appropriate response from legal protection authorities in the enforcement of good practices in the field concerned. The gap between the generality of public procurement principles and concrete solutions of contracting authorities should be closed with the examples of good practice, which the contracting authorities can identify as effective and feasible without the risk of the procedures be repealed. The purpose of this contribution is to illustrate certain possible solutions, which in practice have proved efficient also in the contract implementation phase.

Notes

1 Such a case is the procedure to award a public contract "The Construction of the Markovec tunnel (in relation to the works) at the Koper – Izola motorway)", where due to the low price there was a review claim lodged. The National Review Commission (as the institution responsible for settling disputes in public procurement procedures, whose decisions are final and cannot be appealed against through the courts) rejected the claim based on the argument (No of Decision, 018–163/2009–21):

> In this context, also in practice, the National Review Commission on several occasions stated its position that in case of the lowest price as the sole criterion, only the total tender price may be defined as abnormally low rather than its components respectively individual pro-forma items. It is only the final total tender price as a whole that is relevant while a more detailed structure of the majority of individual items (setting the prices for such items, with the exception of VAT) under the total price is subject to the business policy of each competitor in the relevant market and is exclusively within their jurisdiction. Free pricing is one of the fundamental characteristics of free market competition, where it usually applies that a tenderer may offer an optional high price if accepted in the market or an optional low price if such price still guarantees their existence in the market (is profitable, or at least reduces the impending loss). The relevant legal regulations normally do not prevent the selling price from being lower than own production or purchase price (due to the principle of free pricing, the relevant literature and the case law generally do not consider price reduction unfair respectively consider it unfair only in exceptional circumstances). In practice, it often comes to circumstances where a company is forced to sell goods, perform services or carry out works under its own (production, purchase respectively other) price (due to the end of a season or decreased demand there is a risk of loss, and the company endeavours to reach a new market or be placed in the market as a new company, or introduce a new product or service or is using a joint/mixed price calculation with internal subsidization).

The successful tenderer who the contract was concluded with went bankrupt and the indicated project which was the subject of the contract has until today, after five years not been completed.

2 EU Commission (2011): Commission Staff Working Paper; Evaluation Report Impact and Effectiveness of EU Public Procurement Legislation (SEC(2011) 853 final, 27.6.2011):

> The evaluation finds that the average cost of running each procedure is approximately €28,000. The cost of the procurement process may represent quite a high percentage of the total value of a contract, particularly at the lower end. At the lowest threshold in the Directives, €125,000, total costs can amount to between 18 and 29% of the contract value. At €390,000, the median contract value, costs reach between 6 and 9%.

3 Decision of the Constitutional Court, No U-I-243/96.
4 Minimum Wage Act (*Official Gazette of RS*, No 13/2010), which provides that a minimum wage for a full-time work performed from 1 January 2014 amounts to €789.15 (gross).
5 Jorens, Y., Peters, S. and Houwerzijl, M. (2012): *Study on the protection of workers' rights in subcontracting processes in the European Union Project* DG EMPL/B2 – VC/2011/0015 (Ref. Ares(2012)763789–25/06/2012):

> Another common application obstacle is that the major part of the rules on protection of workers' rights in subcontracting processes only apply to employees and can thus be relatively easily evaded via the concept of self-employed workers. This problem was mentioned for Belgium, Luxembourg, the Netherlands, Norway, Poland and the United Kingdom. The phenomenon of bogus self-employment is well known in Belgium as a means of escaping the protective labour law rules. [...] The attractiveness to be able to work with cheaper self-employed persons and this way avoid that minimal social conditions and standards have to be complied with in the country of temporary employment involves the risk of an increase in (cross-border) bogus self-employment, where persons act as an employee, but are registered as a self-employed person. Moreover, the forms of bogus self-employment have become increasingly sophisticated in the past few years, which is a tendency to be observed in the whole of Europe.

6 Point b) of second paragraph of Article 45 of the Public Procurement Act (Official Gazette of RS, No 12/13-UPB5, 19/14, hereinafter: ZJN-2).
7 Article 630 of the Code of Obligations (*Official Gazette of RS*, No 83/2001 as amended), i.e. Responsibility of Associates, provides that: "A contractor is responsible for persons who were authorised to perform the work taken over as if it was performed by the contractor."
8 *Official Journal of the European Union*, L 134/114, 30. 4. 2004.
9 *Official Journal of the European Union*, L 134/114, 30. 4. 2004.
10 1. A contracting authority may state in the contract documents, or be obliged by a Member State so to state, the body or bodies from which a candidate or tenderer may obtain the appropriate information on the obligations relating to taxes, to environmental protection, to the employment protection provisions and to the working conditions which are in force in the Member State, region or locality in which the works are to be carried out or services are to be provided and which shall be applicable to the works carried out on site or to the services provided during the performance of the contract. 2. A contracting authority which supplies the information referred to in paragraph 1 shall request the tenderers or candidates in the contract award procedure to indicate that they have taken account, when drawing up their tender, of the obligations relating to employment protection provisions and the working conditions which are in force in the place where the works are to be carried out or the service is to be provided. The first subparagraph shall be without prejudice to the application of the provisions of Article 55 concerning the examination of abnormally low tenders.
11 With the indicated provision, the Republic of Slovenia directly transposed Article 55 of Directive 2004/18/EC, which provides that if, for a given contract, tenders appear to be abnormally low in relation to the goods, works or services, the contracting authority shall, before it may reject those tenders, request in writing details of the constituent elements of the tender which it considers relevant. Those details may relate in particular to: [...] (d) compliance with the provisions relating to employment protection and working conditions in force at the place where the work, service or supply is to be performed; 2. The contracting authority shall verify those constituent elements by consulting the tenderer, taking account of the evidence supplied.
12 EU Evaluation Report (2011): Evaluation Report Impact and Effectiveness of EU Public Procurement Legislation (SEC(2011) 853 final, 27.6.2011):

A recurrent concern in the design of public procurement procedures is the cost, complexity and delay. The typical time from the dispatch of an invitation to tender to an award across all procedures is 108 days, but the difference between the top performers and the slowest is approximately 180 days.

13 Luxembourg: Publications Office of the European Union, 2010.
14 Convention No 94 and Recommendation No 84 were adopted in 1949, at the time of the post-Second World War reconstruction, soon after the creation of the United Nations and the World Bank.
15 Judgement 31/87 Beentjes v State of the Netherlands.
16 *Official Journal of the European Union*, L 94/65, 28.3.2014.
17 Article 18 (2): Member States shall take appropriate measures to ensure that in the performance of public contracts economic operators comply with applicable obligations in the fields of environmental, social and labour law established by Union law, national law, collective agreements or by the international environmental, social and labour law provisions listed in Annex X.
18 Article 71 of Directive 2014/24/EU.
19 In case No 018–029/2012, the National Review Commission decided:

> The National Review Commission agrees with the applicant that the Contracting Authority's further requirement: "[…] who is employed with the tenderer" is contrary to the subject of the public contract. The already mentioned provision in point b) of paragraph 2 of Article 45 of ZJN-2 provides that economic operators may prove their technical abilities according to the nature, quantity or importance, and the use of services: "an indication of the technicians or technical bodies involved, whether or not employed with or working at present or in the future for the economic operator […]" allows for various forms of legal or contractual cooperation between the technical person and tenderers, and does not force tenderers to enter into employment contracts, as the contracting authority requires in the present case.

20 In case No 018–116/2012, the Jožef Stefan Institute, the National Review Commission decided:

> The provided documentation shows that the contracting authority on 24 January 2012 during the review and evaluation of tenders established that the price offered by the applicant was substantially lower than the prices offered by other tenderers. Despite the fact that the applicant offered (and included in the calculation) 2 workers more than other participating tenderers, the price is more than 20% lower than the price offered by the successful tenderer and more than 30% lower than the prices offered by the remaining three tenderers. […] The applicant submitted three Tables, which illustrate that labour costs for the first two categories of workers amounted to €969.25 per person per month, while for workers from Bosnia and Herzegovina they amounted to €550.00 per person per month. […] However, it should be taken into account in the present case that the contracting authority explicitly required from the tenderers to include in the necessary workforce only their employees. Since the applicant failed to comply with this requirement respectively did not comply with it (as explained by the applicant) because it provided almost half of the required human resources through an associated company, it was legally excluded by the contracting authority.

21 In case No 018–064/2008, University Medical Centre Maribor, the National Review Commission decided:

> In the Table 3.1 section designated for entering data on the total number of employed workers for the provision of 29.524 h/month, the first applicant entered the number 150, which, in accordance with the Contracting Authority's calculations

set out in the contract notice No SC-49/08 of 27 March 2008, does not correspond to any of the values of the required number of workers for the provision of daily presence of 121 workers at the location of the contracting authority. [...] In order to provide the daily presence of 121 workers at the location of the contracting authority while not violating the labour legislation regarding the permissible maximum working hours, the tenderer had to ensure a minimum quota of workers necessary for the provision of the required presence. Since the applicant failed to provide a sufficient number of workers, the contracting authority excluded the tender as incomplete, which was subsequently confirmed by the National Review Commission, who rejected the applicant's claim for review.

22 In case No 018–386/2012, the public institution Radio Television Slovenia, the National Review Commission, as regards the applicant's complaints about the abnormally low price and non-compliance with the staff conditions by the selected tenderer due to its supposed non-sufficient number of workers, decided:

Based on the fact that the contracting authority failed to determine in the contract notice the minimum required number of cleaners to be provided by respective tenderers but left this choice to tenderers, and on the fact that the standards of the Chamber of Craft and Small Business of Slovenia are not binding and absolute, it is necessary to accept the explanation that the number of workers was set by each tenderer individually, knowing their own cleaning technology and taking into account the specific requirements of the contracting authority. Agreeing with the applicant who based on its own calculations indicates that the selected tenderer does not provide a sufficient number of cleaners, would on the one hand mean non-compliance with the provisions of the contract notice, according to which the sufficient number of workers was set by each tenderer individually, and on the other hand would make the recommendations of the Chamber of Craft and Small Business of Slovenia binding, and hence the exclusion of the tender on the basis thereof would be entirely arbitrary.

23 The duration of annual leave is governed by the provision of the first paragraph of Article 159 of the Employment Relationship Act (*Official Gazette of RS*, No 42/2002 with further amendments, hereinafter: ZDR), which provides that a worker shall have the right to annual leave in an individual calendar year, which may not be shorter than four weeks, regardless of whether he works full time or part time. The minimum number of days of a worker's annual leave shall depend on the distribution of working days within week in respect of an individual worker.

24 Decision, University Medical Centre Maribor, No 018–052/2011–12.

25 http://procureinsightseu.wordpress.com/2014/06/17/getting-outsourcing-right-by-colin-cram/.

26 *Buying Social: A Guide to Taking Account of Social Considerations in Public Procurement*, Directorate-General for Employment, Social Affairs and Equal Opportunities, October 2010. The indicated also means that it is very unlikely that social considerations can be incorporated into consideration of a candidate's "economic and financial standing". This means that in most cases the only way in which social considerations can be used as grounds for not selecting a candidate is if they can be regarded as affecting the candidate's "technical knowledge and/or professional ability". (Incorporating Social Considerations into Procurement, SIGMA, January 2011).

27 CJEU judgment of 20 September 1988 in case 31/87.

28 It was required: "the work-force must be made up of at least 70% long-term unemployed persons employed through the regional employment office."

29

In case C-225/98 Commission v France the CJEU held that contracting authorities can award a contract on the basis of a condition related to eg combating unemployment, provided this condition is in line with all the fundamental principles of EU law, but only where the authorities had to consider two or more equivalent tenders. The Member State in question regarded this condition as an additional, non-determining criterion and considered it only after tenders had been compared on the basis of the other award criteria. Finally, the CJEU stated that application of the award criterion regarding combating unemployment must have no direct or indirect impact on those submitting bids from other EU Member States and must be explicitly mentioned in the contract notice, so that potential contractors were able to know that such a condition existed.

(*Buying Social: A Guide to Taking Account of Social Considerations in Public Procurement*, Directorate-General for Employment, Social Affairs and Equal Opportunities, October 2010)

30

The execution phase of public procurement contracts is not currently regulated by the public procurement directives. In addition, such clauses or conditions must be implemented in compliance with all the procedural rules in the directives, and in particular with the rules on advertising of tenders. They should not be (disguised) technical specifications. They should not have any bearing on the assessment of the suitability of tenderers on the basis of their economic, financial and technical capacity, or on the award criteria. Indeed, "the contract condition should be independent of the assessment of the bidders' capacity to carry out the work or of award criteria"

(Interpretative communication of the Commission on the Community law applicable to public procurement and the possibilities for integrating social considerations into public procurement /* COM/2001/0566 final */)

31 Discussed also by Macfarlane, R. and Collins, A. *Solicitors LLP in report: Tackling poverty through public procurement*, 28 April 2014. www.jrf.org.uk/sites/files/jrf/poverty-procurement-social-mobility-full.pdf.

32 In case No 018–375/2012, the Republic of Slovenia, the Ministry of Infrastructure and Spatial Planning, Slovenian Roads Agency, the National Review Commission repealed the provision of the contract notice, which pertained to the acquisition of workers and obliged the successful tenderer to recruit the workers of the existing tenderer:

Such requirement of the contract notice directly restricts the autonomy of the conduct of economic operators, whereby the current providers of regular maintenance of state roads in certain areas have advantage (are in a privileged position) over those economic operators who endeavour to be awarded a contract for the first time, since the indicated requirement in its content does not apply to the current providers of regular maintenance of state roads.

33 In case No 018–407/2012, the General Hospital Celje, the National Review Commission was deciding on the applicant's review claim, in which the applicant alleged that considering the total tender price offered by the successful tenderer the latter could not provide an appropriate number of employees and that considering the offered price the successful tenderer had not taken into account all the labour and material costs. In the calculation, the applicant overlooked the fact that based on the sample contract the tenderers were required to include in the work process also six workers of the contracting authority.

References

Buying Social: A Guide to Taking Account of Social Considerations in Public Procurement, Directorate-General for Employment, Social Affairs and Equal Opportunities, October 2010.

EU Commission (2011): Commission Staff Working Paper; Evaluation Report Impact and Effectiveness of EU Public Procurement Legislation (SEC(2011) 853 final, 27.6.2011).

EU Evaluation Report (2011): Evaluation Report Impact and Effectiveness of EU Public Procurement Legislation (SEC(2011) 853 final, 27.6.2011).

Jorens, Y., Peters, S. and Houwerzijl, M. (2012): *Study on the protection of workers' rights in subcontracting processes in the European Union Project*, DG EMPL/B2 – VC/2011/0015 (Ref. Ares(2012)763789–25/06/2012).

Labour Clauses Guide (2008): Labour Clauses (Public Contracts) convention, 1949 (No. 94) AND Recommendation (No. 84) www.ilo.org/wcmsp5/groups/public/@ed_norm/@normes/documents/publication/wcms_099699.pdf.

LLP in report: Tackling poverty through public procurement 28 April 2014. www.jrf.org.uk/sites/files/jrf/poverty-procurement-social-mobility-full.pdf.

Part II

Lots – the economic and legal challenges of centralized procurement

4   Colloquium

Giancarlo Spagnolo
Christopher R. Yukins

1 Giancarlo Spagnolo – Paper 1 on Art. 46 of the Directive 2014/24/EU (and the similar Art. 65 Directive 2014/25/EU)

The design of lots is the most important decision in procurement, as it (a) "defines the object" procured, and (b) it "defines the market", who will be able to supply, how much competition there will be, etc. Everything else in procurement is a consequence of that decision, even more than for "market definition" in antitrust. The new Directive tries to clarify some very important aspects related to this crucial decision, and I will focus my attention on what I think is the core of this attempt, Article 46.

The first part of comma 1 of Article 46 states the status quo, in the sense that dividing tenders in multiple lots has always been done without the directive, and now the directive states this is OK. My only comment is that, while I understand that some lawyers and practitioners want to hear this to be completely sure, EU Legislators and National Legislators should not be so prescriptive, and stop stating what contracting authorities can do, which sometimes means stating the obvious, but other times meant prescribing rather weird instruments on which they have no expertise, suggesting implicitly that what is not described/pre-scribed as legal is not so. This hinders innovation, motivation and performance in all fields. Regulators and law makers do not have sufficient knowledge to tell people what they should do, which is typically very different in different situations, and should limit themselves to state what we should not do, like unfairly discriminating, or bundling previously unbundled supplies, while making clear that what is not forbidden is legal.

The second part of the first comma is more interesting, as it requires contracting authorities to "provide an indication of the main reasons for their decision not to subdivide into lots, which shall be included in the procurement documents or the individual report referred to in Article 84." This clarifies that the expectation by the EC and the spirit of these articles are that tenders should be "normally" divided in lots, and only in the case of a single lot a justification is needed. This sounds similar to the US's Small Business Act's requirement of a written justification when larger/more bundled lots are tendered than in the past. The big difference is that here there is no reference to the past, so there is no benchmark for the size of the lots. So, for example, a contracting authority that used to tender a single lot every year and now tenders a single lot of half the original size every six months, is required to justify why it tenders a single lot. An administration that used to tender a certain type of goods or services divided in four lots and repeated every six months, and that now bundles demand and tenders everything divided in two very large lots once a year will not have to justify its bundling choices, because its procurements have two lots. This sounds very much against the general spirit of article 46 that – according to my understanding – aims at fostering unbundling of tenders in smaller lots that are more accessible to SMEs.

More generally, the number and size of lots, together with the frequency of procurement, are choices that directly determine who can participate and who cannot to the procurement auction, and should therefore always be justified and motivated extensively and publicly. Having four instead of 40 lots may have much bigger consequences than having one lot instead of three (Grimm *et al.* 2006).

The second comma also puts down on paper a consolidated practice in procurement aimed at "managing dynamic competition", in the sense of avoiding "one-winner-takes-all outcomes" so as to keep multiple suppliers active in the market. It discusses two practices that have been used in several countries, in the first case with some concerns relative to their full legality and some complaints from the competition authorities.

The first practice is described in the first part of comma 2, stating that "contracting authorities shall indicate, in the contract notice or in the invitation to confirm interest, whether tenders may be submitted for one, for several or for all of the lots." Limiting the number or combination of lots on which suppliers can bid is a very strong intervention in terms of limiting competition and producing inefficiencies. This type of restriction does not even allow potential suppliers to fully express their ability to optimally serve the contracting authority on the various lots. How can then we expect the resulting award to be even constrained efficient?

This intervention may create very large inefficiencies, and is not at all necessary: the tool we discuss below (restricting the number of lots that can be awarded to the same supplier, and not those on which the supplier can bid if qualified) can be used to avoid one-winner-take-all outcomes without need of restricting suppliers' ability to express their full potential. Their positive effects can be easily achieved by restricting the number of lots awarded to a single supplier, without the negative effect of preventing suppliers to bid/communicate what they can do best.

The second part of comma 2 discusses a less inefficient and more interesting tool, that has been used in many contexts to keep more than one supplier active, or to favor smaller or disadvantaged suppliers, as in the case of US's "set asides". The Directive states that

> contracting authorities may, even where tenders may be submitted for several or all lots, limit the number of lots that may be awarded to one

tenderer, provided that the maximum number of lots per tenderer is stated in the contract notice or in the invitation to confirm interest.

Limiting the number (or type) of lots that a supplier can win, without preventing suppliers to fully express their capability to serve all lots, allows the contracting authority to choose among all the best offers for each lot, not only a subset of them, given the constraints about how many lots can be awarded to each player. This allows to maintain multiple winners, which hopefully means having more bidders in the future, but sacrificing a smaller amount of efficiency in the current procurement.

My view, therefore is that the first part of the comma 2, on limiting bidding possibility, is wrong and misleading, and should never have been written, as it encourages the many less well informed contracting authorities to use a very inefficient instrument that can only worsen welfare compared to what can be achieved by limiting the awarded lots, leaving firms free to bid on all of them. The Commission should have written that the first part, restricting bids, is not allowed, while the second part, restricting the number of lots a single supplier can win, can be used to avoid pathological situations in which a single supplier, by repeatedly winning all the lots, drives all other potential suppliers out of the market. Supporting SMEs does not require limiting all suppliers' ability to express their capacity by bidding on all lots either. It is sufficient to reserve one lot to them, or to offer them bid subsidies.

Comma 3, instead, is very good news. It makes clear that combinatorial procurement auctions can be used. These are procurement auctions where offers for a "combination (or package) of lots" can be made, if this possibility was specified in the contract notice or in the invitation to confirm interest. We used combinatorial auctions in a few occasions in Consip, in 2004–2007. The main advantage is their flexibility, and their ability to unveil whether small firms can really be competitive in a market without eliminating the possibility for larger suppliers to exploit strong economies of scale. The point is that, particularly in rapidly changing industries, it is very difficult to know whether small firms could be reasonably effective suppliers. We have heard many times small firms arguing that they could provide the needed goods and services at lower costs and higher quality than the winning large firms, if only the lots would have been smaller and allowed them to participate. But it is hard to substantiate these claims in the absence of data, and to resist the temptation to ask why these firms remain so small if they are so efficient, why don't they grow outcompeting the less efficient larger rivals. And we have heard all too often large firms and procurement agencies arguing for large lots, so that economies of scale could be exploited, to end up with very few large firms that know each other very well and interact repeatedly in many different markets, with many more signs of a collusive market sharing agreement than the famous synergies and economies of scale everybody is so keen in mentioning.

Combinatorial procurement auctions allow us to test these loose claims, one against the other. They admit at the same time many small lots that allow small suppliers to participate and express all they potential efficiency; and at the same time they allow larger suppliers that may enjoy economies of scale, to express these economies by bidding on combinations of lots, forcing them to share these economies – when present – with the contracting authority and the taxpayer, thanks to the competitive pressure from small firms.

Combinatorial auctions become easily complex and require skilled designers. The combinations of lots on which suppliers can bid can, and may have to be restricted by the contracting authority to limit the computational problem of finding the optimal/winning combination of bids and lots. There are different ways to do it and the appropriate one will depend on the specific characteristics of each market and tender. Contracting authorities that plan to use them need to prepare their procurer with somewhat more strategic and economic oriented training than the legalistic "how-to-apply-the-procedure-without-being-blamed" training that is more often offered to public buyer (Dimitri *et al.* 2006).

The last comma of article 46 acknowledges the possibility that some states would make the awarding of contracts in the form of separate lots compulsory. This is a rather unfortunate idea. If we are purchasing, a large amount of micro-chips, the most likely number of suppliers that will come to our procurement auction is two, as two are the main producers of these high tech devices in the world. A law that forces more than one lot would be a disaster in this case, as it would harm taxpayers by inviting the producers to split the market/lots among themselves. Whether to split in lots, in how many lots, etc. is a decision that must depend on the specific characteristics of each market, and may differ from year to year even for the same market (firms enter, exit, fail…). And how would one enforce it? A purchasing authority that buys four times a year computers through single lots procurement auctions, facing a law that forces to split contracts in lots, can simply reduce the frequency and buy twice a year transforming two sequential single lot procurements in one procurement with two simultaneous lots. And nothing will have changed in terms of lots size, apart from having distorted the timing of purchasing.

2 Christopher R. Yukins – Harnessing economics and the law to procure best value

This essay begins by attempting to address what seems a fairly simple question: From a legal perspective, are the procurement rules optimized to ensure that governments can gain best value from their massive purchasing power? This essay (which draws primarily on experience in the United States and the European Union) breaks that overarching question into subsidiary issues:

1   What role do small- and medium-sized enterprises (SMEs) play in government demand aggregation?
2   How should government demand aggregation be structured, organizationally?
3   How should we select goods or services for aggregated procurement?
4   What kinds of procurement contracts should be used?

2.1 What role do SMEs play in government demand aggregation?

Experience in Europe and the United States suggests that SMEs are the "elephant in the room" when it comes to demand aggregation. While contracting authorities may wish to leverage broader demand and reduce transaction costs by awarding larger contracts, the political and competitive need to accommodate SMEs forces contracting authorities to break those larger contracts into smaller "lots."

Language in the procurement directive recently issued by the European Union, Directive 2014/24/EU, which was an important inspiration for this session, illustrated how demand aggregation and SMEs collide, over the issue of lot size. In a number of different contexts, that directive discusses how contracting authorities should structure procurements in smaller "lots" so as to enhance small- and medium-sized entities (SMEs') opportunity to compete.

This reflects an abiding concern, in procurement systems around the world, that aggregating demand – a natural extension of the government's purchasing power – will hurt SMEs' position in public procurement markets. Recital 78 to the recent directive, for example, states:

> (78) Public procurement should be adapted to the needs of SMEs.... To that end and to enhance competition, contracting authorities should in particular be encouraged to divide large contracts into lots. Such division could be done on a quantitative basis, making the size of the individual contracts better correspond to the capacity of SMEs, or on a qualitative basis, in accordance with the different trades and specialisations involved, to adapt the content of the individual contracts more closely to the specialised sectors of SMEs or in accordance with different subsequent project phases.
>
> The size and subject matter of the lots should be determined freely by the contracting authority, which, in accordance with the relevant rules on the calculation of the estimated value of procurement, should also be allowed to award some of the lots without applying the procedures of this Directive...

The recital thus makes it clear that while concern over SMEs drives a commitment to smaller "lots" in procurement, the contracting authorities retain broad authority – discretionary authority that would be difficult to challenge in a remedies proceeding, for example – to reshape (or even abandon) a strategy of smaller lots for smaller contractors.

Article 46 of the directive confirms this, for it leaves contracting authorities with the authority to "decide to award a contract in the form of separate lots and may determine the size and subject matter of such lots." Although contracting authorities are required to document the "reasons for their decision not to subdivide into lots," so long as the decision can be reasonably explained, it will be difficult to challenge.

Evolving US federal procurement policy confirms that "lot size" marks the battleground between SME policy and demand aggregation. While the US government originally addressed this problem by discouraging agencies from unnecessarily "bundling" requirements into larger contracts, see, e.g., 64 Fed. Reg. 72,441 (Dec. 27, 1999) (interim rule); 68 Fed. Reg. 60,006 (Oct. 20, 2003) (final rule, more broadly covering framework agreements), because purchasing agencies' discretion in setting contract size was very difficult to challenge, see, e.g., Ishak Akyuz, Note, *Bundling into the Millenium: Analyzing the Current State of Contract Bundling*, 30 Pub. Cont. L.J. 123 (2000), the regulations were recently tightened, at Congress' insistence, to bar unwarranted "consolidation," 78 Fed. Reg. 61,114 (Oct. 2, 2013). Despite the new term, however, the new rule still left agencies with substantial discretion (as the EU directive does) in setting "lot size," so long as consolidation can be reasonably justified. *Id.* at 61,138 (setting forth new 13 C.F.R. §125.2(d)). This suggests that ultimately the complex problems of "lot size" cannot be solved simply by enforcement of a legal rule.

2.2 How should government demand aggregation be structured, organizationally?

Because of the complex political and policy issues which surround demand aggregation (see, for example, the SME issues discussed above), one logical home for decisionmaking regarding lot size would be a centralized, politically responsive policymaking organ. In the United States, the Office of Federal Procurement Policy (OFPP) has played a central role in guiding the Obama administration's "Strategic Sourcing Initiative," which has consolidated the federal government's demand in several sectors, such as office supplies and online data purchases. (www.whitehouse.gov/omb/procurement_strategic.)

On the other hand, a regulatory regime might be built around having a centralized purchasing agency – a natural leader in demand aggregation – lead the effort. This has not occurred smoothly in the US federal system, however, as the General Services Administration has played more of a facilitating, rather than leadership, role in consolidating demand. Probably most significantly, the General Services Administration has not developed any comprehensive means of tracking purchases, which users could use to leverage aggregated demand and to identify useful past performance information.

The gap in leadership at the centralized purchasing agency has left individual purchasing agencies with responsibility for "lot size." This may explain why both the US and the European regulatory regimes leave so much discretion to the purchaser regarding "lot size" or "consolidation" – with limited data available on overall government demand, the purchasing agency can hardly be expected to develop a sophisticated strategy of demand aggregation.

2.3 How should we select goods or services for aggregated procurement?

The leading example of demand aggregation in the US federal marketplace has been, as noted, the Strategic Sourcing initiative, coordinated by the Office of Federal Procurement Policy (which is part of the White House's Office of

Management and Budget). The OFPP has not disclosed sophisticated systems for identifying goods and services for consolidated purchasing. See Jeffrey Zients, Office of Management and Budget, Memorandum of Dec. 5, 2012 (mapping loose administrative strategy for identifying promising product categories), available at www.whitehouse.gov/sites/default/files/omb/memoranda/2013/m-13–02_0.pdf. In contrast, CONSIP, the Italian centralized purchasing agency, uses an economic analysis to target goods and services to offer through its centralized framework agreements (Albano G. L., 2014).

2.4 What kinds of procurement contracts should be used?

In the US federal system, as in many European nations, framework agreements (known as "Indefinite Delivery/Indefinite Quantity" contracts in the United States) have been used as the preferred vehicles for contract consolidation. Because transparency is incomplete (not all the demand that will be addressed through US framework agreements is publicized, and not all orders are publicized), competition is incomplete (not all orders are truly competed), and accountability is incomplete (not all framework orders are protestable), the legal structure for demand aggregation remains unsatisfactory in the US federal system.

3 Giancarlo Spagnolo – Response to Paper 2

In contrast with the specificity of my comments in the first paper, Prof. Yukins took a very broad perspective to the problem of lots design, which was very useful to put the more specific problems I discussed into perspective.

Let me here focus on a problem that links the broad and the specific perspectives, i.e. the lack of information by the procurer on the optimal level of bundling, and of combinatorial auctions, package bidding as one of the best solution to this core problem of lot design, able to elicit the information necessary to answer the question "which goods or services should be aggregated in larger lots and which not" from a purely static efficiency perspective.

Before tackling that problem, it is important to clarify an issue that is often confusing the debate on SMEs and demand aggregation. Many observers assume that, by bundling demand, the price of supply will automatically fall because of economies of scale, and therefore that the problem of involving SMEs in public procurement is mainly a political one, or at most a "dynamic industrial policy" one (i.e. the need to give an opportunity, even if this is costly in the short run, to new, small firms to get some public contracts, so that they can grow and hopefully become efficient).

This view is incorrect and has always been put forward by large and well connected suppliers to avoid the annoying problem of competing with a large number of smaller and independent firms, rather than colluding with a handful of equally large and well connected oligopolists. We have experienced the disaster of this kind of talk in the US Defense Procurement, in the UK Public Private Partnerships, and in the Italian Global Service case. It is time to learn.

We have strong evidence than in many cases SMEs are considerably more efficient than large firms, so that the issue of how to involve them in government procurement is one of immediate efficiency, not just a political constraint or a costly investment for the future. This evidence is under the eyes of everybody: it is the amount of subcontracting to SMEs that most large suppliers undertake after they win large contracts from bundled procurement. If the large firms were more efficient than SMEs, they would lose money by subcontracting to SMEs, hence we would only observe subcontracting to other large firms. Even if sub-contracting is necessary to complement the limited skills of the prime contractor, as suggested by Prof. Yukins in the debate, if SMEs were so inefficient we would only observe subcontracting to other large firms...

As soon as we observe subcontracting to SMEs in an industry, therefore, we know that SMEs are more efficient than large suppliers in that industry. And given the amount of subcontracting to SMEs going on in many cases after large, bundled contracts are signed with large contractors, and the complaints from large suppliers when limits to subcontracting are imposed by a procurement agency or regulator, we know that this is a rather common case. So we can summarize this in a first conclusion.

Conclusion 1: SMEs are often more efficient in production than large sup-pliers, hence taxpayer gains in terms of value for money could be obtained if we could find the way to involve SMEs directly in public procurement, rather than having large firms playing the role of intermediaries and cashing these efficien-cies themselves, thanks to the limited competition for very large contracts.

The typical problem with directly involving SMEs in public procurement is coordinating their work and ensuring a reliable and constant level of quality, not risking to pay more. Quality problems and coordination problems are important, they should be taken into account, and they are typically solved well by large suppliers who use subcontracting all the time. Therefore, even when SMEs are more efficient, the ability of large suppliers to solve coordination and quality assurance, control problems when dealing with them may still justify bundling demand in larger contracts.

Conclusion 2: Even though SMEs are often more efficient in production than large firms, coordination and quality control problems could be large enough to make it preferable for the government to contract with large firms and let them deal with SMEs as subcontractors.

Therefore, the problem is: how do we know when the difference in produc-tion efficiency between large firms and SMEs that could be captured by the buyer by having smaller lots and direct involvement of SMEs, are larger than the additional administrative, coordination and quality control costs that the buyer will have to incur when there is not a large supplier serving as an intermediary?

Of course, neither SMEs nor large suppliers will tell us their real production costs or their cost of coordinating and controlling subcontractor, if we simply ask them, as that is precisely the private information that allows them to obtain some profits. This lack of information is what makes efficient lot design a big problem.

Empirical methods looking at the past are one important avenue to try understand this, but as any method it has limitations. For example, it can only look at past data; therefore, in the presence of dynamic and innovative markets, it typically fails to capture what is happening currently and what is the best solution today, which may be completely different than yesterday.

An alternative and complementary solution is using "package bidding" or "combinatorial auctions" (Dimitri *et al.* (2006)) to let the market tell us, during the competitive process, whether SME efficiencies are large enough to justify small lots or not. The idea, that we already implemented in a couple of large procurements in Consip and that is implemented all the time all around the world to procure public transportation, e.g. bus routes in large towns, is to have small lots on which everybody can bid, but also allow for bids conditional on winning a large number of lots, a "package" or "combination" of lots. Then efficiencies of SMEs in serving small lots can then be fully expressed, because individual lots are small, so that SMEs can fairly compete with the larger firms. At the same time, larger suppliers can fully express their economy of scale through offers that are only valid if all lots in the "package" are all awarded to that firm. (To take into account the larger coordination cost the buyer would sustain when many small suppliers serve many small lots, a small coordination charge could in principle be introduced on single lot bids).

One problem of combinatorial auctions is the large number of offers they might generate and the connected difficulty of identifying the combination of bids that maximizes value for money for the buyer. This problem can be contained by limiting the number of combinations of lots (of packages) that can be considered in the bidding process. There various methods to do this, several of which are discussed in the Handbook chapter mentioned above.

The main problem of implementing combinatorial auctions in public procurement seems however to be legal. A situation where one SME has offered the lowest price on a first lot, while a large firm has offered the most competitive offer on a group of five lots, including the first one, that overall is preferable to allocating lots separately. This hard to handle in the current legal framework, at least some countries. The reason is that when the combinatorial offer is globally better, the "best bid" on the first lot will not be awarded a contract for that lot. This may create problems of legal acceptability. A legal framework that regulates combinatorial auctions would be most welcome, as would allow us to use safely from a legal point of view this important instrument that allows the market to determine the optimal amount of demand aggregation in each market and at each point in time.

The Directive makes an important step in the right direction. The problem will be then assisting national lawmakers in the implementation of the directive, given the very limited expertise on serious procurement techniques among public procurement legal scholars and law makers.

4 Christopher R. Yukins – Response to Paper 1

In his paper, Professor Giancarlo Spagnolo addresses the "lots" issue head-on: he argues that recent European efforts to tightly regulate the procurement of goods and services in smaller or larger "lots," to encourage competition from smaller businesses or to allow efficiency, may prove a failure. He urges that a better course would be to allow freer innovation in procurement, to accommodate both (1) the efficiencies brought by larger enterprises, and (2) the innovation offered by small- and medium-sized enterprises (SMEs). His recommendations are spot-on, but his recurring complaint – that the law should be nudged out of the path of progress – may overlook some of the subtle interplays of law and practice in the procurement world.

The Guideposts of the Law: Professor Spagnolo's first proposition – that regulators should limit themselves to stating only what procuring officials *cannot* do, not what officials *should* do – seems, on its face, quite reasonable. It seems a restatement of the fundamental, liberty-affirming principle – the principle at the heart of US society, for example – that what is not prohibited, is permitted. Indeed, in keeping with that principle, the Federal Acquisition Regulation (FAR) was amended during the time that Professor Steven Kelman, of Harvard University, served as the Administrator of the Office of Federal Procurement Policy (part of the White House), to state explicitly that the role of each official involved in an acquisition "is to exercise personal initiative and sound business judgment in providing the best value product or service to meet the customer's needs." In exercising that initiative, the FAR now states, officials "may assume if a specific strategy, practice, policy or procedure is in the best interests of the Government and is not addressed in the FAR, nor prohibited by law (statute or case law), Executive order or other regulation, that the strategy, practice, policy or procedure is a permissible exercise of authority." FAR 1.102(d) (amended by 60 Fed. Reg. 4205 (1995)).

Notably, though, Professor Kelman is a political scientist, not a lawyer or even a career procurement official. The idea that the law should set only minimum constraints on human behavior, and that humans (including procurement officials) should be left to their own creative efforts outside of those proscribed corridors of behavior, is a seductive one, but one that does not completely describe reality in many mature administrative systems, such as the procurement system (with roughly $500 billion in annual purchases) in the US federal government.

In these mature systems, the law is more of a guidepost, or set of guideposts, which guide official behavior and shape contractors' expectations – and, in practice, encourage competition, by ensuring that the contractors' investments in procurement are not squandered. (Arrowsmith (1998)) (discussing role of transparent and accessible rules). Administrative behavior may be held close to those guideposts, or may be allowed to swing wide around them – the degree of adherence turns on many factors, such as the clarity of the law, the availability of sanctions or review, public scrutiny, and society's tolerance for indifference, deviance, or even corruption.

What is important to emphasize, though, is that the stakeholders involved – the program officials, the procurement officers, and the contractors, among others – are constantly negotiating with one another, some in an effort to force their opposites to adhere more closely to the guideposts, some to win freedom for greater deviation. Those negotiations can occur informally, or they can be aggressive and confrontational, such as in a remedies process. These negotiations occur largely behind the scenes, and they are the hallmark of a sound system, not because they allow deviation, or countenance chaos, but because they confirm our faith in the system to self-correct – to steer, ultimately, along the trajectory marked out by the guideposts of the law.

Applying the "Guideposts" Theory: Embracing this concept of procurement law in a mature administrative system – that even when highly prescriptive, the law may well provide only guideposts, strictly or loosely followed but always the focal points for stakeholders' straining negotiations – helps confirm many of Professor Spagnolo's suggestions, specifically here with regard to lot size and preferential treatment of small- and medium-sized enterprises (SMEs):

- Overly prescriptive rules may not work: As Professor Spagnolo suggests, in his close analysis of Article 46 of the new European procurement directive 2014/24/EU, the European Union's efforts to closely regulate the use of lot size may be doomed to failure. That has certainly been the experience in the US federal system, where successive attempts to resolve issues of "bundling" and "consolidation" by regulation have not proven truly successful – in part, because ultimately procurement law focuses on process, and agency actions (even if harmful to SMEs) are likely to survive challenge so long as the procedural and planning requirements are met. See, e.g., WIFCON, www.wifcon.com/pd7_107.htm (summary of US Government Accountability Office decisions under FAR 7.107, on bundling and lot size, many of which denied challenges because procedural requirements met); 78 Fed. Reg. 61113 (Oct. 2, 2013) (revised US Small Business Administration (SBA) rules on bundling and consolidation).
- Other forces emerge as more important: Once it becomes clear that rules themselves can't solve all procurement's ills, other forces – the economic and organizational forces that actually drive the hydraulics of the system – become more apparent. In procurement, officials' concerns with reputation and transaction costs appear to be the most important of those forces. Those forces explain, for example, why procuring officials may favor the largest US defense contractors (less reputational risk, lower transaction costs), even if those contractors may cost more. By laying bare those concerns – by pointing out the agency problem, that contracting officials (as agents) may choose inferior solutions from larger contractors, to preserve the officials' reputations and to reduce work – we open the door to Professor Spagnolo's suggestion that SMEs should be given a broader role in government procurement because (in his view) SMEs are (as many argue in the United States) fonts of innovation. But compare Hurst and Pugsley (2011) arguing

that data suggest that assumptions that small businesses drive innovation in the United States are overstated

- Guideposts make systems easier to align: Seeing the law as a set of guideposts for administrative behavior also makes it easier to harmonize procurement regimes, as some have argued (for example) that the European and US federal procurement regimes should be harmonized to reduce artificial, rules-based barriers to trade (Yukins C. R. and Priess H. (2014)). See, e.g., Take, for example, Professor Spagnolo's suggestion that procuring entities should have the legal discretion to award some lots to SMEs (to spur innovation), while awarding other combinations of lots to larger enterprises (if doing so seems more efficient). If we take a step back, and look for the critical (and typical) "guideposts" in the procurement regime – here, for instance, the rules regarding "lot" awards under framework agreements – we can use the US example to show that Professor Spagnolo's suggestion is completely workable. Under the US rules, a procuring agency may issue awards under a standing framework agreement based on "best value," and procuring officials are left with broad discretion in structuring orders (i.e., lots awarded) under existing framework agreements (which are called "indefinite-delivery/indefinite-quantity" (IDIQ) contracts in the U.S. federal system). See, e.g., FAR 16.505(b)(1)(ii) ("The contracting officer may exercise broad discretion in developing appropriate order placement procedure.") Ultimately, this US rule (this "guidepost") can thus be harmonized with what Professor Spagnolo argues is the emerging best practice (and rule) in the European Union.

5 Giancarlo Spagnolo – Conclusions

Professor Yukins is probably right in arguing that I may have been a bit too strong in complaining about the excessive attempts of lawmakers to micro-regulate public procurement processes they do not fully understand and master. We come, however, from very different legal traditions and environments. I would have probably fully subscribed to his more balanced view if I lived in the US or the UK and had not experienced four years of frustration being forced to a lot evidently inefficient with the Italian procurement agency because of the high risk of infringing one of the many components of the complex web of confused and frequently conflicting, prescriptive rules making the Italian procurement legislation.

When, for example, a directive prescribed different possible ending rules for electronic auctions, and plenty of theoretical and empirical studies showed that one was sound, one was not sound but could make sense at least in some situations, and a third was actually pure nonsense, as it guaranteed the failure of the auction, the Italian legislators used their discretion to create legal certainty, and used it to restrict the options only to the latter rule, the one that make no sense whatsoever. These are frequent mistakes, as lawmakers in Europe tend not consult and trust experts from the field they are regulating. For example, it allowed framework agreements with one winning suppliers, or with three or more. Not with two. In other words, it made competition among two preselected suppliers, "dual sourcing", illegal in Europe, allowing everything else, from one (monopolist) winner, to three, four or five. Too bad that there are twenty years of studies highlighting the benefits of "dual sourcing", i.e. of two selected and competing suppliers, which is very often the most efficient solution because it creates some competition minimizing duplication of costs. It is essential that the guideposts of procurement rules remain as open as possible, leaving the competent procurer the option possibility to use the good methodology, at least some times, rather than imposing the use of the bad one or forbidding the very best one.

The decision how to group tasks in service contracts, how to define the geographical coverage of a procurement tender, and how long should a procurement contract of framework agreement last, are obviously among the most crucial and complex decisions in the procurement process. They determine the size and number of lots, what type of supplier will be able to participate and win, as well as the frequency of procurements. The optimal choice along these dimensions will be very different for different markets at different times. Some rules are necessary to have a benchmark for monitoring and evaluating performance, and for discovering malpractices. Rules, however, may or may not be good: they may or may not be informed by accumulated knowledge on the issue, whether they relate to education, health or markets. It would be a great success if conferences like the Interdisciplinary Symposion on Public Procurement, in which public-service-oriented law and economics scholars meet to discuss important new market regulations, could take place one year before the regulation is implemented, potentially influencing their final versions, rather than identifying mistakes already made into binding laws.

Conclusion: The purpose of this innovative symposium is to show that a dialogue between economists and lawyers can help improving the regulation of public procurement markets. I hope the interaction between us showed that very divergent approaches can still converge and lead to productive communication. The "law and economics" approach to regulation common to Anglo-Saxon countries could lead to substantial improvements of European Directives, as well as of their national implementation.

6 Christopher R. Yukins – Conclusions

In his concluding statement, Professor Spagnolo suggests that Italian authorities chose the "worst" form of reverse auctions – which is, ironically, exactly what US procurement officials have consistently done, by implementing reverse auctions which allow customer agencies, after the price auction is over, to select not the lowest price "winner" but rather a higher-priced offeror. The foremost private provider of reverse auctions to the US government describes the award process as follows:

- When proceeding with an award, the FedBid Terms of Use do not obligate a Buyer to make an award to the lowest bid submitted...
- The FedBid Bidding Requirements for each buy include a clause notifying Sellers that an award may be based on factors other than pricing...

- Buyers have the capability to set the terms on each buy posted to the Marketplace.... The reverse auction platform does rank Sellers' bids according to price, but Buyers are able to award based on whatever criteria best fits the procurement strategy/procurement requirement (FedBid).

If public buyers may ignore the low bidder in a reverse auction, and instead decide after the price auction to make award to a higher-priced bidder, this arguably undoes the integrity of the reverse auction, and runs counter to fundamental legal and economic principles of public procurement: that award be based on the criteria clearly stated and understood by all involved in the procurement. See, e.g., FAR 15.204–5, 48 C.F.R. 15.204–5 (solicitation must set forth relative weight of evaluation factors for award). In other words, the leading US reverse auction model, see also Defense Logistics Agency Acquisition Directive (DLAD) 52.215–9023 (adopting model), while has already been the focus of policy scrutiny, see Pub. Law No. 113–291, Sec. 824 (Dec. 2014) (calling for new Defense Department regulations on electronic reverse auctions); (recommending reforms to improve competition in reverse auctions), arguably remains a classic example of a procurement process at odds with basic legal and economic principles.

As this example shows, policy in public procurement (on both sides of the Atlantic) would benefit from continuing, sound input from both economists and lawyers. The question, then, is whether economists and lawyers can speak to the regulators, as well as the rules – and when, and how, those conversations should occur.

References

Albano, G. L. (2014): *Performance Indicators for Centralized Public Procurement* (Istanbul, May 28, 2014) (on file with author).

Arrowsmith, S. (1998): Towards a Multilateral Agreement on Transparency in Government Procurement, 47 Int'l & Comp. L.Q. 793, 797 (1998).

Dimitri, N., Pacini, R., Pagnozzi, M., and Spagnolo, G. (2006): Multi-contract tendering procedures and package bidding in procurement, Ch. 8 of the *Handbook of Procurement*, (Dimitri, Piga and Spagnolo Eds.), Cambridge University Press, 2006.

FedBid: *Can I Award to a Seller Who Is Not in the Lead on a Buy?*, available at http://fedbid.custhelp.com/app/answers/detail/a_id/49.

Government Accountability Office (2013): Reverse Auctions: Guidance Is Needed To Maximize Competition and Achieve Cost Savings, GAO-14–108 (Dec. 9, 2013), available at www.gao.gov.

Grimm, V., Pacini, R., Spagnolo, G., and Zanza, M. (2006): "Division into lots and competition in procurement," Ch. 7 of the *Handbook of Procurement*, (Dimitri, Piga, and Spagnolo (eds)), Cambridge University Press, 2006.

Hurst, E., and Pugsley, B. W. (2011): *What Do Small Businesses Do?* (August 2011) www.brookings.edu/~/media/Files/Programs/ES/BPEA/2011_fall_bpea_papers/2011_fall_bpea_conference_hurst.pdf.

Yukins, C. R., and Priess, H. J. (2014): *Breaking the Impasse in the Transatlantic Trade and Investment Partnership (TTIP) Negotiations: Rethinking Priorities in Procurement*, 56 Gov. Contr. 235 (July 23, 2014), available at http://ssrn.com/abstract=2471653.

5 Size matters

Exploring the rules, practices and rationale behind splitting and combining of administrative requirements under India's public procurement frameworks

Sandeep Verma[1]

1 Introduction

Contract splitting, or the division of administrative requirements into "lots" for the purposes of individual procurement or contracting actions, is a commonly invoked technique used in multiple jurisdictions worldwide. The United States' Federal Acquisition Regulation (FAR) recognises that "bundling"[2] of administrative requirements could lead to measurable benefits such as: (i) cost savings or price reduction; (ii) quality improvements that will save time or improve or enhance performance or efficiency; (iii) reduction in acquisition cycle times; or (iv) better terms and conditions of contract; but it also nevertheless mandates procuring officials[3] to "unbundle" procurement actions so as to maximise small business participation – an important responsibility that needs to be viewed in context of mandatory set-asides of below-threshold procurement contracts to small businesses in the US.[4] France has a similar approach: public procurement contracts need to be split into small volumes; and outright purchase from foreign sources is possible only if procurement officials cannot split contracts any further.[5] At the regional level, Germany has also had a long-standing rule on award of contracts in lots,[6] and the percentage of contracts being advertised in lots has been as high as 19 per cent.[7] Finland seems to take a middle-of-the-road approach; the public procurement law includes a prohibition to artificially subdivide or combine contracts: no public contract may be divided into lots, severed or calculated using artificial methods with the intention of excluding it from the scope of Finnish procurement laws; a public supply or service contract may not be combined with a works contract; and neither may contracts be otherwise artificially combined to prevent them from coming with the scope of domestic procurement laws (Kaijalainen and Luoma, 2014).

The reasons for contract-splitting can themselves thus be numerous and diverse: smaller contracts are typically more efficient in terms of the speed of procurement, thereby resulting in greater user-satisfaction; and smaller contracts can also typically attract greater competition from smaller participants and prevent cartel-formation amongst sellers in the process, at least in the short run (Grimm *et al.*, 2006), particularly in the case of *Commercial-Off-The-Shelf* (COTS) items procurement. Procurement in small lots can also serve important public policy objectives by ensuring that abuse of bid protest and bidder complaint/grievance redressal processes by unscrupulous bidders can be minimised, de-risking the attainment of public objectives because of the government not "putting all its eggs in one basket".

In terms of international practices, the overall mood in the EU has been for nudging public procurement officials to divide contracts into lots by default as part of European efforts to encourage greater participation of small and medium European enterprises; although under the latest EU directives, procurement officials are merely required to provide an explanation where contracts are not divided into lots (Semple, 2014). The tensions with procurement in lots in the EU are similar to those with extension of EU tendering rules to award of subcontracts by PPP concessionaires – PPP prime contractors tend to be big, leaving little space for smaller businesses to fully participate in the procurement process – but the EU debate could not result in concrete proposals on transparent and competitive award of subcontracts by PPP concessionaires,[8] similar to what has eventually happened to proposals for mandatory division into lots.

Interestingly though, this division into lots in the EU takes place without compromising the mandatory publication and competition requirements imposed under EU procurement directives that would have applied to the sum-total procurement contract had such division into lots not taken place (Semple, 2014. p. 10). The EU guidance allows contracts not to be divided into lots for reasons such as: (i) chances of restricting competition as a result of division into lots; (ii) potential for rendering the execution of the contract excessively technically difficult or expensive because of such division; or (ii) that the need to coordinate the different contractors for the lots could seriously risk undermining the proper execution of the overall administrative requirements.[9]

However, from alternative perspectives, contract splitting can sometimes be viewed negatively, as it may dis-incentivise participation of bigger players capable of "better-quality" deliveries, while also resulting in costlier procurement by preventing economies of scale from kicking-in. Contract splitting almost invariably results in lowering of the level at which financial sanctions would need to be issued; and at least in the Indian context, this outcome seems to be the primary reason for discouraging contract splitting in public procurement in India – essentially a case of oversight and accountability objectives overriding other procurement desiderata such as contract efficiency, user satisfaction and (sometimes) competition. Separately, from a political economy perspective, unscrupulous state entities may be more inclined to centralise procurement so as to ensure greater visibility on contract volumes, costs and resultant "benefits" that may become available to higher political and bureaucratic levels with vested interests in over-centralisation of administrative needs for conducting public procurement actions.

2 Rules and practices on splitting and combining of administrative requirements in India

Collaborative public procurement through centralised combination of procurement volumes by various government entities, or through the more "decentralised" use of common framework agreements, is not only expressly permitted under procurement regulations in India,[10] but has indeed been encouraged by the Government in a variety of cases for reasons of public interest.[11] The following section explores rules on various permissible forms of such collaboration and/or centralisation of public procurement actions by government procuring agencies in India.

2.1 Rules on pre-bid quantity splitting and agglomeration

Pre-RFP splitting (or agglomeration) of administrative requirements has two important features in India from procurement regulations perspectives. Procurement actions are largely decentralised amongst different hierarchies of government offices – ministries and departments have been delegated full powers to make their own arrangements for procurement of goods[12] under the *General Financial Rules 2005* (hereafter "GFR") that apply to ministries and government departments at the federal level in India; and this delegated procurement authority gets further sub-delegated under administrative procedures of respective ministries and departments. However, within this delegated authority, a particular procuring official or agency is encouraged to agglomerate required quantities into one single tender rather than conduct procurement through separate smaller lots. More specifically, the GFR require that under Rule 148 of the GFR that apply to public procurement actions of ministries and government departments at the federal level in India, a demand for goods should not be divided into small quantities to make piecemeal purchases to avoid the necessity of obtaining the sanction of higher authority required with reference to the estimated value of the total demand.[13] The (subsidiary) *Manual on Policies and Procedures for Purchase of Goods* (hereafter MoPPPG) imposes a similar requirement: a demand should not be split into small quantities for the sole purpose of avoiding the necessity of taking approval of the higher authority required for sanctioning the purchase of the original demand[14]; as does the other *Manual on Policies and Procedures for Procurement of Works*, according to which no project or work will be split up to bring it within the sanctioning powers of a lower authority.[15] However, the GFR also simultaneously require procuring officials to exercise care so as to avoid procuring quantities in excess of (current and near future) requirements, so as to avoid inventory carrying costs.[16] State rules in India tend to echo similar concerns, for instance, the General Financial and Accounts Rules of the (State) Government of Rajasthan require that procurement should not be done in a piecemeal approach or be split to avoid sanction of higher authorities,[17] together with an almost identical caveat that store purchases should not be undertaken in advance of actual requirements, if purchases are likely to prove "unprofitable" to the Government.[18]

Procurement processes in India also rely on a "rate contract" method of procurement – essentially a case where a Central Purchase Organisation (hereafter "CPO") so declared by the Government of India sets up basic framework agreements[19] against which different ministries and departments can directly place independent indents with enlisted suppliers. Where departments and ministries desire the Directorate General of Supplies and Disposals – one of the biggest, and perhaps the only CPO at the federal level in India – to undertake the procurement action on their behalf, the DGS&D's rules require that competent purchasing officers in the DGS&D can combine demand of several departments and place a consolidated supply order,[20] although bulking of demands between "urgent" indents and "ordinary" indents is not permissible.[21]

2.2 *Rules on pre-bid bundling and unbundling*

Executive guidance on bundling (commonly understood in India as combining two related or unrelated contracts into one, different from simply combining of the same administrative requirement) in India is practically non-existent. Even for the case of maintenance of sophisticated and costly machinery and equipment, the GFR merely enable a procuring agency to enter into maintenance contract with the supplier for post-warranty maintenance,[22] rather than specifically stating that supply, warrant and maintenance aspects can be clubbed together into one single contract. To that extent, the GFR, in fact, allow the maintenance aspects to be split from the supply part of an administrative requirement, allowing procuring agencies to either enter into a separate maintenance contract with the supplier of the original equipment, or with any other competent firm, not necessarily the original supplier of goods. Interestingly, within a separate policy framework for contract design of Public–Private Partnership (PPP) concessions in India, the applicable legal framework allows both related[23] and unrelated[24] activities to be contracted under the same concession where such combinations could be leveraged for greater efficiency and for attracting greater bidder participation.

2.3 *Rules for contract splitting (post-bid evaluation)*

An extremely interesting feature of procurement regulations in India, perhaps without exact parallels in most international practices, is a very real possibility of splitting of quantities by a procuring agency amongst different bidders *post evaluation of bids*, even though the original RFP could be a single one for the combined quantities. The regulations merely require that such possibility of splitting of quantities, once competing bids have been evaluated, should be explicitly stated in the original single RFP, alongwith possible proportions of permissible split.

More specifically, as per standard procurement procedures in India, each schedule of requirement incorporated in the bid enquiry documents is required to be awarded to the lowest (in price) responsive bidder for that schedule without dividing the same; and a bidder who does not quote for the complete schedule as required is normally to be treated as unresponsive and ignored. However, the procurement rules provide for an exception on special occasions of purchase of very large quantities of goods which are beyond the capacity of a single bidder, and when the lowest responsive bidder is unable to take the load of the entire quantity.[25] In such cases, the remaining quantity may be ordered on the second lowest responsive bidder at the rates offered by the lowest responsive bidder. If required, the rules allow for negotiation to be held with the second lowest responsive bidders to reach an agreement for delivery at the lowest bid prices.[26] As an extension of this concept of quantity splitting post evaluation of bids, in certain high-volume cases, it may also become necessary to divide the require-ment under a schedule by placing multiple contracts for part quantities on more than two responsive bidders, the only caveat being that such an eventuality should normally be foreseen by procuring officials and provided for in the *Notice Inviting Tenders* (NIT, also understood as a *Request for Proposals* or an RFP). The rules also require that the proposed formula to be adopted for allocation of orders to multiple (responsive) bidders should be clearly brought out in the NIT/ RFP; and that splitting of order by purchasing organisation should be an excep-tion rather than a rule.[27]

Such post-bid evaluation splitting of contracts, other than the general provi-sions contained in the Manual, also gets mandatorily activated under certain cir-cumstances for fulfillment of certain socio-economic objectives. For instance, the *Public Procurement Policy for Micro and Small Enterprises (MSEs) Order, 2012* provides a price preference to micro and small enterprises, provided they have been otherwise technically qualifies and the quoted prices are within a price band of (lowest price bid) + 15 per cent. Subject to such MSE bidders matching the lowest bid price, they shall also be allowed to supply a portion of require-ment, up to 20 per cent of total tendered value.[28] In case of more than one such MSEs falling within the lowest price band and matching the lowest quoted price, the order requires that the supply amongst such MSEs shall be shared propor-tionately to the tendered quantity, although it is not clear how such MSEs not quoting for the full quantities required under the RFP can be treated as techni-cally compliant and responsive.[29] Similar provisions for post-bid evaluation splitting of supply order are contained in the *Policy for Preference to Domesti-cally Manufactured Electronic Products* in India, which requires procuring offi-cials to normally specify the percentage of procurement value in a particular bid document that would be awarded to the lowest-priced technically qualified domestic manufacturer of electronic products, subject to price matching with (a non-domestic manufacturer) the lowest bidder.[30] Further splitting of orders amongst several domestic manufacturers may be possible, if and as provided for in the bid documents, subject to price matching requirements.[31]

The State of Tamil Nadu in India provides for a unique situation of post-bid evaluation splitting of supply orders against the same principal bid document: in cases where two or more tenderers quoted the same price, the tender (bid) accepting authority is mandatorily required to split the procurement among such bidders taking into consideration their experience and credentials; and where such splitting is not possible or cannot be done equally, the procuring authority shall record reasons for the same.[32] The Tamil Nadu guidance to procuring officials for mandatory splitting of contract volumes contrasts sharply with the position under the competition law (anti-trust law) in India, where the latter requires a thorough examination of such cases of identical quoted prices for possible collusion and cartelisation amongst unscrupulous bidders (CCI, 2010; Vaid, 2013).

2.4 Other processes facilitating (de facto) combinations

Combinations or splitting can take place in a variety of other ways under India's procurement regulations, quite apart from rules on agglomeration and bundling outlined above. Two of such important methods of procurement are: (i) rate contracts[33]; and (ii) setting of standard (or minimum) technical specifications, the latter being done generally for ensuring inter-operability of equipment and platforms across different procurement and user agencies. An interesting feature of both these methods is that the empanelment of suppliers (in case of rate contracts) or specification of standard technical specifications is done centrally, while procurement and supply orders are carried out in a decentralised or localised fashion. In some case, the second stage – decentralised procurement or placement of supply orders – could be followed by de facto centralisation of supply orders with a single or a small number of suppliers, or even a large number of suppliers acting in a coordinated fashion with potential risks of collusion. In either of these two cases, the negotiating capacity of procuring agencies gets diluted vis-à-vis suppliers through dispersal of procurement volumes into a large number of small, individual supply orders.

On a more positive note, many states have started centralised procurement of drugs and diagnostic and treatment services that are distributed through government hospitals as part of policies on health assurance, particularly for poor and marginalised groups. The model followed is one of centralised laying down of technical specifications of drugs and diagnostic services, followed by centralised empanelment and procurement: one that is quite distinct from the rate contracting system followed by the DGS&D or mechanism centred on common and centralised technical specification-setting but decentralised procurement.

2.5 Some emerging practices on quantity agglomeration

An important development in India of recent origins relates to combination of quantities by a group of state procurement agencies that are have separate and distinct legal identities, culminating in the outcome that one nominated procuring agency undertakes the complete procurement as one single contract, even though the user agencies themselves are separate and geographically spread out, to the point of being *even competitors amongst themselves* in specific product or services marketplaces. This form of collaboration amongst competitors engaged in public services delivery is relatively new in India, and quite distinct from the normal forms of collaboration amongst public entities through pooling of procurement volumes or through common framework agreements hitherto practiced. More specifically, the Government of India have shown forward action on joint tenders by *Central Public Sector Enterprises* (CPSEs)[34] and "Public Sector Banks" (PSBs) in a few cases, although cases of different government departments bundling their requirements have otherwise been largely minimal. This appears to have been done in exercise of general constitutional authority of the Government, rather than specifically invoking particular provisions of the GFR or any relevant procurement rules of concerned entities or specifying the underlying statutory/constitutional authority of the Government.

In one case, the collaboration was ordered through *plain administrative orders* by the concerned administrative Department (as in the case of joint tendering for *Automated Teller Machines* – ATMs – by PSBs), and on a few other occasions through *policy decisions* of the Government. In order to appreciate the legal position better, it may therefore be worthwhile to examine the procurement rule position, as well as the competition law position, relating to joint purchasing agreements in India.

2.5.1 The procurement rule position

The MoPPPG contains an enabling provision for rate contracts (simplified framework agreements as explained in an earlier section), whereby a designated *Central Purchase Organisation* (CPO)[35] can enter into common rate contracts for user items frequently needed in bulk by various Ministries and/or Departments.[36] The provision has two important underlying features: (i) that the placement of supply orders by a user organisation against a common rate contract is completely voluntary and at the *option* of the user/procuring organisation; and (ii) that the provision does not appear to allow one user organisation to place supply orders against rate contracts established by *other* user organisations, but *only* against a rate contract established by a CPO. Separately, the Central Vigilance Commission or the CVC (2012) that performs an important oversight functions in terms of procurement integrity in India, issued some recent guidance to the effect of discouraging indiscriminate placement of direct supply orders by one state procurement entity on another, in cases where such direct purchase orders are followed up by single source procurement by the receiving agency without any "value-addition" in the process. On a closer reading, these two independent instructions appear to have a small area of divergence: as per the CVC, one government department or state agency can nominate another government department or state agency for undertaking its procurement activities so long as the receiving agency or department conducts its procurement in an open and competitive manner (presumably also through open and competitive framework agreements); whereas the MoPPPG allows centralise procurement through a designated CPO alone, rather than placement of supply orders by requiring entities on *non-designated* CPOs.

2.5.2 The competition law position

The position in law governing horizontal co-operation in India is quite rigid, and any agreement entered into between enterprises or associations or any other enterprises, which, inter alia: (i) directly or indirectly determines purchase prices; (ii) limits of controls the production, supply, markets or technical development of services; (iii) shares markets by way of allocation of geographical area or number of customers; or (iv) directly or indirectly results in bid rigging or collusive bidding, is *presumed* to have an appreciable adverse effect on competition and is void,[37] with the exception of agreements by way of joint ventures if such agreements increase efficiencies in acquisition of goods or services.[38] Such collaborative procurement through joint ventures, if such arrangements increase efficiency in acquisition of goods or services, are not presumed to have an appreciable adverse effect on competition, and therefore need to be analysed for potential anti-competitive effects under a "Rule of Reason" approach.[39] Also, joint purchasing agreements that contain elements of exclusive supply agreements and "refusal to deal" agreements are void[40] under Indian law if they can be shown, under a "Rule of Reason" approach, to result in appreciable adverse effect on competition in India. In respect of vertical co-operation, the competition law in India prohibits, inter alia: (i) imposition of unfair or discriminatory conditions in purchase or sale of goods or services, or imposition of unfair or discriminatory price in purchase of goods or services; (ii) arrangements that result in denial of market access in any manner; and (iii) use of the dominant position of one enterprise or group to enter into another relevant market[41]; and joint purchasing agreements that incorporate these elements are therefore anti-competitive under a "Rule of Reason" approach.

Extending this rule to collaborative procurement amongst competitors by way of joint purchasing agreements through a joint tender – an exercise that *inherently* involves the fixation of a common price of procurement of supplies by participating members – it would appear that joint purchases as in the case of ethanol procurement by OMCs shall presumed to have an appreciable adverse effect on competition and is void under a per se approach.[42]

3 Analysing the potential legal, economic and public policy implications of Indian public procurement frameworks

A quick review of the rules and practices on splitting and bundling of administrative requirements in India reveals a rather interesting position. On the one hand, for routine procurements as well as for infrastructure PPP concessions, the rules and practices generally seem to encourage agglomeration of quantities, bundling of contracts and centralisation of procurement actions by public contracting entities; whereas for technical items procurement with more limited number of suppliers, the rules and practices appear to de facto encourage agglomeration and centralisation of sales at the suppliers' end, with a huge mix and variety of procurement strategies somewhere in between these two positions.

3.1 Quantity agglomeration

In the case of routine procurements, for instance, current rules encourage procuring entities to combine required quantities, and the (primary) underlying rationale seems to be that in the absence of any such guidance, procuring entities would attempt to split procurements so as to avoid the need for obtaining administrative sanctions from higher authorities: clearly a case of oversight and accountability objectives overriding other equally important desiderata[43] such as greater user satisfaction that could be achieved with smaller and decentralised procurements with timely availability of supplies and services to user agencies, or simply because of a limitation that the user agencies may not have adequate inventory carrying capabilities that may be necessary for larger volumes of supplies. Another important concern behind this encouragement for quantity agglomeration is the expectation that such agglomeration would result in more competition through an open procurement process, whereas smaller lots could be processed by procuring entities through a limited (restricted) tendering route; but once again, this rationale for quantity agglomeration does not adequately factor into account: (i) the fact that the thresholds for using limited/restricted tendering in India are rather low, and therefore limited tendering can be undertaken by procuring agencies in a really handful of cases; (ii) the nature of supplier positions with resultant large value contracts – whether an overreach on quantity agglomeration could actually reduce competition through cartelisation amongst bigger players or by creating barriers to small business participation. The latter is especially important in view since in certain cases, the rules themselves allow post-bid evaluation splitting of contracts, ignoring the competition-discouraging and small business participation-discouraging effects of agglomeration in the first instance.

3.2 Post-bid evaluation splitting of quantities

The rationale behind post-bid evaluation splitting of RFP quantities amongst the best offeror and the next one or more, the latter subject to price matching with the best offeror, is stated to be providing a preference to procurement from indigenous sources or from small businesses, depending upon the rules framework in operation. In the case of the policy for preferential procurement from small businesses, the rationale therefore essentially presumes that small businesses will bid for the entire quantity required under an RFP and be ready to supply the entire quantity required should they emerge as the best offeror, or at least a significant part of the required quantity should they emerge within a certain price band of the best offeror and provided they are willing to match the price offered by the best offeror. In the absence of published data regarding number or value of cases where either of these two eventualities happens, it is difficult to assess the effectiveness of the underlying strategy, but it is otherwise easy to see that the expectation that a small business will be willing to supply the entire quantity under the RFP may be difficult to achieve in practice, both on account of smaller supply/production capabilities, as well as their relative lack of economies of scale. A similar assessment can perhaps also be made in the case of preferential procurement from indigenous manufacturers, given that the underlying procurement strategies are identical in the two cases.

Perhaps a more effective strategy would be utilising the outright set-aside strategy that is followed in the US, both for small businesses as well as in the case of indigenous suppliers/manufacturers: in case of small businesses, all contracts below identified thresholds are mandatorily set aside, providing them surety of award if they are willing to supply the (smaller) quantities required under an RFP; whereas small businesses are given a simple price preference, without expectations of price matching, for higher-than-threshold procurements. In the case of indigenous manufacturing, irrespective of value, a contract can be set aside for domestic competition if such as set aside is necessary for developing/mobilising the domestic industrial base.

3.3 Bundling of administrative requirements

India's regulatory frameworks on public procurement do not contain extensive guidance on bundling of related contracts, beyond the limited provisions mentioned earlier allowing entering into maintenance contracts with original equipment suppliers. The provision has been drafted more from a financial/budgetary perspective since capital expenditure and revenue expenditure are booked under separate heads of accounts, rather than from a contracts efficiency perspective that would require bundling of related contracts into one single RFP at the time of original competition to maximise value-for-money for the Government and for avoiding problems with subsequent vendor lock-in.

Insofar as bundling of unrelated contracts is concerned (as in the case of airport concessions with real estate development), the practice has been perhaps more influenced by the need to keep airport user charges artificially low through cross-subsidisation from real estate operations, resulting in minimising public opposition to airport privatisation, rather than ensuring transparency through visibility on the real costs of airports privatisation. In addition, the practice could also have an untended effect of reducing competition in public contracting by requiring dual skills from bidders in terms of eligibility criteria: a subject for further study and research from competition in procurement perspectives.

3.4 Collaborative public procurement

In the context of anti-competitive effects of quantity agglomeration, two emerging cases of agglomeration of ATM procurements by PSBs and joint ethanol procurement by OMCs are of particular interest. The ATM case was initiated by an administrative order of the concerned Department, but could potentially have ignored the position that the State may perhaps not have had the authority for issuing such an order in the first instance. The case was initiated by concerns on different rates for ATMs being procured by different PSBs, although it is not known if the fluctuations were wide enough and unrelated to different specifications and/or capabilities of the machines themselves, and whether such agglomeration could have encouraged cartelization amongst ATM suppliers or ATM-services providers rather than attracting greater competition through larger business volumes. The ATM case did not reach finality; the procurement process was abandoned after a few months of procurement planning and issue of RFPs, and had an unintended effect of adversely affecting PSB capabilities to reach out to their customers with adequate depth and range of services necessary in a highly competitive marketplace such as banking services' markets. In the latter case of joint tenders for ethanol, the regulator's orders have created an interesting situation because of the divergence between the competition law and the case law in India. The India Glycols case, for instance, probably contained a significant number of important tender design issues with potentially anti-competitive effects as commonly understood in academic literature on the subject, for instance: (i) dominance of buyers in both input markets as well as in output markets; (ii) consumer expectation of competition between the dominant buyers in the commercial market place (the downstream market); (iii) mandatory (involuntary) participation of dominant buyers in the scheme with pre-fixed purchasing commitments; (iv) sharing of commercially sensitive information amongst the members of the buying group; (v) artificial geographical market segregation and similar unilateral restrictions imposed on suppliers during the contract finalisation process; (vi) denial of responses to tender queries by the purchasing entities unless such queries were jointly raised by suppliers; (vii) invitation of expressions of interest from suppliers without intimating in advance intended purchase prices or specific quantities to be allocated to each participant, and subsequent restrictions on future participation of any respondents who choose not to sign final contracts if the purchase prices unilaterally mandated or quantities unilaterally allocated by the OMCs were unacceptable to ethanol suppliers; and (viii) arbitrary and non-monitorable restrictions on use of transport assets by suppliers during return trips.[44] And yet, the case law arising out of orders of the competition regulator and the appellate authority contain little legal substance to be of use for meaningful academic research on potentially harmful competitive effects of state-enforced joint purchasing agreements.

4 Conclusions

The aforesaid section lists different rules and practices in India on splitting and bundling of administrative requirements by public procuring entities within themselves, as well as on collaborative purchasing agreements amongst separate public procuring entities in India. To the extent that quantity agglomeration, bundling and joint purchasing are some of the important ways that affect contract values and bidder eligibility for posing meaningful competition, it is clear that size definitely matters in public procurement when it comes to acquisition planning using any one or more of these devices in the country. Depending upon the context within which they are employed, quantity agglomeration, bundling and joint purchasing could increase economy in contracting or reduce competition; they could enhance contract efficiency or make procurement more risky from a buyer perspective; and they could definitely enhance small business participation or drive them out of competition. The underlying legal and economic implications of contract splitting are therefore not only related to merely one of the important desiderata – namely, socio-economic preferences through small business participation – but have profound impact on a full range of public policy objectives, from efficiency and competition to integrity and risk-aversion. To that extent, the regulatory developments under Indian frameworks identified in this short chapter could perhaps inform practices and rules in other jurisdictions as well, given the complexity of policy objectives that could unravel only upon a closer study of the underlying small print and resultant policy, legal and economic implications. As stated earlier in this chapter, the tensions with mandatory procurement in lots within the EU have been similar to those with EU's green paper consultations on extension of EU tendering rules to award of subcontracts by prime PPP concessionaires, issues that resonated before High Courts in India[45] as well but did not attain finality given the complex legal issues involved, just as they failed to find adequate traction within the EU itself. At a subsequent stage of analysis, it may therefore be of considerable research and practical interest to compare Indian strategies and resultant implications on public procurement in lots, bundles or collaboration, with those currently being practiced or under consultation in the EU and in other important national frameworks as the US FAR and elsewhere, even if to only attempt a fuller discussion of advantages, risks and concerns with contract agglomeration, bundling and joint purchasing arrangements that are fast evolving both in India and internationally.

Notes

1 © 2014, *Sandeep Verma. Not to be cited or reproduced without prior approval of the Author. This draft is presently under submission to the (forthcoming) 2nd Public Procurement Symposium 2014, Budapest (Hungary).* The author is a civil servant and holds an LLM with highest honours, having specialised in Government Procurement Law from The George Washington University Law School, Washington DC. Views contained in this short academic paper (working draft) are purely personal; and do not reflect the official position or policy of the Government of India or any of her departments or agencies.

2 FAR 2.101 defines "bundling" as consolidating two or more requirements for supplies or services, previously provided or performed under separate smaller contracts, into a solicitation for a single contract that is likely to be unsuitable for award to a small business concern due to: (i) the diversity, size, or specialised nature of the elements of the performance specified; (ii) the aggregate dollar value of the anticipated award; (iii) the geographical dispersion of the contract performance sites; or (iv) any combination of the above factors.

3 FAR 7.103(u)(2) read with 7.107(a). See, also, National Oceanic and Atmospheric Administration, *FAR Requirements for Bundled Contracts*, available online www. easc.noaa.gov/APG/Planning/Plan_Docs/FAR-Requirements-for-Bundled-Contracts. pdf.

4 FAR 19.502–1.
5 European Tender Information System (2006), *Public Procurement in France*, available online www.etisys.com/uploads/media/France.pdf.
6 European Tender Information System (2006), *Public Procurement in Germany*, available online www.etisys.com/uploads/media/Germany.pdf.
7 Royal Institute of British Architecture (2012), *Comparative Procurement: Procurement Regulation and practice in Germany, Sweden and the UK*, available online www.architecture.com/Files/RIBAHoldings/PolicyAndInternationalRelations/Policy/PublicAffairs/2012/ComparativeProcurement.pdf.
8 See e.g. EU Communication (2005) and Green Paper (2005).
9 European Council (2014), Directive 2014/24/EU, ¶78.
10 For instance, Indian procurement rules envisage the creation of a *Central Purchasing Organisation* to bring in rate contracts for common user items frequently needed in bulk by various Ministries/Departments; 1.1.3(iii), *Manual of Policies and Procedures for Purchase of Goods*, p. 4, http://finmin.nic.in/the_ministry/dept_expenditure/acts_codes/MPProc4ProGod.pdf).
11 Recent instances in India include an attempt by public sector banks to jointly procure ATM services (*State Bank of India led state-run bank's consortium to install 40,000 ATMs by March 14*, http://in.finance.yahoo.com/news/state-bank-india-led-state-120603813.html) and the ongoing joint industry tenders for ethanol procurement by Oil Marketing Companies (OMCs) for blending with retail petrol marketed by them; *PIB Press Release*, November 22 2012, www.pib.nic.in/newsite/erelease.aspx?relid=89270. Current proposals also include creation of a *Special Purpose Vehicle* for direct aviation fuel imports where the *Airports Authority of India*, OMCs and airlines will have equity participation (*AAI to create common infra for direct aviation fuel imports*, Business Standard, June 07 2013, www.business-standard.com/article/companies/aai-to-create-common-infra-for-direct-aviation-fuel-imports-113060600692_1.html), as well as a proposed joint venture company promoted by public sector oil companies for streamlining crude oil imports into India (*Panel moots joint venture of PSUs for smooth crude oil imports*, The Hindu Business Line, May 08 2013, www.thehindubusinessline.com/companies/panel-moots-joint-venture-of-psus-for-smooth-crude-oil-imports/article4696154.ece).
12 Government of India (2005), *General Financial Rules*, ¶140.
13 Ibid., ¶148.
14 Government of India (2006), *Manual on Policies and Procedures for Purchase of Goods*, ¶2.2.2.
15 Government of India (2006), *Manual on Policies and Procedures for Procurement of Works*, ¶1.2.1(e).
16 GoI, *supra* n.13, ¶137(i).
17 Government of Rajasthan (2011), *General Financial and Accounts Rules – Part II*, ¶64(ii).
18 Ibid., ¶64(iii).
19 Rate contracts as practiced in India are essentially closed framework agreements with prices fixed as part of the main framework contract itself – essentially a list of empanelled suppliers with price and technical aspects of various goods fixed in advance, and requiring ministries and departments merely place supply orders for quantities required by them a pre-fixed prices and technical specifications.
20 Government of India (1999), *DGS&D Manual*, ¶7.14.3.
21 Ibid., ¶7.23.
22 GoI, *supra* n.13, ¶156.
23 Government of India (2009), *Public Private Partnership in Greenfield Airports – Model Concession Agreement*, ¶¶17–20. These clauses allow the bundling of operations and maintenance aspects with airport construction under the same principal concession.

24 Ibid., ¶¶ 27. The clause permits bundling of real estate development with airport con-
    striction and maintenance under the same principal concession.

25 GoI, *supra* n.15, ¶11.7.5.

26 Ibid.

27 Ibid.

28 Government of India (2012), *Public Procurement Policy for Micro and Small Enter-
    prises Order*, ¶6(1).

29 Ibid., ¶6(2).

30 Government of India (2013), *Policy for Preference to Domestically Manufactured
    Electronic Products*, ¶4.2.2.

31 Ibid.

32 §10(5), The Tamil Nadu Transparency in Tenders Act, 1998 (Tamil Nadu Act No. 43
    of 1998).

33 *Supra*, n.20.

34 The traditional international terminology for such enterprises is *State-Owned Enter-
    prises* (SOEs).

35 As stated earlier, the *Directorate General of Supplies and Disposal* (DGS&D) under
    the Ministry of Commerce is one such CPO; see www.dgsnd.gov.in.

36 *Manual*, ¶1.1.3(iii), p. 4, *supra* n.2.

37 §3(3), Competition Act 2002 (Act No. 12 of 2003).

38 *Proviso* to §3(3), *supra* n.50.

39 See, generally, CCI (2012): Competition Commission of India (2012), *Cartels*, www.
    cci.gov.in/images/media/Advocacy/Cartels2012.pdf.

40 §3(4), ibid.

41 §4(2), ibid. See, also, CCI (2012).

42 This legal position under Indian law is not different from the legal position for joint
    tenders in South Africa; Fiandeiro *et al.*, *supra* n.23.

43 For an in-depth understanding of the entire range of policy objectives in public
    procurement; see, Schooner, S.L. (2002), See also, Schooner *et al.* (2008).

44 These possibilities have been extrapolated by the author from a joint reading of the
    underlying purchasing framework on ethanol purchase by OMCs (www.pib.nic.in/
    newsite/erelease.aspx?relid=89270) and a subsequent joint EOI issued by OMCs, spe-
    cifically, EOI No. Ethanol/Industry/2012–2013 (copy available with author), presum-
    ing that similar tender design defects would have existed in the relevant joint EOI
    invitation as well. The identified potential competition design defects in the joint
    EOI listed earlier are *in addition to* other procurement design defects noticed in the
    EOI, for instance, the EOI under reference contained the following elements that
    could be problematic from a purely procurement rule perspective: (i) invitation of
    expressions of interest from suppliers without intimating in advance intended pur-
    chase prices or specific quantities to be allocated to each participant; (ii) non-
    specification of the pricing formula that would govern ethanol supplies upon changed
    specifications; (ii) non-specification of specific delivery schedules other than mention-
    ing the total annual requirement per annum at various depots; (iii) restrictions on offe-
    rors to make any individual queries, presumably even genuine ones; (iv) seemingly
    contradictory clauses on supplier responsibility in the event of non-issue of movement
    permits by State Excise authorities; (v) prohibitions on sub-letting of the contract
    eventually awarded but permission to execute an irrevocable power of attorney to be
    executed by suppliers allowing de facto sub-letting of the supplier's performance
    obligations under contract; and (vi) permitting individual OMCs to recover pending
    dues/penalties of other, unrelated contracts executed by a supplier with the same or
    any other OMC while receiving payments for supplies against the ethanol contract(s).
    In addition, the majority order in the *India Glycols* case notes that the *Cabinet Com-
    mittee on Economic Affairs* is the *apex body for deciding the prices of commodities
    for procurement and supply by the Government of India* – a statement that is different

from the procurement rule stipulation in India assigning this role specifically to desig-nated *Central Purchase Organisations* – a problem that could get further compounded in view of the fact that procurement in the *India Glycols* case was not being under-taken by departments or offices of the Government of India, but by *government-owned commercial companies incorporated as distinct legal entities*. For a more detailed review of collaborative public procurement; see, Verma, S. (2013).

45 *Flemingo Duty-Free Shop Pvt. Ltd. & Vivek S. Bhatt versus Union of India & Others*, Bombay High Court (Writ Petition No. 617 of 2007, orders dated June 05, 2008), available online http://indiankanoon.org/doc/1799553/. See, also, *Flemingo Duty-Free Shops Pvt. Ltd. versus Union of India & Others*, Karnataka High Court (Writ Petition No. 14070 of 2008, orders dated December 19, 2008).

References

CCI (2010): Competition Commission of India (2010), Public Procurement: Achieving Best Value Through Competition, available online www.cci.gov.in/menu/backgNote091210.pdf.

CVC (2012): Central Vigilance Commission (2012), Transparency in Works/Purchase/Consultancy Contracts Awarded on Nomination Basis – Reg., http://cvc.nic.in/181212_12122012.pdf.

EU Communications (2005): Communication from the Commission to the European Par-liament, The Council, The European Economic and Social Committee and the Com-mittee of the Regions on Public Private Partnerships and Community Law on Public Procurement and Concessions, available online http://eur-lex.europa.eu/legal-content/EN/TXT/PDF/?uri=CELEX:52005DC0569&from=EN.

Green Paper (2005): Report on the Public Consultation on the Green Paper on Public–Private Partnerships and Community Law on Public Contracts and Concessions, Com-mittee Staff Working Paper, SEC(2005)629.

Grimm, V., Pacini, R., Spagnolo, G. and Zanza, M. (2006): Division in Lots and Com-petition in Procurement (Preliminary Version), SSRN, available online http://papers.ssrn.com/sol3/papers.cfm?abstract_id=896734.

Kaijalainen, T., and Luoma, R. (2014): Getting the Deal Through: Public Procurement – Finland, available online www.peltonenlmr.fi/sites/default/files/getting_the_deal_through_-_public_procurement_2014_pp. 2014_finland.pdf.

Schooner, S.L. (2002): Desiderata: Objectives for a system of Government Contract Law, SSRN, available online http://papers.ssrn.com/sol3/papers.cfm?abstract_id=304620.

Schooner, S.L., Gordon, D.I. and Clark, J.L. (2008): Public Procurement Systems: Unpacking Stakeholder Aspirations and Expectations, SSRN, available online http://papers.ssrn.com/sol3/papers.cfm?abstract_id=1133234.

Semple, A. (2014): New EU Procurement Directives: Comparing the Final Text to Earlier Versions, Public Procurement Analysis, available online www.procurementanalysis.eu/resources/New+EU+procurement+directives+-+comparing+the+texts.pdf.

Vaid, S. (2013): Research Paper on Bid Rigging in Public Procurement, available online http://cci.gov.in/images/media/ResearchReports/Bid%20Rigging%20in%20Public%20Procurement.pdf.

Verma, S. (2013): Collaborative Public Procurement: A Comparative Review of Inter-national Best Practices and the Indian Position on Pooled Procurement from Competi-tion Law Perspectives, IICA Working Paper 01/2013, SSRN, available online http://papers.ssrn.com/sol3/papers.cfm?abstract_id=2308290.

6 Conditions on lots

Practical desirability versus legal acceptability

Jan Telgen, Niels Uenk, Wouter Lohmann and Elisabetta Manunza[1]

1 Introduction

Conditional tendering is shorthand for a technique in which a tender is divided into separate lots, while the award procedure contains conditions that restrict the number of possible tender outcomes (assignments of lots to bidders). A simple example is a tender in two lots with the additional condition that both lots cannot be awarded to the same supplier. Conditional tendering is a well-known technique that is applied frequently and is highly regarded in major private companies, especially in large tenders. The reasons for applying conditions may vary from the desire to use dual sourcing to the limitation of the total number of contracted suppliers and from concentrating supplier and contract management efforts to preventing a dominant position in the supply market.

Contrary to the private sector, conditional tendering is not used (frequently) in the public sector. We consider the legal acceptability of the technique. One of the concerns in this matter is that the use of conditions may imply that the best bid on a specific lot is not awarded the contract. This situation occurs for example when one supplier submits the best bid on multiple lots, while a condition determines suppliers can only win one lot.

The current European Directives do not contain regulations on lots in general or on conditional tendering. The new directives (2014/24/EU), however, do cover lots in Article 46 and allow for one condition: contracting authorities may limit the number of lots that may be awarded to one tenderer. This and other provisions in the new EU directives provide the basis for our analysis of the legal acceptability of conditional tendering.

2 Conditional tendering

Conditional tendering[2] is a technique that may be used when a tender is divided into separate lots. Its main feature of this technique is the use of conditions that affect the awarding of the lots to bidders. Many different conditions may be applied, such as 'no one bidder can win all lots', 'the total number of lots won by any supplier may not exceed X' or 'the total number of suppliers that win a lot is not more than Y'. Conditions may be used by a buyer who does not want

Table 6.1 Three bids on three lots

Bidder	Lot 1	Lot 2	Lot 3
A	€1	€3	€5
B	€3	€2	€6
C	€5	€5	€3

its suppliers to become too powerful or who wants to limit the number of suppliers the buyer has to manage.

The conditions may vary greatly as exemplified by the examples given above. Their common characteristic is that they somehow tie the various lots together: the awarding of the lots to a bidder cannot be done for each lot separately. The assignment of lots to bidders is a matter of mutual dependency: the lots have to be considered in combination.

Consider an example where three bidders compete for three lots, under the condition that we do not want to have more than two suppliers. Table 6.1 shows the offers in costs quoted by the bidders. We want to evaluate the offers on lowest cost.

Obviously, without the condition, we would award lot 1 to bidder A, lot 2 to bidder B and lot 3 to bidder C. With the condition however, the best solution is to award lots 1 and 2 to bidder A and lot 3 to bidder C. So even though bidder B is best on lot 2, he does not get that lot awarded.

The numerical example given above uses lowest cost, but similar examples can be given for awarding to the Most Economically Advantageous Tender (MEAT).

This result does not pose any mathematical or economical problems. Here we analyze the legal acceptability of conditional tendering.

3 Practical applications

The practical applications of conditional tendering are numerous. We give some real-life examples.

A large European FMCG-company needs carton packaging in all their factories in a large number of countries. The company wants to tender for the carton packaging and decides to use separate lots per type of packaging and for each country. Assuming 50 different types of packaging are used in 20 different countries, the result is 1000 lots. As the company does not want to deal with 1000 suppliers each supplying just one type of packaging to one factory, it will introduce conditions. One obvious condition is to limit the total number of suppliers. Another one is to limit the number of suppliers per country or per type of packaging, thereby limiting the transportation movements per factory or providing economies of scale in producing the packaging.

A second example involves a large manufacturing company that produces and sells in Europe and North America. For its trans-Atlantic transportation, the company hires shipping companies for 50 different routes back and forth. The manufacturing company tenders with each route as a separate lot and adds conditions on the total number of suppliers it wants to deal with. Additionally, the bidders are allowed to add conditions to their offers as well. For example, a bidder may offer a discount on its fares when it wins both the outbound and the inbound lot. Alternatively, a bidder may be willing to supply on any two routes, but not on three or more as its vessel capacity is insufficient. The bidder may put in a bid for all routes, but adds the condition it can't take on more than two routes.

Finding the best solution in conditional tendering is not an easy task. Only in very small scale examples it is possible to do this 'by hand'. Mathematically finding the best solution requires the application of linear programming (LP) or integer programming (IP); techniques that are widely available. For relatively simple problems an add-in in MS Excel or freely available software may suffice, but for more complicated cases specialized software is required. Several companies provide extensive software packages that can optimize tenders with many lots and conditions. For example, Trade Extensions[3] and Sciquest-Combinenet[4] have conducted such tenders for large private companies like Unilever, Procter and Gamble, BP and Mars. The involvement of this type of company illustrates the (economical) benefits of conditional tendering. Applications in public sector however are rare.

4 Considerations

Applications of conditional tendering in the public sector have caused some debate on LinkedIn fora. In the debate objections against using conditional tendering were raised based on the legal provisions in the EU directives and European case law. The objections can be grouped under two main arguments.

The first argument concerns the legal requirement that all detailed rules of the award procedure should be related to the subject matter of the contract. Opponents of conditional tendering argue the conditions in conditional tendering generally do not refer to the subject matter of the tender itself. The conditions refer to additional arguments like limiting the number of suppliers, guaranteeing a minimum number of suppliers or avoiding dependence on one supplier etc. All of these conditions refer more to the market situation and the position the contracting authority wants to take in that market, than to the subject matter of the contract itself. The argument continues by stating that the conditions cannot be applied in a tender since they are not related to the subject matter of the contract. As a consequence it is argued conditional tendering is not allowed under the directives.

The second argument is that, using conditional tendering, any specific lot may be awarded to a tenderer who did not submit the best bid for that lot. Simple examples of such a situation are tenders in which no supplier may win more than a specified number of lots or where two specific lots may not be won by the same supplier or when there is a maximum number of suppliers over the total number of lots. If awarding each lot individually to the best tenderer would mean violating such a condition, at least one lot has to be awarded to a tenderer who did not submit the best bid. This seems to be at odds with the objective of the award procedure and the principles of equal treatment and transparency as clarified in the case law of the EU Court of Justice Note that this argument is valid for both awarding on lowest price and awarding to the Most Economically Advantageous Tender.

5 Analysis

The previous section concludes that applying conditions on awarding lots – however useful it may be – might conflict with the EU directives on public procurement. In this section we analyze the issue in more detail against the new (2014) EU procurement directive 2014/24/EU (henceforth: the directive).[5]

5.1 Lots and conditions in new directive

According to Article 46 of the directive contracting authorities are allowed to award a contract in the form of separate lots. Actually, throughout the recitals and the directive itself it becomes apparent that division of contracts into lots is strongly encouraged. Recital (78) states: 'Public procurement should be adapted to the needs of SMEs (small and medium size enterprises). [...] To that end and to enhance competition, contracting authorities should in particular be encouraged to divide large contracts into lots.'

Furthermore, Article 46 actually requires contracting authorities to motivate in the procurement documents their decision not to subdivide into lots. This indicates dividing a contract into lots is the default option.

Paragraph two of Article 46 contains provisions regarding what contracting authorities shall and may do, when awarding a contract in the form of separate lots. The first part of paragraph 2 states: 'Contracting authorities shall indicate, in the contract notice or in the invitation to confirm interest, whether tenders may be submitted for one, for several or for all of the lots.'

This means, if a contracting authority wishes to limit the number of lots to be awarded to an individual tenderer, one option is to limit the number of lots for which tenderers may submit a tender. This same goal can be reached by conditional tendering: allowing each tenderer to submit a tender for multiple or all lots, and deciding which tenderer is awarded which lot(s) in the award phase of the procedure. This latter approach is preferred from an economic point of view. If a contracting authority limits the amount of lots it awards to individual tenderers, these tenderers are still allowed to tender for more lots. Tenderers may in fact tender for all lots, leaving the contracting authority with more options from which it selects the combination that fulfills its conditions and is economically most advantageous. If a contracting authority only allows tendering for a limited number of lots, by definition there uwill be less tenders per lot for the contracting authority to choose from – and therefore less potential to achieve the actual economic optimum. Limiting the number of lots to tender for is a rather crude way to achive a similar result as with conditional tendering. However it is clear that form an economic point of view for contracting authorities limiting the number of lots to tender for is suboptimal.

Bearing this economic advantage for conditional tendering in this specific example in mind, we continue the analysis of paragraph 2 of Article 46. The second part of this paragraph reads:

> Contracting authorities may, even where tenders may be submitted for several or all lots, limit the number of lots that may be awarded to one tenderer, provided that the maximum number of lots per tenderer is stated in the contract notice or in the invitation to confirm interest.

The directive furthermore states that the contracting authority shall indicate the objective and non-discriminatory criteria or rules they intend to apply to determine which lots will be awarded. This is a clear example of applying a condition regarding the awarding of lots that is explicitly allowed by the directive.

Reviewing the corresponding recitals for this article confirms this. Recital (79) states:

> contracting authorities should, for instance in order to preserve competition or to ensure reliability of supply, be allowed to limit the number of lots for which a tenderer may tender, they should also be allowed to limit the number of lots that may be awarded to any one tenderer.

To complete the analysis of Article 46, which is of such importance for the subject of lots, the third paragraph states that Member states may provide that contracting authorities may award contracts combining several or all lots where more than one lot may be awarded to the same tenderer. Again, to comply with the principles of transparency and equal treatment – contracting authorities must specify the possibility of doing so in the contract notice or invitation to confirm interest, and indicate the (groups of) lots that may be combined.

5.2 Are conditions in general allowed?

In the previous section we conclude that at least one condition on the awarding of lots is explicitly allowed in the directive: limiting the amount of lots to be awarded to individual tenderers. The question now is whether this means other conditions on awarding lots are allowed as well. What if, for example, rather than limiting the number of lots that any one supplier may be awarded, the contracting authority wishes to deal with a maximum number of suppliers? Or what if the contracting authority for strategic reasons requires different suppliers for specific lots? These are distinct goals that constitute a certain (economic) value to the contracting authority and these goals can be achieved using conditions on awarding lots as well. However, the conditions to achieve these goals are different. For example instead of limiting the number of lots awarded to individual tenderers, a contracting authority may in contrary limit the number of different suppliers all lots are awarded to.

Unfortunately, neither the directive nor the recitals provide a conclusive answer to this question. Applying conditions to awarding lots is not explicitly recognized or discussed as such. However, we can review the arguments against the use of conditions in the light of the explicitly allowed condition of limiting the amount of awarded lots to tenderers.

The main argument against the use of conditions is that they do not relate to the subject matter of the contract. In the next section we discuss whether this is indeed problematic for applying conditions by reviewing relevant articles and recitals of the directive covering this relation to the subject matter of the contract.

5.2.1 Relation with the subject matter of the contract

The new directive provides detailed provisions on the circumstances under which an award criterion is considered to be related to the subject matter of the contract. Article 67.3 of the directive states:

> award criteria shall be considered to be linked to the subject matter of the public contract where they relate to the works, supplies or services to be provided under that contract in any respect and at any stage of their life cycle [...]

To understand what the European Commission has in mind when it mentions 'in any respect and at any stage of their life cycle', we turn to the recitals. Recital (97) states that

> the use of the award criteria relating to the works, supplies or services to be provided under the public contract in any respect and at any stage of their life cycle from extraction of raw materials for the product to the stage of disposal of the product, including factors involved in the specific process of production, provision or trading and its conditions of those works, supplies or services or a specific process during a later stage of their life cycle, even where such factors do not form part of their material substance.

It is clear that this definition of the required relation with the subject matter of the contract extends beyond award criteria in at least one aspect; Article 70 stipulates contract performance conditions should be linked to the subject matter of the contract within the meaning of Article 67(3). Other articles that mention the link to the subject matter requirement – like Article 42 on Technical specifications – however do not refer to the Article 67 definition of this concept.

5.2.2 *Conditions related to subject matter of contract?*

Considering this broad view on the relation of award criterion, we argue that conditions on the awarding of lots are in fact related to the subject matter of the contract by giving three arguments.

A first indication for the relation between conditions and the subject matter of contracts is that conditions reflect a certain (economic) value to the contracting authority in the light of the execution of the contract. This value reflects for example in reduced supply risk by requiring different suppliers for different lots, or in contrary in reduced contract management efforts and transaction costs by limiting the number of different suppliers. These factors are not part of the 'material substance' of the contract but they are directly related to the execution of the contract and (economic) consequences for the contracting authority – at least in any respect at any stage of the life cycle such as Article 67.3 requires.

A second argument for the existence of a relation between conditions on awarding lots and the subject matter of the contract is the fact that these conditions will typically be different for every tender. Conditions on awarding contracts are tailored to minimize risks or maximize opportunities related to the specific subject matter of the contract. No (sensible) contracting authority would apply generic conditions to different contracts.

Finally, and perhaps the most compelling argument to consider conditions on awarding lots as related to the subject matter, is the explicit allowed example of limiting the number of lots awarded per tenderer. Clearly the European Commission recognizes the relation between at least this condition and the subject matter of the contract.

Concluding this section: we identify one example of conditional tendering, which is mentioned and allowed explicitly in the directive. We analyze this example in light of potential objections against the use of conditions, and based on this analysis we argue other conditions are allowed as well.

5.3 *How to apply conditions?*

If conditions on the awarding of lots are allowed under the new directive, the final question is how to apply conditions in a tender from a technical point of view. The directive only deals with one specific condition – limiting the number of lots that may be awarded to any one tenderer – explicitly. Paragraph 2 of Article 46 indicates that contracting authorities can simply mention this condition clearly in the contract notice or invitation to confirm interest, together with the objective and non-discriminatory criteria or rules the contracting authority will apply to determine which lots will be awarded to which tenderers.

The directive does not discuss conditions in general, or other examples such as a maximum total number of suppliers for all lots. If our analysis is correct, and other conditions – provided that they comply with this directive and the principles of equal treatment and transparency in general – are allowed, there is one means that may be very well suited.

Article 70 of the directive allows contracting authorities to apply special conditions to the performance of the contract. This article states:

> contracting authorities may lay down special conditions relating to the performance of a contract, provided they are linked to the subject matter of the contract within the meaning of Article 67(3) and indicated in the call for competition or in the procurement documents. Those conditions may include economic, innovation-related, environmental, social or employment-related considerations.

The intention and motivation for using conditions in awarding lots seems to fit the description and the goal of conditions described in this Article 70 very well. Examples of conditions we provide have an economic motivation in general, and in the previous section we argue the presence of a relation with the subject matter of the contract.

6 Conclusion

Conditional tendering is a well-known technique that is frequently used and highly regarded in major private companies, especially in large tenders. The reasons for the conditions may vary from the desire to use dual sourcing to the limitation of the total number of contracted suppliers and from concentrating supplier and contract management efforts to preventing a dominant position in the market.

In this chapter, we analyze the use of conditions on awarding lots in tenders against the new EU directive 2014/24/EU on public procurement. We consider the relevant provisions on dividing contracts into lots, determining the lots, awarding these lots in tenders, and more specifically the provisions on the relation of criteria (and conditions) to the subject matter of the contract. We conclude at least one specific condition is allowed, as this is specifically stated in the directive. Based on an analysis of this condition and the relevant provisions, we conclude conditions on awarding lots can very well be considered to have a relation to the subject matter of the contract. When applying conditions on the awarding of lots, obviously this should be done transparently, objectively and should not discriminate against any one of potential tenderers. The contracting authority should state the use of conditions in the tender documentation or contract notice, and should include the objective and non-discriminatory criteria or rules they apply to determine the award of lots within the bounds of the condition. As such, conditions can be considered as special conditions relating to the performance of a contract as described in Article 70 of the directive.

In addition to this legal analysis we take a more economic approach to the question at hand. The technique of conditional tendering – widely used in private sector procurement – is an economically sensible technique. Moreover, using this technique actually supports achieving some of the goals of the directives; achieving the best value-for-money for the contracting authority, preserve competition, adapting public procurement to the needs of SMEs, and supporting economic progress.

Notes

1 All authors are associated with the Public Procurement Research Centre: a cooperation between the University of Utrecht and the University of Twente, the Netherlands. Address for correspondence: j.telgen@utwente.nl.
2 See also Dimitri, Piga and Spagnolo, *Handbook of Procurement*, Cambridge University Ptress (2006), Ch. 7 and 8.
3 www.tradeextensions.com.
4 www.sciquest.com.
5 http://eur-lex.europa.eu/legal-content/EN/TXT/PDF/?uri=CELEX:32014L0024&from =EN.

Part III

Innovation through innovative partnerships

7   Colloquium

Elisabetta Iossa
Christopher H. Bovis

1   Elisabetta Iossa – Procuring innovation: why, when and how

There is growing attention in Europe on the use of the use of public procurement to achieve an innovative, intelligent and sustainable growth. Public procurement of works, goods and services currently accounts for about 19 per cent of GDP in the EU, and using public demand to stimulate investment in new technologies can help achieve a twofold objective.[1]

First, new technology developments have created great opportunities to improve the efficiency of public services and face societal challenges related to population aging, climate change and social inclusion. Public procurement of innovative works, goods or services can thus help exploitation and further development of these new technologies in order to face these societal challenges, and provide higher quality and more cost effective public services.

Second, innovation can increase a country's competitiveness and stimulate its growth, thus helping to address wider macroeconomic challenges. Public procurement is then seen as a potential instrument to boost the incentives of the private sector to invest in R&D, and thus reduce the market failure that arises because of firms' insufficient incentives to invest.

Insufficient private R&D incentives arise for a number of reasons, which have been discussed by the economics literature on innovation. (Scotchmer, 2004) The production of an innovation requires that the potential demand for an innovative product or service meet the potential supply of it. This in turn comes with three necessary requirements:

a   The existence of a potential demand for the resulting innovative product/ service;
b   The presence of innovation capacity among suppliers;
c   The potential social benefit (including knowledge creation) from the innovation are greater than the potential cost of researching and developing the innovation.

These conditions are self-explanatory; they are necessary but not sufficient: even when they are satisfied, a number of factors can still impede private investment from taking place.

First, the information about the potential demand may be dispersed and not reach potential suppliers. Think for example of public administrations with similar needs but located in different geographical areas or different countries. Joint procurement is still a difficult practice to implement because of coordination problems. Potential buyer may also be unable to formulate and communicate their needs in a way that allows the potential demand to be identified.

Second, project risks may be perceived as excessive by firms with innovation potential, especially if these are small and medium size firms (SMEs), or if there is an imperfect capital market which denies credit for such risky projects.

Third, suppliers may not be able to appropriate all of the benefits of their investment. Knowledge is a public good with elements of non-rivalry and non-excludability that make it difficult for the innovator to appropriate fully the social benefit from its innovation, even when the intellectual property right (IPR) on the resulting innovations can be relatively well defined. Imperfections in IPRs systems and their legal enforcement can also be a problem.

The resulting market failure requires government intervention, and this is well understood by policy makers. What is instead less clear-cut is how this market failure can be best addressed.

Typically, supply-side policies have been the main instrument governments have relied upon in order to develop innovative markets, to revive traditional segments and so on. Regulation, competition policies or standard monetary policies are natural examples of these supply-side policies. Fiscal channels, mainly through taxes or subsidies are other examples of how policy intervention may foster innovation via the supply-side of the market.

The basic idea underlying these supply-side policies is that, supporting a particular market or a particular segment of firms, which constitutes a potential and fruitful path for research activities, may spur innovation. Supply-side policies thus presume that firms are able to identify the potential demand for an innovation, recognizing unsatisfied needs, but may instead lack sufficient innovation capacity, e.g. because of lack of human capital or of physical capital, or of the required funds. Support to R&D investment, tax credit for R&D investment or support for training and innovations, the main supply-side policies, can then compensate firms for their insufficient capacity, raising their incentives to invest.

Alternative, sometimes complementary policy, are demand-side policies which are the centre of current debate and policy at European level. Demand-side innovation policies presume that there is a problem (or there may also be a problem) on the demand side. Even if firms have sufficient innovation capacity, they may have insufficient incentives to invest because they are uncertain as to whether there is a potential demand for their innovation.

Demand-side innovation policies then aim to reduce all the barriers that may cause a potential demand for innovation not to materialize, and to provide the market with a demand for innovation, by reducing the uncertainty that surrounds users and administration needs and thus favouring the information aggregation and transmission of users needs. This is turn can be done by favouring the exchange of information among users, so as to aggregate information on the potential demand, and by coordinating procurers to aggregate their demand and those of the citizens they represent.

In the EU 2020 strategy, a key role among demand-side policies is played by public procurement.[2] Among the procurement mechanisms, Pre-commercial Procurement (PCP) and Innovation Partnerships (IP) are viewed as key institutions that may help the public sector to foster private investment, by procuring innovations that satisfy public needs.

Pre-commercial procurement aims to identify the best value for money solutions to address a specific procurement need, by making use of competitive development in phases and risk-benefit sharing under market conditions. Under PCP, the public authority procures R&D activities, from the solution exploration phase to prototyping and testing, but reserves the right to tender competitively the newly developed products or services in a separate Public Procurement of Innovation (PPI).

An alternative instrument is the Innovation Partnership, introduced by the new Procurement Directive 2014/24. Under an IP, development and production are procured through one single tender, the innovator also obtaining the contractual right to produce the innovation. The procedure allows contracting authorities to establish a long-term innovation partnership for the development and subsequent purchase of new, innovative products, works and services, provided they can be delivered at agreed performance levels and costs. The partnership is structured in successive stages following the sequence of steps in the research and innovation process, possibly up to the manufacturing of the supply or the provision of the services.

Despite the great attention on these policies, there does not exist a clear understanding of the potential pros and cons of the different mechanisms used in practice. First, it is not clear when demand side policies should be used, and what it should be expected; neither is it clear under which conditions a public authority should choose pre-commercial procurement or an innovation partnership. As a result, there is still little understanding of how these mechanisms can be adequately implemented, and how, when, and to which extent, they can be effective.

Understanding these issues remains a challenge in itself.

2 Christopher H. Bovis – Innovation and regulatory trends in Public–Private Partnerships

Innovation as a principle underpins the notion of public procurement through Public–Private Partnerships. The Euro 2020 Strategy proclaims a need for strategic procurement where the private sector will be engaged alongside the public sector as a partner, as a financier, as a risk sharer and as an innovator in the delivery of public services. Public–Private Partnerships denote a contractual format between public authorities and private sector undertakings (Blanc-Brude, Goldsmith and Valila, 2007). Such relations aim at delivering infrastructure projects, as well as many other schemes in areas covering transport, public health, education, public safety, and waste management and water distribution and have the following characteristics (Deloitte, 2006): the relatively long duration of the relationship; the funding source for the project; the strategic role of the private sector in the sense that it is expected that to provide input into different stages of the project such as design, completion, implementation, and funding and finally the distribution of risks between the public and private sectors and the expectation that the private sector will assume substantial risk (Poschmann, 2003). At European Union level, as part of the Initiative for Growth, the European Council has approved a series of measures designed to increase investment in the infrastructure of the trans-European transport networks and also in the areas of research, innovation, and development,[3] as well as the delivery of services of general interest.[4] Pre-commercial Procurement (PCP) and Innovation Partnerships (IP) will play a major role to foster private investment, by procuring innovative solutions to deliver public services. The evolution of the interface in Public–Private Partnerships will focus on regulatory standardisation which will have recourse to both hard law and soft law. Hard law will utilise normative acts of public law character in order to ensure a safeguard for competition, procurement, and selection of private sector partners; contractual issues such as terms and conditions, guarantees, and dispute resolution; and corporate structures between public and private sectors. The role of international organisations will be pivotal in shaping such instruments of hard law which will be applicable to both developed and developing nations. Their standardisation will augment legal certainty amongst public and private sectors and the society at large. On the other hand, soft law in the form of guidelines will create the appropriate consultative environment in the fields of risk management, risk assessment, financing, securitisation, and debt treatment of Public–Private Partnerships. Regulatory standardisation Public–Private Partnerships will emit best practice in transparency and consistency in public services, ensure innovation and quality in the delivery of public service and articulate on constantly developing issues such as the competitive environment in delivering public services, as well as issues relevant to the financing, investment, control, and exit of private actors from such relations.

2.1 Public–Private Partnerships as public service instruments

Public–Private Partnerships can be viewed as public service instruments. As such, the state opts for an externalised model in the delivery of public services and heralds a departure from an asset-based to an enabled-based format in public services. Through risk transfer mechanisms, the public–private partnership is treated as an emanation of the state and reveals a different ethos in public sector management, that of the state as enabling and facilitating agent. However, the strategic role of private actors in financing and delivering infrastructure facilities and public services by providing input into the various phases such as finance, design, construction, operation, and maintenance, reflect the need for longevity of the relations between public and private sectors. The often lengthy duration of

Public–Private Partnerships is justified on the basis of affordability for repayment on the part of the public sector and on the basis of the ability of the private sector to recoup its investment profitably. Nevertheless, this could potentially result in market foreclosure. There is a pertinent need to address the competitiveness of Public–Private Partnerships before and after the procurement process of the private actor.

2.2 Public–Private Partnerships as investment instruments

Public–Private Partnerships can be viewed as investment instruments. Financing for a Public–Private Partnership can take one of the following forms: (a) a stand-alone project, where the funding raised is for only one specific project; (b) a Special Purpose Vehicle (SPV) as the borrower, where an independent legal vehicle is created to raise the funds required for the project; (c) a high ratio of debt to equity through either gearing or leverage, where the newly created project company usually has the minimum equity required to issue debt for a reasonable cost; (d) private lending based on project specific cash-flow and not a corporate balance sheet, where the project company borrows funds from lenders. The lenders look to the projected future revenue stream generated by the project and the project company's assets to repay all loans; and (e) various financial guarantees, where the guarantees are provided by the private sector partners, often limited to their equity contributions. As a result, the lender receives its payment from the income generated from the project or directly from the public sector. A Public–Private partnership can be also financed by securitization of claims on future project revenues. In a typical Public–Private Partnership securitization operation, the public sector would sell a financial asset – its claim on future project revenues – to an SPV. The SPV would then sell securities backed by this asset to private investors, and use the proceeds to pay the public sector, which in turn would use them to finance the Public–Private Partnership. Interest and amortisation would be paid by the SPV to investors from the public sector's share of project revenue.

2.3 Structure regulation of Public–Private Partnerships

The development of two distinctive legal structures/models will assist the evolution and delivery of Public–Private Partnerships. First, the contractual model, where the interface between the state and the private actors reflects on a relation which is based solely on contractual links. Under this model and structure, it is unlikely that there would be any element of exclusive asset exploitation or end-user payments levied by the private actor. However, mechanisms of profit sharing, efficiency gain sharing as well as risk allocation between the public and private partners distinguish contractual Public–Private Partnerships from traditional public contracts for works or services. The contractual model of Public–Private Partnerships assumes that the private sector partner will provide the financing for completing the project and the public sector partner will pay back by way of "service or unitary charges" which reflect payments based on usage volumes or demand (i.e. payments in lieu of fees or tolls for public lighting, hospitals, schools, roads with shadow tolls).

Second, the institutional model of public private partnerships involves the establishment of a separate legal entity held jointly by the public partner and the private partner. The joint entity has the task of ensuring the raising of finance and the delivery of a public service or an infrastructure project for the benefit of the public. The direct interface between the public partner and the private partner in a forum with a distinctive legal personality allows the public partner, through its presence in the body of shareholders and in the decision-making bodies of the joint entity, to retain a relatively high degree of control over the development and delivery of the project. The joint entity could also allow the public partner to develop its own experience of running and improving the relevant public services, while having recourse to the support of the private partner. An institutional Public–Private Partnership can be established either by creating an entity controlled by the public and private sector partners, or by the private sector taking control of an existing public undertaking or by the participation of a private partner in an existing publicly owned company which has obtained public contracts or concessions.

2.4 Risk treatment and its regulation in Public–Private Partnerships

A significant regulatory trend which has emerged as a result of the strategic role of the private sector and its long-term engagement in delivering infrastructure and public services reflects on the legal treatment of risk distribution between the public and private sectors within Public–Private Partnerships and in particular, the allocation and pricing of construction or project risk, which is related to design problems, building cost overruns, and project delays; financial risk, which is related to variability in interest rates, exchange rates, and other factors affecting financing costs; performance risk, which is related to the availability of an asset and the continuity and quality of the relevant service provision; demand risk, which is related to the ongoing need for the relevant public services; and residual value risk, which is related to the future market price of an asset. Risk transfer from the public sector to the private sector has a significant influence on whether a Public–Private Partnership is a more efficient and cost-effective alternative to public investment and publicly funded provision of services (Moss, 2002).

The case for the success of Public–Private Partnerships rests on the relative efficiency of the private sector. However, this efficiency must demonstrate itself in a dynamic mode, reflecting the need for competition in the provision of the relevant services through the Public–Private Partnership. In traditional public contracting, public procurement through tendering secured the repeated competition for a market which is inherently oligopolistic yet contestable by new entries or offerings. However, the scope for competition in the activities undertaken by Public–Private Partnerships is more limited, because they tend to be less contestable for reasons relevant to the longevity of the engagement between public and private sectors, for reasons under which social infrastructure remains undervalued and economic infrastructure involves large sunk costs. For Public–Private Partnerships to operate in a global competitive environment, safeguard the principles of transparency, and accountability in public sector management, incentive-based regulation is paramount. Where a private sector operator can sell public services to the public, but there is little scope for competition, the public sector must regulate the prices for the relevant public services. However, the challenge is to design well-functioning regulation which increases output towards the social optimum, stabilises prices in a sustainable manner, and limits monopoly profit while preserving the incentive for private sector to be more efficient and reduce costs.

This challenge is translated in the legal interface of the developed and developing nations pose some considerable questions in relation to the role and scope of private actors in delivering public services, the regulatory compatibility between norms of anti-trust and exclusivity of private actors in delivering public services, questions relevant to the expectations of private actors both in financial, operational and strategic perspectives, questions in relation to compliance and enforcement of Public–Private Partnerships relations in the process of delivering public services, and finally, questions in relation to risk treatment arising out of such relations.

3 Elisabetta Iossa – Response to Paper 2

Consider the Innovation Partnership (IP), the new procedure introduced by Art. 31 of the Procurement Directive 2014/24 to help the public sector foster private investment, by procuring innovations that satisfy public needs.

The procedure allows contracting authorities to establish a long-term partnership for the development and subsequent production of innovative products, works and services, provided they can be delivered at agreed performance levels and costs. The partnership is structured in successive stages following the sequence of steps in the research and innovation process, possibly up to the manufacturing of the supply or the provision of the services.

In particular, the main characteristics of IPs can be briefly summarized as follows:

- Bundling of phases (R&D plus production): the award procedure establish a long-term partnership for the development (R&D) and subsequent purchase (production) of an innovative solution, not yet available on the market. Thus, a key aspect of this procedure is that there is bundling of R&D and production, which are allocated to the same firm (or consortium of firms).
- Multiple-stage procedure: the procedure provides for multiple stages following the sequence of steps in the research and innovation process, up to the manufacturing of the supply or the provision of the services. There are intermediate targets to be attained by the bidders who are remunerated in

appropriate instalments. Based on those targets, the contracting authority may decide after each stage to terminate the partnership and launch a new procurement procedure for the remaining phases, provided that it has acquired the relevant intellectual property rights.

- The contract shall be awarded in accordance with the rules for a competitive procedure with negotiation (Article 27). Contracting authorities shall negotiate with tenderers the tenders submitted by them to improve the content of the offers in order to better correspond to the award criteria and minimum requirements.
- Possibility of multiple partners. The contracting authority may establish a partnership with more than one firm (or consortium of firms) so that it is possible to have multiple partnerships at both the R&D stage and the production stage.

These characteristics of IPs suggest that IPs may be particularly beneficial when the following circumstances arise:

i   There is a great potential benefit from the bundling R&D and production because there are extensive spillovers across the two phases. Spillovers may in turn arise because there are economies of scope that make it cheaper or more effective for the innovator to also be a contractor, or because bundling provides incentives for the developer to put more effort into the R&D stage, anticipating future benefits in terms of e.g. lower development costs at development stage.[5]
ii There is potential benefit from using the competitive procedure with negotiation, because the public authority has identified minimum solution requirements but it may benefit from negotiation with the firms (on an equal and transparent terms) during the multi-stage process to understand the best way for demand to meet supply.

We note however that there are many aspects of the procedure that the Directive has left unregulated, and which play a crucial role in determining its potential impact.

In particular, the following aspects need attention:

- There is no bound on the value of the contract to be allocated or on the duration of the IP relationship.[6]
- There is no restriction on the number of awardees, which implies that a single may be selected.
- There is no indication of how project risks and intellectual property rights will be allocated.

It follows that the risks of using an IP are therefore clear: We may have generated a monster which will allow public authorities to choose a single partner for a large contract for a long period of time, and to transfer all IPRs from the product commercialization to this awardee, whilst keeping most of the risks. We should then not be surprised to observe as a result market foreclosure, SMEs exclusion, and firm's lock-in, with long term effects.

So is the IP a beauty or a beast? To answer this question, we shall need to wait to see how the Directive will be transposed into national legislations. As emphasized by for Christopher H. Bovis for the case of Public–Private Partnerships in his symposium's first paper, for Innovation Partnerships the evolution of the interface must also involve a regulatory standardization that makes recourse to both hard law and soft law. Hard law must ensure a safeguard for competition, by covering procurement and contractual issues such as terms and conditions, IPRs, risk allocation; and number of final awardees. The soft law in the form of guidelines must be created so as to learn from the experience and disseminate best practice, innovation and quality in the R&D procurement of innovations.

4 Christopher H. Bovis – Response to Paper 1

Innovation is one of the most desirable features of the production process. It feeds competitive advantages for firms by reducing costs and improving quality and equally allows the consumer to benefit from advanced products and services. Innovation has been an imperative yet silent feature in procurement regulation. Innovation is not allowed to function fully in the procurement acquis. For traditional public contracts, innovation rarely plays a role. For complex contractual formats between public and private sectors, such as concessions and Public–Private Partnerships, innovation is a distinctive feature. The European acquis on procurement regulation displays a dysfunctional picture on the treatment and expectations of innovation.

On the one hand, innovation as a concept is underpinning the intellectual support of procurement regulation in the European Union which draws inferences from economic theories. Regulating public sector and utilities procurement aims at bringing the respective markets in parallel to the operation of private markets and at establishing conditions similar to those that control the operation of private markets. Innovation is a most significant feature in private markets. Public sector and utilities procurement markets, which are referred to as public markets, reflect an economic equation where the demand side is represented by the public sector at large and the utilities, whereas the supply side covers the industry.

Public markets tend to be structured and to function in a distinctive way, where innovation is not the evident priority. Their structure reveals monopsony characteristics and cyclical dynamics, where the state and its organs often appear as the sole outlet for an industry's output. In terms of its origins, demand in public markets is institutionalised and operates mainly under budgetary considerations rather than price mechanisms. It is also based on fulfilment of tasks, mainly the pursuit of public interest, and it is single for many products. Supply also has limited origins, in terms of the establishment of close ties between the public sector and industries supplying it and there is often a limited product range. Products are rarely innovative and technologically advanced and pricing is determined through tendering. The purchasing decision is primarily based upon the life-time cycle and costing, reliability, price and policy considerations.

However, innovation is silently reflected in the procurement process. The lowest offer as an award criterion of public contracts is a quantitative method of achieving market equilibrium between the demand and supply sides. The supply side competes in costs terms to deliver standardised works, services and goods to the public sector. Price competition is bound to result in innovation in the relevant industries, where through investment and technological improvements, firms could reduce production and/or distribution costs. The lowest offer criterion could be seen as the necessary stimulus in the relevant market participants in order to improve their competitive advantages.

The welfare gains emanating from public procurement regulation encapsulate the actual and potential savings the public sector (and consumers of public services at large) would enjoy through a system that forces the supply side to compete on costs (and price). These gains, however, must be counterbalanced with the costs of tendering (administrative and evaluative costs born by the public sector), the costs of competition (costs related to the preparation and submission of tender offers born by the private sector), the costs of innovation, research and development and finally litigation costs (costs relevant to prospective litigation born by both aggrieved tenderes and the public sector).

Innovation can also feature in the most economically advantageous offer award criterion, which includes a series of factors other than price chosen by the contracting authority, which are relevant to the subject matter of the contract. However, innovation as a concept, contradicts the legal fundamentals of procurement regulation. Innovation is in conflict with standards and specifications for products and services, upon which the procurement process is based and organised. Innovation could be legitimately considered only if variants are allowed in parallel to accepted standard-compliant bids. Further, innovation is expensive in capital and resources terms. Innovation can only be assessed in procurement procedures when it is most economically advantageous to the demand side. If is induced externally, it would be the result of demand-driven pressures, or regulation. Mostly, innovation is risky because of potential failure or of the unknown results.

European Institutions have assumed that by encouraging the public and the utilities sectors in the European Union to adopt a homogenous purchasing behaviour which is based on the principles of openness, transparency and non-discrimination, and allows for innovative solutions, products and services, the result will be the achievement of efficiency gains and the stimulation of industrial restructuring in the Member States. Budget constraints confronting European governments and the widespread assumption that private sector know-how will benefit the delivery of public services appear as the main policy drivers[7] for selecting a public private partnership route (OECD, 2008). The principal benefit from involving the private sector in the delivery of public services has been attributed to the fact that the public sector does not have to commit its own capital resources in funding the delivery of public services, whereas other benefits include quality improvement, innovation, management efficiency, and effectiveness, elements that are often underlying private sector entrepreneurship (Grout, 1997). Consequently, the public sector receives innovative solutions and value-for-money in the delivery of public services, while it can also be maintained that through this process the state manages in a better, more strategic way the public finances. Value for money denotes a concept which is associated with the economy, the effectiveness and the efficiency of a public service, product or process, i.e. a comparison of the input costs against the value of the outputs and a qualitative and quantitative judgment of the manner in which the resources involved have been utilised and managed (Kay, 1993).

The challenge is three-fold: how innovation will be captured and assessed in market testing and pre-procurement exercises; how innovation will be quantified and measured in the procurement process; how innovation will benefit stakeholders in the delivery phase of public services. Elisabetta Iossa provided a critical assessment of the need to address innovation in public procurement and demonstrated the capacity and limits of the envisaged mechanics for procuring innovation, in the form of Innovation Partnership as award procedure. Mostly, her position revealed the threats arising from the application of the innovation partnership, namely the unintentional market foreclosure and exclusion of SMEs, both threats resulting from the need for pre-procurement engagement and the associated resources required by the private sector to produce innovative solutions destined for public services.

5 Elisabetta Iossa – Conclusions

The previous discussion has emphasized how Innovation Partnerships (IP) have the potential to exploit the economies of scale and spillovers that may arise from the bundling R&D and production, which may give rise to stronger research incentives and lower research costs. It may also help public authorities to negotiate with the firms during the multi-stage process in such a way to understand the best way for demand to meet supply.

Innovation Partnerships, however, also expose the public authority to decisions that may seem suitable in the short term but that have instead long term anti-competitive effects. To avoid this, soft or hard law should put clear constraints on the value of the contract to be allocated or on the duration of the IP relationship, on the number of awardees, and the allocation of project risks and intellectual property rights.

It will therefore be very important to provide public authorities with sufficient training so as to understand the issues at hand, and to make an informed choice as to which procedure to use, knowing the pros and cons of each of the available alternatives. A mere application of the law will be detrimental: authorities should recognize that their tender decisions have short and long run effects on market competition, and should therefore take into account both legal and economic factors when making their choices. In this respect, a crucial role in the procurement of innovation will be played by the alternatives available, such as pre-commercial procurement, which do not exploit economies of scope but can be more pro-competitive than an Innovation Partnership.

6   Christopher H. Bovis – Conclusions

Can innovation in public–private relations be regulated? In her elaborate discussions, Elisabetta Iossa showed the potential and opportunities from correctly applying Innovation Partnership as award procedure in procuring innovation for delivering public services. Emphasis is placed on pre-commercial procurement, which could allow market optimisation without anti-competitive outcomes. The synergies of such market optimisation from applying correctly Innovation Partnership are evident in PPPs, as a modality to deliver public services over and above the thrust of traditional public contracts.

The desirability of innovation in PPPs and public contracts is counterbalanced with the difficulty of its regulation, because innovation is aspirational and not tangible and cannot fit into the procedural uniformity in the award of public contracts and concessions. Public procurement is a decision-making process which is based on objective, transparent, and uniform procedures for selecting contractual partners in order to deliver public services. Innovation is a concept which will emerge after the procurement process, in the delivery phase of public services. It will most likely appear in PPPs and not in traditional public contracts. The PPP relation is conducive to development processes and systems which create new ground and advanced delivery and finance methods. Partner motivation in PPPs creates an environment which is conducive for innovation.

Environmental conduciveness in PPPs for innovation exhibits a balancing exercise of factors such as price, cost, risk, quality, performance, and continuous improvement which underpins the value for money (VFM) principle in public service delivery. The VFM is supported through incentivisation in PPPs, by mechanisms which create profit or revenue driven notions such as gain and profit sharing and through value engineering, for the determination of specifications and standards and the development of solutions utilising R&D functions of the private partner.

The challenge of the European aqcuis is twofold: first, to introduce innovation in traditional public contracts and mimic the collective motivation relations between public and private sectors which are found in PPPs; second, to capture innovation during the procurement process and allow it to influence the selection process and be a decisive factor in the award of public contracts. Public procurement regulation is channelled through three phases: selection, tendering, and award. Innovation could possibly emerge in the award phase, as the selection phase is confined to objectively determined and standardised processes. Innovation could also emerge in the tendering phase when utilising negotiations between public and private sectors in competitive dialogue and innovation partnerships award procedures.

The regulatory success of PPPs rests on the relative efficiency and innovation capacity of the private sector. This efficiency must demonstrate itself in a dynamic mode, reflecting the need for competition in the provision of the relevant services. Innovation can provide for such efficiency. In traditional public contracts, the inherently oligopolistic yet contestable market is ripe for innovation as a feature which will facilitate new entries or offerings.

To safeguard the principles of transparency and accountability in public sector management, an incentive-based regulation is the benchmark. The challenge for the EU policy and law maker is to design a system which increases output towards the social optimum, stabilises prices in a sustainable manner, limits monopoly profit while preserving the incentive for private sector to be more efficient and reduce costs.

Notes

1 http://ec.europa.eu/enterprise/policies/innovation/policy/public-procurement/index_en.htm.
2 See the communication "Innovation Union" – SEC(2010) 1161 which highlights the strategic use of public procurement to promote research and innovation.
3 See Conclusions of the Presidency, Brussels European Council, 12 December 2003, Council of the European Union, Brussels, 5 February 2004, 5381/04. See Communication from the Commission to the Council and to the Parliament "Public finances in EMU 2003," published in the European Economy No 3/2003 (COM (2003) 283 final).
4 See COM (2003) 270.
5 On the benefit of bundling subsequent stages in procurement, see Bennett and Iossa (2006), *Building and Managing Facilities for Public Services*, Vol. 90, pp. 2143–2160; and Iossa and Martimort (2014), The Simple Micro-economics of Public–Private Partnerships, *Journal of Public Economic Theory*, forthcoming.
6 The Directive only provides for the estimated value of the contract to "not be disproportionate in relation to the investment required for their development."
7 See Communication from the Commission of 23 April 2003 "Developing the trans-European transport network: innovative funding solutions – interoperability of electronic toll collection systems," COM (2003) 132, and the Report of the high-level group on the trans-European transport network of 27 June 2003.

References

Blanc-Brude, F., H. Goldsmith and T. Valila (2007): Public–Private Partnerships in Europe: An Update, Economic and Financial Report, 2007/03, Luxembourg: European Investment Bank (2007).

Deloitte (2006): Deloitte Closing the Infrastructure Gap: The Role of Public–Private Partnerships, Deloitte Research Study, (2006) London.

Grout P. (1997): The Economics of the Private Finance Initiative, in 13 *Oxford Review of Economic Policy* 53–66 (1997).

Kay J. (1993): Efficiency and Private Capital in the Provision of Infrastructure, in Infrastructure Policies for the 1990s, Organization for Economic Co-operation and Development (1993).

Moss D. (2002): *When All Else Fails: Government as the Ultimate Risk Manager*, Harvard University Press. 2002.

OECD (2008): *Public–Private Partnerships: In Pursuit of Risk Sharing and Value for Money*, Paris: OECD.

Poschmann F. (2004): Private Means to Public Ends: The Future of Public–Private Partnerships, C.D. Howe Institute Commentary No. 183, (June 2003)

Scotchmer S. (2004): *Innovation and Incentives*, MIT Press.

8 Stretching the limits for innovative and sustainable public procurement

Innovative and sustainable clothing for hospitals as a show case for innovative procurement in healthcare

Oana Pantilimon Voda and Shirley Justice

1 Introduction – rationale for public procurement of innovation

In cases where no solutions exist yet on the market, innovative procurement enables public purchasers to get technologically innovative solutions developed according to their specific needs.[1] By steering product development upstream in the product development process, public purchasers are better positioned to improve the quality, effectiveness and efficiency of their public services, while the private business sector shall operate within an increasingly competitive environment, including also more innovative Small and Medium Enterprises ("SMEs"). Such an approach contributes to achieving best value for money as well as wider economic, environmental and societal benefits in terms of generating new ideas, translating them into innovative products and services and thus promoting sustainable growth.[2]

European competitiveness in the global marketplace is a top priority for Europe. The European Union strongly supports the public procurement of innovative solutions through a number of policy documents linked to Europe 2020 strategy for smart, sustainable and inclusive growth.[3] Instrumental in achieving this objective is to enhance European innovation. A renewed emphasis on innovation as an instrument of industrial policy was developed at the end of the twentieth century as a result of an increasingly competitive nature of the international economic arena and the correlated structural changes (Georghiu 1996, pp. 359–377).

Public authorities, utility companies and care providers have the obligation to provide citizens (tax payers) with services of public interest of the best possible quality. At the same time, however, there seems to be a "market failure" in the sense that, on one hand, the demand is not able to encourage the market to answer its needs by failing to give the right signals, while on the other hand, the offer is not known.[4] A collaborative approach whereby the combination of skills and the sharing of costs and risks are correlated with government support to compensate for market failure (Georghiu 1996, pp. 359–377) is needed. This is where the public purchasing power can play a role to make a difference (Georghiu 1996, pp. 359–377). Market uptake of innovative products and services could be enhanced by employing innovative public procurement practices.

This chapter provides an overview of a new approach to support and enable the development of a sustainable and innovative prototype for hospital clothing by technology vendors represented by SMEs in co-operation with purchasing bodies (hospitals), by means of employing a co-operative procurement methodology ("Care Project"). It shows how innovative and sustainable procurement approaches could be addressed in a European single market that aims at being competitive, fair, transparent and non-discriminatory, within the framework shaped by the World Trade Organization ("WTO") rules, the recently passed new public procurement legal package, the recently adopted state aid rules, and Corporate Social Responsibility ("CSR") instruments[5] embedded in the Organization for Economic Co-operation and Development ("OECD") Guidelines for Multinational Enterprises,[6] ISO 26000 and the United Nations Global Compact.[7] The chapter is structured as follows: a first section describing the Care Project, followed by a presentation of the main institutional forces designing the legal framework within which the Care Project is developed, and further going into the depths of creating innovative procurement tactics, with specific focus on market consultations, sustainability issues, the tender procedures to be used and the key elements to consider in a public procurement of innovation strategy.

2 Case study – presentation of the Care Project in the Netherlands

Traditionally, the procurement of hospital uniforms was conducted based on drawing up a limited amount of specifications and selecting on lowest price. The common approach undertaken by hospitals interested in buying hospital uniforms is to purchase items from priced catalogues rather than through engagement and discussion of needs with the supply chain actors or the end-users. Environmental and social sustainability issues hardly ever play a role. The more innovative concepts of output based specifications or life-cycle costing, customary to public procurement of innovation, are largely unknown.[8] In this setting, the Care Project is developed by MVO Nederland ("CSR Netherlands")[9] together with three academic hospitals and a healthcare institution[10] from the demand side and, respectively, a group of seven SMEs working in the textile sector from the supply side. The objective of the Care Project is to develop a sustainable, circular and innovative prototype for hospital uniforms produced in developing countries,[11] in a co-operative approach between hospitals and SMEs in the Netherlands. Its purpose is to serve as a show case for the health sector of value creation by means of innovative, sustainable public procurement and to stimulate innovation among SMEs in the textile sector, especially with respect to encouraging production in developing countries.

Work uniforms are relevant to serve as show case for several reasons. From a sustainability point of view, the textile sector faces many challenges, especially concerning working conditions of (unskilled) workers in developing countries. This is partly due to the focus in Western countries on lowest price which puts production costs under great pressure. Furthermore, the environmental performance of the working uniforms can be optimized by circular design and by developing a circular business concept. At its core, a circular economy aims to "design out" waste. Products are designed for disassembly and reuse – either entirely, or parts thereof – whilst being supported by a shift towards licensing "performance" over selling "products".[12] The Care Project thus explores business cases for circular hospital uniforms. Finally, the technical design of the hospital uniforms can be highly improved by adding different functionalities, e.g. with respect to physical (e.g. spine) support of the user, a functionality which is already used in the sport sector but not in the health sector. Other examples are antibacterial functions or bacterial detection functions which can be added to the fabric.[13] These functionalities will have a positive impact on the performance of the employees (lower absenteeism through illness) and can reduce infection risks. It is expected that all these improvements will not only lead to a more innovative and sustainable product, but will also improve the image of the hospitals towards their employees, their patients and the society as a whole. In this respect, raising awareness among management, employees, patients, visitors and other healthcare institutions is an integral part of the project. Several other contracting authorities and private companies have already expressed interest in the outcome of the project. Scaling up the project will be considered at a later stadium. The project is divided into three phases: (1) the development of a CSR strategy and subsequently demand for circular uniforms at the hospitals, (2) research into a circular and technical innovative clothing design and the development of a prototype, (3) innovative and sustainable procurement of uniforms by the hospitals. The approach undertaken in this chapter will focus on the third phase and entails the consideration of available innovative procurement instruments within the more general policy- and legal-related frameworks, coupled with an analysis of the material requirements for innovative procurements, customized for the implementation of the Care Project.

3 The institutional forces – a legal framework supporting the public procurement of innovative solutions

Innovative and sustainable procurement in the health sector and specifically in what regards sustainable clothing for hospitals is a rather complex matter which requires careful consideration of applicable regulations, rules and recommendations. Whereas there is no specific and unique piece of legislation governing the procurement of sustainable clothing for hospitals, several legal deeds and policy documents available at both international and European level are applicable, as further provided below.

3.1 International trade playing field

Procurement-wise, the WTO Government Procurement Agreement ("WTO GPA")[14] is an international agreement between several signatory parties which have agreed to open their public procurement markets towards each other, in full compliance with the principles of non-discrimination, equal treatment and fairness and the procedural rules agreed to this end.[15] When a public institution does the procurement from a GPA signatory country,[16] this institution may be mandated to allow competition from other signatory countries. This depends on whether the respective public institution is covered by the GPA, the value of the procured contract and whether the object of the contract falls within the scope of the GPA. According to the GPA, the European Union is not restricted in regulating its own internal market, but rather to comply with certain obligations towards non-EU parties to the GPA. In this respect, the European Union did not draft separate rules to be applied for non-EU GPA signatories, but suggests the application of the EU public procurement directives to both EU and GPA bidders.[17]

As regards the CSR instruments, the core set of internationally recognized principles and guidelines regarding CSR are the OECD Guidelines, ISO 26000 and the UN Global Compact together with the United Nations Guiding Principles on Business and Human Rights and the International Labour Organization's ("ILO") Conventions. They have a common normative basis as all aim to stimulate responsible business practices. Without going into too much detail on these international instruments, it is worth mentioning that they are all sets of voluntary recommendations and guidance for corporations in the fields of labour, human rights, the environment, economic aspects and other corporate responsibility issues they need to account for in their daily business conduct. Whereas the main issues covered by these instruments are equally addressed in each of them, differences exist in terms of applicability, outreach and enforcement mechanisms, legal status and government endorsement (Theuws, van Huijstee 2013). These instruments, especially the OECD Guidelines, form the CSR framework within the Care Project and will be considered when defining the specific CSR requirements in the procurement.

3.2 State of play in the European Union – the new procurement package

At the European level, the legal framework for public procurement of innovative solutions is defined by the provisions of the Treaty for the Functioning of the European Union ("TFEU") and by the EU Procurement Directives, namely the Directive 2004/18/EC of the European Parliament and of the Council on the coordination of procedures for the award of public works contracts, public supply contracts and public services contracts ("Old Procurement Directive"). More recently, a new procurement directive was passed.[18] While safeguarding the requirements of transparency, equal treatment, competition and non-discrimination, the New Procurement Directive opens new opportunities for the public procurement of innovative solutions, provided they are conducted proportionately and that compliance with the new State Aid Framework for research and development and innovation ("R&D&I")[19] is ensured. Innovative procurement entails innovative approaches in both practices and procedures (Bos and Corvers 2006). Both dimensions are equally addressed in the New Procurement Directive which encourages the employment of innovation friendly approaches including, inter alia, the conduct of market consultations, the possibility to include social and environmental considerations in the tender specifications, the use of life-cycle costing approach, the use of the most economically advantageous tender criteria ("MEAT") as award criteria and the acceptance of variant offers. New procedures have been added, specifically the innovation partnership[20] and the competitive procedure with negotiation, of particular relevance for public purchasers envisaging the purchase of innovative products. Moreover, SMEs are ensured better access to tender procedures through a number of changes to selection processes and documentation requirements. Additionally, new explicit rules on joint procurement are aimed at facilitating cooperation between public purchasers, thus potentially encouraging risk and benefit-sharing for innovative projects and demand pooling. Consequently, the New Procurement Directive sets the scene for a more strategic approach by public purchasers toward public procurement as a mean to identify and support innovation and thus deliver better solution to their needs.

3.3 The new State Aid Framework for R&D&I

According to the 2014 State Aid Communication, no state aid within the meaning of article $107(1)$[21] of the TFEU is deemed to be awarded to undertakings delivering relevant services as long as an open or restricted procedure for the public procurement is carried out in accordance with the provisions of the New Procurement Directive. The same applies when public purchasers procure innovative solutions from a preceding R&D procurement, or non-R&D products and services that are delivered to a performance level requiring a product, process or organizational innovation. In all other cases, including Pre-commercial Procurement, the Commission will consider, a priori that, in principle, no state aid is awarded to undertakings where the price paid for the relevant services fully reflects the market value of the benefits received by the public purchaser and the risks taken by the participating providers.[22] The 2014 State Aid Communication voices the European Commission's intent to propose new measures to further promote R&D&I, ensure consistency with the Europe 2020 strategy which identifies R&D&I as key driver for achieving the objectives of smart, sustainable and inclusive growth, boost competitive markets and properly address market failures, cover financial gaps and promote risk-taking and experimentation. As currently drafted, the 2014 State Aid Communication seems to cover not only Pre-commercial Procurement, but also the Public Procurement of Innovation and the Innovation Partnership, the new star procedure under the New Procurement Directive.[23] Whereas the 2014 State Aid Communication is saluted by all relevant stakeholders in the innovation world, we note that failure to meet the requirements aforementioned would lead to the conclusion that the undertakings delivering the relevant services do not fall outside the state aid exemption rule and will thus be subject to notifying the Commission accordingly or to facing the consequences for failing to comply with state aid regulations.

4 Designing innovative procurement methodologies

Legally, Public Procurement of Innovation (PPI) refers to a public procurement implemented according to the applicable European and national legislations, in which public procurers, possibly in cooperation with additional private buyers, act as early adopters by procuring innovative solutions that are new arrivals on the market but not yet available on a large-scale basis (Bos and Corvers 2006). In addition to meeting the needs of individual public sector players by the conduct of individual procurements, there is also the potential for PPI to be co-operative and to be conducted jointly. Cooperative procurement is intended to provide an innovative solution of interest for both public purchasers and end-users (Edquist and Hommen 2000).

Four key aspects have been identified in relation to the design of public procurement strategies promoting innovation, entailing both interactive and evolutionary issues (Cave and Frinking 2003), namely: the relation between public and commercial demand; the reasons for public intervention; the kind of innovation involved; and the choice of modalities. We will further detail each of the four aspects, as steps to be taken in the design of the procurement strategy, covering both the pre-tendering stage, as well as the tendering phase.

4.1 Relation between public and commercial demand – co-operative procurement

4.1.1 General considerations

The relation between public and commercial demand plays an important role, in terms of how public demand influences commercial demand and the other way around. Three categories of modes of interaction have been identified: a public purchaser could conduct a procurement procedure to fulfill an unmet unique need of its own ("direct procurement"), to develop an innovative solution of interest to both the procuring entity and the end users ("co-operative procurement") or to develop a solution aimed at achieving a public goal of the contracting authority ("catalytic procurement") (Edquist and Hommen 2000). This matter should also be regarded from the perspective pertaining to the interaction between users and producers, fundamental to product innovation and the modes of interaction in public procurement of innovation (Lundvall 1985). An overview of the three modes of intervention is provided in Table 8.1 below. They are described by reference to three parameters: interactive learning, which is deemed to occur in various contexts and within different networks, demand structure, in

Table 8.1 Modes of interaction

Modes of interaction	Aspects of user–producer interaction		
	Interactive learning context (networks)	*Demand structure*	*Needs addressed*
Direct procurement	*Development pairs* (simple networks or dyadic relationships)	*Monopsony* (markets with a single buyer)	*Intrinsic needs* (pertaining solely to buyer organizations)
Co-operative procurement	*Knowledge networks* (horizontally extended)	*Oligopsony* (markets with several buyers)	*Congeneric needs* (shared by buyer and other organizations)
Catalytic procurement	*Trade networks* (vertically extended)	*Polypsony* (markets with many buyers)	*Extrinsic needs* (pertaining to other actors than buyer organizations)

Source: Hommen and Rolfstan 2006.

which user–producer communication plays an important role to promote innovation and the needs addressed, namely the ultimate aim of the procurement. It was argued that "when public procurement of innovation addressed this wide range of actors, needs and interests, coordination becomes essential. It becomes necessary to maximize complementarity of diverse initiatives through close interaction of firms, consumers and public authorities" (Meyer-Krahmer 2001).

4.1.2 Co-operative procurement and market consultation

Several authors have argued that the combination of public and private demand to stimulate private sector innovation is a preeminent rationale for co-operative procurement (Brody 1996; Fukasaku 1999). Co-operative procurement takes place in a horizontally extended knowledge network. In order to ensure the best outcome of the Care Project, a broad consultation, taking the form of a structured dialogue (market consultation) with the widest possible cross-section of experts and stakeholders in the concerned field is needed, including participants from the health sector (university hospitals, healthcare institutions) and technology vendors (SMEs).

Market consultation is a powerful instrument that helps bridging the gap between supply and demand and is vital as means to create and increase awareness of the market relating to the needs of public authorities, by bringing all relevant stakeholders at the same table. The Old Procurement Directive was rather scarce in providing guidance on the opportunity for public authorities to conduct market consultations. The New Procurement Directive, however, contains specific provisions regarding the conduct of market consultations,[24] which are used to provide knowledge on whether a specific product/technology is ready available on the market or still needs to undertake development or whether a product requires customization which has not been previously performed. They also shed light on several paramount issues for the success of a project, including project feasibility, the ability of the market to accomplish what is needed, the capacity of the market to achieve it in a time and cost efficient manner. It is most suitable to address these issues at the pre-tendering phase.

In the first phase of the Care Project, CSR Netherlands introduced the participating hospitals and healthcare institution to innovative SMEs and technical experts in the entire value chain of clothing, (i.e. from raw materials, spinning, weaving, knitting and dyeing to garment confection). Several meetings took place, aimed to explore the sustainable and technical possibilities with respect to work uniforms and matching these possibilities with the needs and wishes of the hospitals and of the healthcare institution. To provide a relevant outcome, engaging with stakeholders from the health sector includes hospitals and a healthcare institution that have different attitudes and experiences towards sustainable procurement, thus covering a wide range of issues that are stringent and need innovative solutions. Furthermore, engaging with technology suppliers follows the same principles as above. The main objectives of engaging suppliers are to determine whether they understand the issues surrounding sustainable procurement of hospital uniforms, to ascertain their opinion on the feasibility of the project and, most importantly, to organize the dialogue in view of getting the best answer from the technology vendors' side and identifying the best solution to serve the purpose of the Care Project. The overarching objective is to create a relevant network of buyers and support the supply chain in healthcare organizations. In this regard, the use of the co-nomination procedure (Georghiu 1996), by which the representatives of various stakeholder categories involved could nominate other representatives deemed to have a relevant contribution to the entire exercise, might also be considered.

A sustainable market consultation model is paramount for the success of the Care Project. The involvement of representatives of both the public and commercial sectors is crucial. In addition to involving the main participants mentioned above, there are reasons to argue that the consultation is also extended to the medical personnel ultimately wearing the new uniforms. A similar approach was successfully taken by the Rawicz County Hospital in Poland, in a pilot project implemented thereby with the ultimate scope of introducing new innovation procurement methods. The project team began by consulting the nurses who would wear the new uniforms, "an empowering and novel experience for the staff, which resulted in feedback that informed the outcome based specifications" (Kautsch 2013). Moreover, hospital staff was involved in the testing of the prototypes and in discussions with suppliers. According to the staff feedback, the new uniforms had to be functional, attractive, user-friendly, easy to clean, durable and cost effective. The same method was used in UK, where staff attitudes to uniforms aimed at being sustainably procured were also considered.[25]

Whereas various methods to engage the market exist, including market survey, "meet the buyer" events or industry days, the organization of an industry platform could be a good solution in case of the Care Project. Several things need to be kept in mind:

- the demand side needs to pro-actively communicate its needs and market requirements to potential suppliers; this ensures a good feedback from the market;
- the participation of a previously consulted company must not affect competition within the future tender procedure; any information which a company may receive as result of its prior involvement must be shared with other participants;
- legal assurances must be put in place that suppliers' intellectual property rights ("IPRs") will be protected, or that they will be compensated if it is used in conjunction with another supplier;
- market engagements require compliance with the principles of transparency, non-discrimination and equal treatment; no advantage/disadvantage should be given to any supplier to the detriment of others;
- it is mandatory that suppliers understand that the competitive phase of the public procurement procedure is conducted separately and all suppliers are treated equally; this statement should be included in any invitations to open discussions.

A well conducted market consultation will provide the necessary basis for the initiation of the procurement process, as further detailed under section 4.2 below.

4.1.3 Forward commitment procurement

In case the outcome of the market consultation shows that no required technology is in place at present, another option that the contracting authorities in the Care Project could contemplate is to commit to procure the solution developed by the market in an attempt to respond to the buyers' needs. This approach qualifies as "forward commitment procurement" ("FCP"), a procurement model that can be used to deliver cost effective products and services to the public sector and can help to create the market conditions in which the innovative goods and services can thrive.[26] In other words, it involves alerting the market to the future procurement needs of a purchasing authority and further allowing the market a sufficient amount of time to develop a solution at previously agreed quality and price levels, while committing to purchase the product in the future against a specification that products currently on the market fail to meet. Although initially designed to address particular barriers to market faced by environmental innovations, the FCP is now being used in other sectors such as healthcare and sustainable development.[27] FCP is argued to be a risk and practical supply chain management tool, creating the conditions for the delivery of innovative products and the necessary incentive to unlock private investments for these products in situations in which the private sector does not hold sufficient information regarding the size and nature of future markets.[28] It addresses the investment risk, not the investment costs. Through FCP, a contracting authority does not invest in R&D, but leaves it to the private supplier.[29] Based on the above, it could be argued that FCP seems to be suitable in cases when, for the development of the desired solution, it is sufficient to signal the intention to buy the developed solution to determine the private suppliers to invest in the development thereof. Alternatively, for cases in which the private suppliers are not ready to invest or lack the potential to invest in the development of an innovative solution, the Pre-commercial Procurement followed by the procurement of innovative solutions or, alternatively, the Innovation Partnership procedure, as detailed under section 4.4 below, could be contemplated as potential solutions.

4.2 Reasons for public intervention – from conventional EU GPP criteria towards increased environmental and social responsibility in the procurement of sustainable hospital uniforms

4.2.1 General considerations

The second key element in designing innovative procurements regards the reasons for public intervention. This element is important from the perspective of the needs involved and aimed to be addressed by means of innovative procurement. As stated above, when a wide range of needs must be addressed, effective co-ordination is required. This seems to be the case when procurements are initiated in areas such as environmental and social sustainability and, based on its characteristics, in case of the Care Project, as well. As previously mentioned, the Care Project aims at the development of a sustainable and innovative prototype for hospital clothing and ultimately buying a product that has lower environmental, social and economic impact compared to others already available on the market. Whereas this article does not attempt to steer the focus on analysing the sustainability issues pertaining to the procurement of innovative hospital clothing or provide the detailed tender documentation for the procurement of such a prototype, several issues pertaining to the textile sector and related sustainability issues are worth of due consideration and are relevant for the coordination within the supply chain.

The European Green Public Procurement ("EU GPP") criteria, developed since 2007,[30] serve as guideline for contracting authorities purchasing sustainable products and services. However, the EU GPP criteria for textiles do not encompass the full life cycle socio-economic and environmental impacts of clothing, but are rather rooted in the growth and production of fibres and focusing on excluding certain chemicals.[31] Taking the CSR framework defined in section 3.1 as starting point, sustainability issues should focus on the social, environmental and economic impacts (also referred to as "People, Planet, Profit") during the whole life cycle of hospital uniforms (i.e. including production, use and disposal) (Kautsch 2013).[32] In a nutshell, first, social sustainability and ethical considerations cover issues regarding compliance with labour standards in terms of working age and labour conditions (which is often questionable in case of home-based workers and unskilled workers in developing countries).[33] As a consequence of an increasing demand for ethical clothing, industry players in the clothing industry have developed CSR policies and supply chain initiatives with impact on the garment outsourcing and/or their relations with suppliers (Goworek 2011, pp. 74–86). Second, environmental issues in the textile industry differ throughout the life-cycle of the products – manufacturing and finishing processes, maintenance and cleaning processes, disposal and supply chain.[34] In the manufacturing development, certain processes may be applied to the fabric, such as chemical treatments to create the anti-bacterial property, which trigger a high level of energy consumption. Further down the life-cycle of the medical uniform, the maintenance or cleaning processes entail washing, cleaning, disinfecting, sterilizing and drying procedures which again lead to high levels of water and energy consumption, as well as to toxic emissions. Moreover, in the disposal stage, the discarding of clothes in a hospital environment could trigger significant risks from a (hazardous) waste management perspective. Additionally, in the overall supply chain, significant waste could result from packaging materials. A circular approach should cover all of these environmental issues. Third, economic sustainability issues concern the business efficiency, productivity and profit. These sustainability issues all need to be properly addressed in the market dialogue conducted with all stakeholders involved in the Care Project (as described in section 4.1 above) in order to deliver a clear understanding of the purchasing bodies' needs and, respectively, the options available from the industry side. This approach will ensure clear, well-defined and comprehensive parameters designing the output based specifications to form the basis for the tender procedure. Outcome-based specifications will give the supply chain the opportunity to respond on quality, durability, functionality and life-cycle costs.[35]

4.2.2 Setting clear requirements and technical specifications based on the market consultation outcome

The European procurement legislation does not contain any limitations as regards the definition of a contract subject matter. Contracting authorities enjoy a great freedom to choose what they wish to procure. The only limitations provided for under the applicable legislation regard the way in which the desired product/services/work is procured, in order to ensure compliance with the principles of transparency, non-discrimination, equal treatment, proportionality and fair competition. In defining the subject matter of the contract to be awarded in the Care Project, the contracting authorities will conduct the market consultation described above in order to identify innovative solutions to minimize, for example, the environmental impact of the hospital uniforms. The market consultation will offer a clear image of what the market can offer (e.g. in the field of circular business concepts).

Selection criteria must focus, in addition to the economic and financial standing of the bidders, on their ability to perform the contract. The Old Procurement Directive provides that "the selection of bidders be done in accordance with objective rules and criteria which are available to interested economic operators."[36]

In assessing this ability under the Care Project, contracting authorities would look into specific experience and competence relevant to the subject matter, such as: whether the bidders have previous experience with the type of the tendered contract or in conducting R&D activities; if the bidders have access to or employ personnel with the required educational and professional background; if the bidders have access to the necessary technical equipment or whether the bidders have experience in employing ethical and socially responsible approaches, focusing on sustainability. Nevertheless, in recent projects, some public purchasing bodies have decided that addressing ethical/CSR matters by including them under selection criteria in a tender procedure may prove less effective than including them in the award criteria[37] and thus opted for the second solution. The decision was grounded on the fact that

> using a selection criterion would be a less effective way of ensuring a commitment to social responsibility, as all potential suppliers were to found either their own code of conduct, a supply management system or a certificate proving compliance with CSR instruments.

Consequently, bidders were evaluated on the merits of each system and were required to provide a statement on how they built and implemented a system to verify social standards within the supply chain.[38]

To ensure clarity and avoid any doubt regarding what the contracting authorities envisage when including them in tender documentation, technical specifications[39] should be formulated with reference to European, international or national standards[40] and/or in terms of performance or functionality.[41] Technical specifications may also refer to appropriate specifications that are defined in eco-labels[42] and EU GPP criteria. In order to encourage innovation, it is important not to be over prescriptive in demands. Functional specifications give the opportunity to the suppliers to differentiate their products on factors other than price.[43] Thus, requirements should be framed in terms of performance and not be technically descriptive. This approach will allow suppliers to provide innovative and creative solutions to meet performance targets, possibly expressed in several variants of the same offer. In fact, the use of variants is also encouraged in innovative procurements[44] as a mean to introduce greater flexibility in the specifications of the procedure. Last but not least, the European legislation allows the formulation of technical specifications in terms of environmental performance of a material, product, supply or service.[45] Notwithstanding the above, the obligation of transparency incumbent upon contracting authorities in the conduct of tender procedures implies that technical specifications and the fact that variants are accepted are always clearly indicated in the contract notice and the tender documentation.[46]

4.2.3 Award criteria

Under the Old Procurement Directive, contracting authorities could compare offers on the basis of the lowest price or could choose to award the contract to the most economically advantageous offer. The New Procurement Directive mentions only the MEAT award criteria, in an attempt of the legislator to ensure better value for money and higher quality of the products/works/services procured.[47] Award criteria must, however, be linked to the subject matter of the contract and must not confer a restricted freedom of choice. It must also be suitable of objective, transparent, proportionate and non-discriminatory evaluation, comply with Community law and must not qualify as selection criteria. When variants are allowed, MEAT criteria should always be used.

4.3 Kinds of innovation involved – combining circular and life-cycle costing approaches

As regards the kind of innovation involved, it is important to stress the forms of innovations (i.e. product innovation and/or process innovation) and the relationship between them. In case of the Care Project, product innovation and process innovation are, in fact, interrelated. Product innovation is required to meet the need to develop a sustainable, innovative prototype for hospital clothing, whereas process innovation translates into undertaking a circular approach[48] (see Figure 8.1 below) to meet the aforementioned primary need. Both approaches are built upon the circular approach of the sustainability dimensions occurring throughout the life cycle of a hospital uniform development, as described under section 4.2 above.

The circular economy approach should be complemented by a life-cycle costing ("LCC") approach. There is no specific legislation in Europe requiring LCC to be taken into account in procurement procedures, but the MEAT mechanism introduces it in the New Procurement Directive. While maintaining existing instruments (technical specifications expressed in terms of functional requirements, variants etc.), the New Procurement Directive encourages companies to develop their capacity for innovation. Thus, all procedures may take account of the total life-cycle cost of purchases when tenders are being evaluated

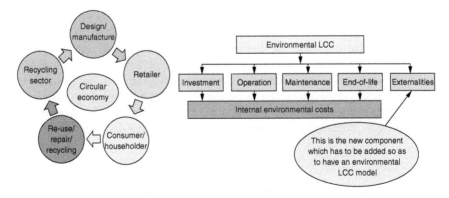

Figure 8.1 Circular economy[49] and life-cycle costing structure.[50]

and innovative bids may be awarded more points in the light of their long-term financial benefits.

LCC, also known as whole-life costing, is a methodology to assess the total cost performance of a product over time, including the acquisition, maintenance and disposal costs.[51] This means internal costs (costs borne by the contracting authority or other users), as well as costs related to environmental factors.[52] In other words, internal costs include costs for research and development, acquisition, production, transport, consumption of energy, maintenance and end-of-life disposal, where externalities may include the emission of greenhouse gases, pollution caused by the extraction of raw materials used in the product or caused by the product itself or its manufacturing. At the level of the European Union it was argued that the LCC brings significant benefits as it is a key element in the assessment of environmental sustainability of products, it provides a tool for economic evaluation of alternative sustainability options unveiling different capital, operating costs or resource usage, it provides methods for evaluating the cost benefits of incorporating more sustainable options into the development of innovative products, it improves awareness of total costs and it helps evaluating competing options (whether they regard the entire product or just parts thereof).[53] Whereas this approach was mainly justified in the sustainable construction sector, we do not see any barrier to employ it also in the development of a sustainable, circular innovative hospital uniform.

As regards the stages in the procurement process when the LCC methodology could be employed, it could be argued that it can be used either at the specification phase, or at the award stage. In the first case, we note that both the Old and the New Procurement Directives allow the use of performance specifications, as well as of sustainability and environmental issues to be included in the technical specifications forming the selection criteria. These specifications can also include requirements for low or optimum levels of life-cycle costs. Alternatively, at the award stage, LCC methodology is relevant in case the MEAT criteria are used.[54] The award criteria are the best opportunity to include LCC in the award process and this could be achieved by including quality and life-cycle costing requirements as main criteria in the award process. According to the New Procurement Directive, when contracting authorities assess the costs using a life-cycle costing approach, they shall indicate in the procurement documents the data to be provided by the bidders and the method which it will use to determine the life-cycle cost on the basis of those data.

The application of the LCC methodology can be a rather complex task and the lack of trained and qualified professionals within the contracting authority could hinder the knowledgeable and successful employment of a LCC method. Another thing to consider is the need to agree on the components of a LCC calculation (which the contracting authority must be able to check objectively) in order to have an effective model, especially in complex projects aimed at the development of sustainable products where a circular approach is envisaged. Consequently, the effectiveness of using a LCC approach should be given due consideration, by employing a joint appraisal thereof from legal, economic and financial perspective.

4.4 Choice of modalities – PCP, PPI and innovation partnership: brief considerations on joint procurement.

4.4.1 General considerations

The fourth key element in designing innovative procurement methodologies is the *choice of modalities*, namely the overall strategy employed to facilitate innovation by the organization of the procurement process. This translates into the selection of the tender procedure, the design of the specifications, the number of suppliers used (Hommen and Rolfstan 2006), the possibility to use variants. Whereas the matters pertaining to the design of the specifications and the use of variants have already been touched upon in above sections, this section will focus on the options available for choosing the tender procedure.

As a general rule, two possibilities could be contemplated as regards the conduct of PPI. Accordingly, in case of procurement of innovative solutions that require R&D, a Pre-commercial Procurement procedure shall be employed, falling outside the Procurement Directives, followed by the conduct of a PPI, fully covered by provisions under these enactments (Wert 2012). Alternatively, in case of procurement of innovative solutions that do not require R&D, a PPI taking the form of regular procurement procedures regulated by the Procurement Directives shall be conducted.

In light of the above and based on the characteristics of the Care Project, two main possibilities are further considered for the implementation of the Care Project: Pre-commercial Procurement, a procedure that falls outside the scope of the procurement directives, to be followed by a PPI procedure covered by the procurement legislation and, respectively, the Innovation Partnership, a newly introduced procedure in the European public procurement framework.

4.4.2 Pre-commercial procurement followed by PPI – does it answer procurers' needs?

Pre-commercial Procurement ("PCP")[55] is an approach for procuring R&D services, which enables the public demand side to identify the best value for money solutions on the market to address a specific procurement need. In the innovation cycle designing the transformation of an idea into a marketable product or service, PCP entails the use of competitive development in phases, risk-benefit sharing under market conditions, and a clear separation between the procurement of R&D services (via the PCP) and the potential public procurements of innovative solutions focusing on deployment of commercial volumes of end-products. The latter will always be subject to the provisions of the European procurement legal framework. PCPs that are implemented in line with these key characteristics fall outside the scope of the EU public procurement directives, the WTO Government Procurement Agreement, and the State aid framework. In a PCP, the public purchasers, as technologically demanding first buyers, share with private sector suppliers the risks and benefits of moving research developments from their early stages to products ready for commercialization. A PCP refers to innovation up to and including a first pre-commercial volume batch of products and/or services validated via field test (Bos and Corvers 2006). It is usually designed as a three-phase process, with evaluation sessions after phase 1 and phase 2 (see Figure 8.2 below).[56]

Phase 1 involves solution exploration, the scope thereof being

> to verify the technical, economic and organizational feasibility of the proposal against the pros and cons of potential alternative solutions, as well as its ability to solve the problem of public interest. The output includes a technology evaluation, as well as an organizational plan and an estimated economic impact of the proposed solution.
>
> (Bos and Corvers 2006)

Phase 2 entails the development of a prototype by the best suppliers selected based on the R&D results achieved during phase 1. The output of phase 2 should

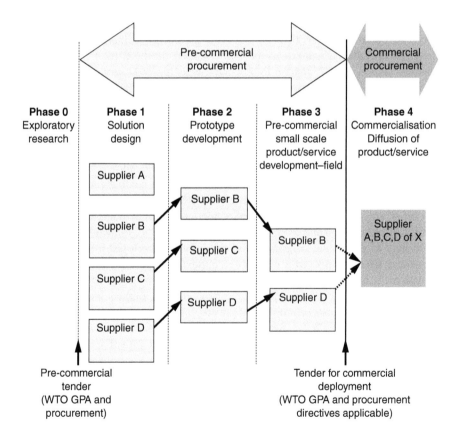

Figure 8.2 PCP process overview – a phased shared risk/shared benefit approach.

include product specifications, a tested prototype, a production plan and a business plan. Last but not least, phase 3 covers test series conducted by the best suppliers (minimum two) selected based on the results of phase 2, the production of a first batch of products/services, the testing thereof in relevant environments and the incorporation of the results of the field testing in a limited series of products, meant to demonstrate the suitability for large scale production, taking the form of classic public procurement. The outputs of this phase are refined production and business plan.[57]

As a general rule, the public procurement legal framework does not generally allow the direct uptake of the solutions developed following the conduct of a PCP procedure, as the PCP covers only the applied R&D part of the typical innovation cycle. As an exception to this rule, both the Old[58] and the New[59] Procurement Directive contain provisions which could be argued to justify the direct purchase of the innovative products/services resulting from PCP. Accordingly, the contracting authority may follow a negotiated procedure without the prior publication of the contract notice in case this is necessary for the protection of exclusive rights, including IPR. Nevertheless, the scope of application of these provisions is rather restrictive and, according to applicable jurisprudence developed by the European Court of Justice, the "simple possession of IPR would not justify direct negotiations with one specific participant, unless the contracting authority can show that there are no other substitutes to the PCP solution on the market".[60] Moreover, whereas in case of PCP, support to procurers' calls for R&D services comes from grants provided to encourage industry and academic researchers to take more risks in developing innovative solutions, processing new technologies and their applications, PPI is mainly driven by the demand of public customers, targeting the development of readily applicable solutions to meet their needs.[61] In this context, PCP and PPI are separate but complementary procurements where PPI does not cover the procurement of R&D. A split between PCP and PPI allows companies that have developed products through other means than a Pre-commercial Procurement (e.g. through SME funding instruments, other R&D grants, own company R&D resources) to still compete for PPI deployment contracts, avoiding issues of foreclosing of competition and crowding out of private R&D investments.

In light of the above, the purchase of the solution developed following a PCP procedure need to undergo a procedure conducted in full compliance with the procurement legal framework. Whereas this approach is grounded by the desire to preserve EU-wide competition in the procurement markets and also ensure compliance with the WTO GPA rules, it may also be a disincentive for public purchasers to conduct PCPs (Apostol 2012).

In order to address this pitfall, the New Procurement Directive seems to grant public purchasers more discretion in order to stimulate their engagement in the procurement of R&D and boost the uptake thereby of innovative solutions to societal problems. To this end, the new "star" procedure regulated by the New Procurement Directive is the Innovation Partnership, which allows for the direct purchase of products/services developed within the framework of an R&D public private partnership.[62]

4.4.3 Innovation partnership – the answer to promote innovation uptake?

The New Procurement Directive provides for and regulates a new procedure aimed at offering contracting authorities a tool to act as demanding customers and early adopters of desired innovation, namely the Innovation Partnership. This new procedure allows the set-up of a structured, long-term partnership by the contracting authority with one or several private undertakings, with the aim to concurrently perform R&D activities and subsequently purchase of commercial volumes of resulting products, services or works (large deployment), provided they correspond to the initially agreed levels of quality and costs.[63] As regards the procedure to be followed, the New Procurement Directive provides that the Innovation Partnership shall be structured in successive phases following the sequence of steps in R&D process, which may include the manufacturing of the products, the provision of the services or the completion of works. However, it is not clarified whether these steps correspond to the R&D phases in a PCP process and no definition of R&D is provided. Furthermore, the Innovation Partnership must set intermediate targets to be attained by the partners and provide for payment of the remuneration in appropriate instalments. It is based on these targets that the contracting authority may decide, after each phase, to terminate the innovation partnership with several partners, to reduce the number of partners by terminating individual contracts. The only obligation incumbent upon the contracting authority in this regard is to clearly mention these possibilities in the tender documentation.

The rules for establishing an Innovation Partnership involve the use of the competitive procedure with negotiation. The conduct of negotiations could occur in stages. The contracting authority shall negotiate with the bidders the initial and subsequent tenders submitted thereby, except for the final tender, fully observing the equal treatment, non-discrimination, proportionality and transparency principles. However, in an attempt to address the industry's concerns regarding the leakage of business information, the New Procurement Directive imposes upon the contracting authority the obligation to preserve the confidential information communicated by a bidder participating in the negotiations unless express consent for the sharing of information is provided by the latter. In the same line of reasoning, specific provisions regarding the safeguarding of IPR rights have also been included. Accordingly, the contracting authority must define the arrangements applicable to IPR rights in the procurement documents. Specifically in case of a partnership with several partners, the contracting authority must not reveal to the other partners solutions proposed or other confidential information communicated by a partner in the framework of the partnership without that partner's express consent.

Whereas the Innovation Partnership seems to be an alternative to the PCP procedure, the two are quite different in scope and effects. First, whereas PCP fall outside the scope of the procurement legislation, the Innovation Partnership falls within its scope and the contract must be awarded in accordance with the rules for a competitive procedure with negotiation regulated by the New Procurement Directive. Additionally, unlike PCP, the Innovation Partnership allows the purchase of the products, services or works resulting after the conduct of the R&D activities in this respect, aiming at large scale deployment of solutions within the same procedure. However, it could be argued that the provisions regulating Innovation Partnerships are rather poorly drafted (Apostol 2012) as they are limited to mentioning that the estimated value of supplies, services or works shall not be disproportionate in relation to the investment required for their development, without providing any information as to what is considered to be disproportionate. In the absence of more clarifications, the proportionality test will most probably be assessed by the European Court of Justice on a case-by-case basis. Moreover, this subsequent purchase is not limited in time or to first products or services, but seems to encourage large deployments thereof, on a long term basis and, potentially, harm competition as the contracting authorities will no longer be stimulated to act as first customers and pull innovative products or services to the market (Apostol 2012). Finally, the New Procurement Directive does not specify in case of partnerships concluded with several industry players, what solution should be employed in case more operationally viable products are developed and whether a competition among the companies having successfully developed such products should be carried out.

Despite the aforementioned criticism, the Innovation Partnership procedure could be welcomed among public authorities. It is an instrument that has the potential to strongly stimulate the investment by public purchasers in R&D activities, provided they have the opportunity to directly purchase the resulting products, services or works without the burden of organizing a new procedure to this end. In order to minimize any potential risks deriving form an arguably poor regulation of the Innovation Partnership and also given the lack of practice and case law due to the novelty of the regulation, the employment of this new procedure should, however, be based on the following minimum recommendations: the purchasing bodies must ensure full compliance with the principles of transparency, equal treatment, proportionality and non-discrimination governing the public procurement arena, while also ensuring the safeguarding of confidential information and trade secrets communicated by the bidders throughout the conduct of the procedure; the tender documentation should be drafted in a comprehensive manner, covering in detail all the aspects of the procedure (e.g. selection and award criteria, the duration and value of the different phases of the procedure and the envisaged stages of negotiation, arrangements applicable to IPRs, the draft framework agreement etc.); considering the risk of distorting competition by allowing a large deployment of products, services or works, the contracting authorities could envisage limiting the purchase of products, services or works resulting from the conduct of R&D activities, to a limited number, such as, potentially, the first batch thereof; the Innovation Partnership ought to not be used by contracting authorities in such a way as to prevent, restrict or distort competition and setting up partnerships with several partners could contribute to avoiding such effects[64] – to this extent, clear rules to be followed by the contracting authority to choose which products to purchase in case more products will be successfully developed by several partners at the end of the R&D phase within the partnership are recommended to be included in the tender documentation; finally, in order to ensure full compliance with the 2014 State Aid Communication, a potential notification of the innovation partnership procedure to the Commission for investigation thereby could also be contemplated.

In light of the above, the Innovation Partnership seems to be a potential solution for the Care Project. However, the healthcare sector involved in the project from the purchasing bodies' side entails the participation of several entities. In this respect, we note that the provisions under the New Procurement Directive regarding Innovation Partnerships are silent as regards whether the contracting authority should encompass a single entity or could include several entities. Nevertheless, as previously mentioned, the New Procurement Directive regulates, for the first time, the possibility of two or more contracting authorities to agree to perform certain specific procurement jointly.[65] In the absence of specific provisions under the article regulating Innovation Partnerships in this respect, it could be argued that such provisions could be read in conjunction with the ones covering joint procurement. Several considerations in this respect are provided below.

4.4.4 *Joint procurement*

In an attempt to shed light on the uncertainties regarding the conduct of joint procurements, the New Procurement Directive provides a new approach, whereby joint procurement is deemed possible, provided certain conditions are met. Pursuant to the provisions under article 38 thereof:

> Two or more contracting authorities may agree to perform certain specific procurements jointly. Where the conduct of a procurement procedure in its entirety is carried out jointly in the name and on behalf of all the contracting authorities concerned, they shall be jointly responsible for fulfilling their obligations pursuant to this Directive. This applies also in cases where one contracting authority manages the procedure, acting on its own behalf and on the behalf of the other contracting authorities concerned. Where the conduct of a procurement procedure is not in its entirety carried out in the name and on behalf of the contracting authorities concerned, they shall be jointly responsible only for those parts carried out jointly. Each contracting authority shall have sole responsibility for fulfilling its obligations pursuant to this Directive in respect of the parts it conducts in its own name and on its own behalf.[66]

Joint procurement can take different forms, ranging from coordinated procurement through the preparation of common technical specifications for works, supplies or services that will be procured by a number of contracting authorities where each authority conducts a separate procurement, to cases where the contracting authorities concerned conduct one procurement procedure jointly. In this second case, two possibilities exist, namely the case in which the contracting authorities act together in the form of a consortium, and, respectively, the second case, in which they entrust one contracting authority with the management of the procurement procedure on behalf of all contracting authorities.[67]

The New Procurement Directive is pending implementation in the Member States. We also note that the new provisions specifically allowing for the conduct of joint procurements do not include any criteria to be taken into account on how to conduct them, but are rather limited to decrypting liability issues.[68] Furthermore, no case-law has been yet developed at the level of the European Union detailing and clarifying these new legal provisions and their practical applicability. Consequently, whereas it is to be reasonably expected that the approach mentioned in the New Procurement Directive will be followed by (national) courts when deciding on similar matters, it could be argued that these provisions will be read in line with the more explicit national legislation in this regard, where such legislation exists.[69]

5 Conclusions

Public procurement of innovative solutions aims at closing the gap between revolutionary technology and processes and the public sector purchasers or users benefiting there from. Sharing risks, costs and gains are all important parts of the PPI, whereas a number of available options to structure the partnerships between the public and the private sectors in this regard are provided under the procurement legal framework. When conducted according to the main principles governing its implementation in the healthcare sector as discussed under this article, PPI will ensure significant benefits for public purchasers and suppliers of innovative hospital uniforms, as well as for the society. Public authorities will be delivered solutions to their needs or challenges, enjoy cost savings on the short, medium and long term, meet higher levels of staff and user satisfaction and successfully contribute to environmental and social policy targets. Suppliers, especially SMEs, will understand public sector challenges and priorities and thus gain access to valuable public sector clients, have the opportunity to apply research and commercialize innovative ideas, achieve higher exposure to PCP and PPI procedures and thus increased chances of winning future contracts and also enjoy positive publicity and reputational gains. Finally, the society will benefit from better public services, improvements in their quality of life and the sense of efficient and smarter spending of public money, while taking into account the interests of workers in developing countries. The outcome is a win–win for all the actors involved in the new arena of public procurement of circular and sustainable innovative solutions.

6 Further debates

Whereas this chapter has focused on the instruments available to design an innovative and sustainable model for the procurement of medical uniforms, the impact measurement aspect of such a methodology should also not be left aside. This is often an aspect that is barely taken into account when introducing innovative procurement strategies. However, without disaggregated data on innovation output it will be difficult to further develop detailed policies on innovation and sustainability (Edquist 2013). Methodologies for impact measurement therefore need increased attention and should be fully integrated into the procurement strategies from the very beginning. How else could contracting authorities assess that their needs are actually met?

Notes

1 Public purchasers may procure research and development services from undertakings through both exclusive development and pre-commercial procurement procedures. See the Communication and associated staff working document – Communication from the Commission to the European Parliament, the Council, the European Economic and Social Committee and the Committee of the Region, "Pre-commercial procurement: driving innovation to ensure sustainable high quality public services in Europe", COM(2007) 799 final, 14.12.2007.

2 See Recital 47 of the Directive 2014/24/EU of the European Parliament and the Council of 26 February 2014 on public procurement and repealing Directive 2004/18/EC.

3 Communication COM (2010)2020 final, *Europe 2020, A strategy for smart, sustainable and inclusive* growth. See also the Europe 2020 flagship initiative Innovation Union Initiative, available at www.bit.ly/innovation-union-initiative.

4 See "Public Procurement – Public purchasers as First customers", available at http://ec.europa.eu/enterprise/policies/innovation/policy/public-procurement/index_en.htm.

5 ISO 26000, the international standard providing guidelines for CSR was developed in 2010. Its goal is to contribute to global sustainable development, by encouraging business and other organizations to practice social responsibility to improve their impacts on their workers, their natural environments and their communities. It was prepared by ISO/TMB Working group on Social Responsibility and released on 1st of November 2010. The International Standard ISO 26000 provides guidance on understanding, implementing and continuously improving the social responsibility of organizations, which is understood as the impacts of an organization's actions on society and the environment. See www.iso.org.

6 See OECD (2010) *The OECD Innovation Strategy: Getting a Head Start on Tomorrow*; OECD and Eurostat (2005) *Oslo Manual: Guidelines for Collecting and Interpreting Innovation Data* (3rd edition). The OECD Guidelines for Multinational Enterprises are recommendations from OECD governments to multinational companies operating in or from adhering countries. They provide an instrument to address corporate misconduct by means of a grievance mechanism. The OECD Guidelines, the UN Global Compact and ISO 26000 are often referred to as "core set of internationally recognized principles and guidelines regarding CSR". See also European Commission, "Communication from the Commission to the European Parliament, the Council, the European Economic and Social Committee and the Committee of the Regions: A Renewed EU Strategy 2011–14 for Corporate Social Responsibility", (Brussels, 25 October 2011), pp. 6–7 and MVO Platform, CSR Frame of Reference, (April 2012).

7 The UN Global Compact's ten principles in the areas of human rights, labour, the environment and anti-corruption enjoy universal consensus and are derived from The Universal Declaration of Human Rights, The International Labor Organization's Declaration on Fundamental Principles and Rights at Work, The Rio Declaration on Environment and Development; The United Nations Convention Against Corruption.

The UN Global Compact asks companies to embrace, support and enact, within their sphere of influence, a set of core values in the areas of human rights, labor standards, the environment and anti-corruption. See www.unglobalcompact.org/.

8 Case study: Introducing innovation procurement methods: Rawicz County Hospital, Poland, available at http://lowcarbon-healthcare.eu/cms/resources/uploads/File/Case%20Study_Rawicz.pdf.

9 CSR Netherlands is a the network organization and Centre of Excellence for companies in the Netherlands with ambitions in the field of CSR. CSR Netherlands has a partner network of over 2000 Dutch companies and trade associations and through different activities and media the organizations has contact with 1000s of companies more. The network involves large, medium and small companies. CSR Netherlands works together with employers' and trade associations, trade unions and NGOs. CSR Netherlands is a non-profit foundation and carries out projects for both the public and private sector (about 2/3 and 1/3 of the turnover respectively). Its objective is to inspire, connect and empower companies, trade associations and other relevant stakeholders in supply chains to take further steps in the field of CSR.

10 In the Netherlands academic hospitals are considered public authorities in the meaning of the EU procurement Directives. The participating healthcare institution is not. However, since this is a national related legal aspect, we will not touch upon it in this chapter, as the latter is deemed to offer an overall innovative approach in the healthcare sector in Europe.

11 In fact, since the project is partly subsidized by the Dutch government, it has a wider focus than the "traditional" developing countries and focuses on the so-called Private Sector Development countries (PSD-countries), defined by the Dutch government.

12 Ellen MacArthur Foundation, www.ellenmacarthurfoundation.org/circular-economy/circular-economy/towards-the-circular-economy.

13 The documentary The Next Black gives a good illustration of innovative techniques being developed in the textile/fashion sector: www.youtube.com/watch?v=XCsGLWrfE4Y.

14 WTO GPA (Government Procurement Agreement) available at www.wto.org/English/tratop_e/gproc_e/gp_gpa_e.htm.

15 The procedural rules are laid down in the Annexes to the GPA.

16 The Agreement on Government Procurement (GPA) consists of 15 parties covering 43 WTO members (counting the European Union and its 28 member states, all of which are covered by the Agreement, as one party). Another 28 WTO members and four international organizations participate in the GPA Committee as observers. Ten of these members with observer status are in the process of acceding to the Agreement. For more information, see www.wto.org/english/tratop_e/gproc_e/memobs_e.htm.

17 Article 25 of the New Procurement Directive.

18 Directive 2014/24/EU of the European Parliament and of the Council on public procurement and repealing Directive 2004/18/EC ("New Procurement Directive").

19 Commission, "Framework for state aid for research and development and innovation" (2014 State Aid Communication) C(2014) 3282.

20 The innovation partnership procedure provided for under article 31 of the New Procurement Directive needs to be distinguished from the European Innovation Partnerships (EIPs). See www.bit.ly/european-innovation-partnerships.

21

Save as otherwise provided in the Treaties, any aid granted by a Member State or through State resources in any form whatsoever which distorts or threatens to distort competition by favoring certain undertakings or the production of certain goods shall, in so far as it affects trade between Member States, be incompatible with the internal market.

22 Several additional conditions need to be met, including: the conduct of R&D services procurements via open, transparent and non-discriminatory procedures, based on objective selection and award criteria provided upfront in the tender documentation; the upfront provision of contractual arrangements describing all rights and obligations of the parties, including with regard to Intellectual Property Rights (IPR); strictly avoiding giving any of the participant providers any preferential treatment in the supply of commercial volumes of the final products or services to a public purchaser in the member State concerned. Additionally, it is required that all results which do not give rise to IPR be widely disseminated and any IPR are fully allocated to the public purchaser. Alternatively, any service provider to which results giving rise to IPR are allocated is required to grant the public purchaser unlimited access to those results free of charge, and to grant access to this parties, for example by way of non-exclusive licenses, under market conditions.

23 This is only applicable in case the open or restricted procedures are used.

24 Article 40 under the New Procurement Directive states:

> Before launching a procurement procedure, contracting authorities may conduct market consultations with a view to preparing the procurement and informing economic operators of their procurement plans and requirements. For this purpose, contracting authorities may for example seek or accept advice from independent experts or authorities or from market participants. That advice may be used in the planning and conduct of the procurement procedure, provided that such advice does not have the effect of distorting competition and does not result in a violation of the principles of non-discrimination and transparency.

25 Department for Environment, Food and Rural Affairs, "Sustainable Clothing Procurement – Uniforms in the NHS" (2011), available at www.brooklyndhurst.co.uk/sustainable-clothing-procurement--uniforms-in-the-nhs-pilot-_146.html.

26 The model was conceived and developed by the UK Government's Environmental Innovation Advisory Group (EIAG) (2003–2008) to address a key market failure, namely the lack of a market pull for environmental innovations. It involves providing the market with advance information of future needs in outcome terms, early engagement with potential suppliers and – most importantly – the incentive of a Forward Commitment: an agreement to purchase a product or service that currently does not exist, at a specified future date, providing it can be delivered to agreed performance levels and costs.

27 Environmental Innovations Advisory Group, 'Environmental Innovation: Bridging the gap between environmental necessity and economic opportunity' (2006).

28 Department for Business Innovation and Skills, "Forward Commitment Procurement: Practical pathways to delivering innovation". Available at https://procurement-forum.eu/resource/download/190/FCP_Overview-1.pdf.

29 See www.bis.gov.uk/policies/innovation/procurement/forward-commitment.

30 See EU GPP criteria for textiles available at http://ec.europa.eu/environment/gpp/pdf/criteria/textiles.pdf.

31 See EU GPP criteria for textiles available at http://ec.europa.eu/environment/gpp/pdf/criteria/textiles.pdf.

32 Department for Environment, Food and Rural Affairs, "Sustainable Clothing Procurement – Uniforms in the NHS" (2011), available at www.brooklyndhurst.co.uk/sustainable-clothing-procurement--uniforms-in-the-nhs-pilot-_146.html.

33 See http://sustainabilityskills.net.au/sustainability-skills-resources/sustainability-sector-guides/sustainability-issues-clothing/.

34 Department for Environment, Food and Rural Affairs, "Sustainable Clothing Procurement – Uniforms in the NHS" (2011), available at www.brooklyndhurst.co.uk/sustainable-clothing-procurement--uniforms-in-the-nhs-pilot-_146.html.

35 Case study: Introducing innovation procurement methods: Rawicz County Hospital,

Poland, available at http://lowcarbon-healthcare.eu/cms/resources/uploads/File/Case%20Study_Rawicz.pdf.

36 See article 48 of the Old Procurement Directive.

37 ICLEI – Local Governments for Sustainability, "The Landmark Project – Moving towards socially responsible procurement, Success stories in socially responsible public procurement: using public spending to drive improvements for workers in global supply chains" (2014).

38 ICLEI – Local Governments for Sustainability, "The Landmark Project – Moving towards socially responsible procurement, Success stories in socially responsible public procurement: using public spending to drive improvements for workers in global supply chains" (2014).

39 Technical specifications serve a dual purpose: (i) they are used to describe the contract to the market in order to allow potentially interested bidders to decide whether it is of interest to them or not, whether they have the required capability and capacity to perform the object thereof and also help determine the level of competition; and (ii) they provide measurable requirements against which tenders can be evaluated, provided they are clear, correct and conveyed in such a way as to ensure understanding thereof by the bidders.

40 Standards can take several forms, from full European standards (ENs) to European or national technical approvals, common or national technical specifications, international standards and other technical reference systems established by European standard bodies. Reference to technical standards can be included directly in the specification defining the contract subject matter. When reference to a standard is used, it must be accompanied by words "or equivalent". See article 23 (3) of the Old Procurement Directive and article 42 of the New Procurement Directive.

41 See article 23 of the Old Procurement Directive and Recital 74 of the New Procurement Directive, according to which performance-based specifications are appropriate means to favour innovation in public procurements.

42 See Recital 29 of the Old Procurement Directive and article 43 of the New Procurement Directive.

43 ICLEI – Local Governments for Sustainability, "The Landmark Project – Moving towards socially responsible procurement, Success stories in socially responsible public procurement: using public spending to drive improvements for workers in global supply chains" (2014).

44 Recital 48 of the new Procurement Directive states that "because of the importance of innovation, contracting authorities should be encouraged to allow variants as often as possible".

45 Annex VI of the Old Procurement Directive.

46 See Case 225/98 *Commission* v *France*, in which technical specifications defined solely by reference to classifications in French legislation were found to be indirectly discriminatory.

47 See Recital 37 and article 18(2) of the New Procurement Directive.

48 Commission, "Communication from the Commission to the European Parliament, the Council, the European Economic and Social Committee and the Committee of the Regions: Towards a circular economy: A zero waste programme for Europe", COM(2014) 398 final.

49 www.waste-management-world.com/articles/2013/02/reuse-recycling-targetef-by-circular-economy-100.html.

50 A potential approach to employ LCC could be found in the environmental LCC structure available at http://ec.europa.eu/environment/gpp/lcc.htm.

51 See article 68 of the New Procurement Directive.

52 See http://ec.europa.eu/environment/gpp/lcc.htm.

53 See "Towards a common European methodology for Life-cycle costing (LCC) – Guidance Document", available at http://ec.europa.eu/enterprise/sectors/construction/files/compet/life_cycle_costing/guidance_case_study_en.pdf.

54 See "Towards a common European methodology for Life-cycle costing (LCC) – Guidance Document", available at http://ec.europa.eu/enterprise/sectors/construction/files/compet/life_cycle_costing/guidance_case_study_en.pdf.

55 Commission, "Pre-commercial Procurement: Driving innovation to ensure sustainable high quality public services in Europe" COM (2007)799 final. See also Commission, "Example of a possible approach for procuring R&D services applying risk-benefit sharing at market conditions, i.e. pre-commercial procurement" (PCP Staff Working Document) SEC (2007) 1668.

56 Commission, "Pre-commercial Procurement: Driving innovation to ensure sustainable high quality public services in Europe" COM (2007)799 final. See also Commission, "Example of a possible approach for procuring R&D services applying risk-benefit sharing at market conditions, i.e. pre-commercial procurement" (PCP Staff Working Document) SEC (2007) 1668.

57 National IST Research Directors Forum Working Group on Public Procurement in support of ICT Research and Innovation, "Pre-commercial Procurement of Innovation: A Missing Link in the European Innovation Cycle" (2006).

58 Article 31(1)(b) of the Old Procurement Directive.

59 Article 32(2)(b) of the New Procurement Directive specifically states that:

> The negotiated procedure without prior publication may be used for public works contracts, public supply contracts and public services contracts [...] where the works, supplies or services can be supplied only by a particular economic operator for any of the following reasons: (i) the aim of the procurement is the creation or acquisition of a unique work of art or artistic performance; (ii) competition is absent for technical reasons; (iii) the protection of exclusive rights, including intellectual property rights. The exceptions set out in points (ii) and (iii) shall only apply when no reasonable alternative or substitute exists and the absence of competition is not the result of an artificial narrowing down of the parameters of the procurement.

60 *Commission of the European Communities* v. *Greece* (C-394/02) 2 June 2005; *Commission of the European Communities* v. *Italy* (C-385/02), 14 September 2004.

61 Procurement of Innovation Platform, "Guidance for public authorities on Public Procurement of Innovation" (2014), available at www.innovation-procurement.org.

62 Article 31 of the New Procurement Directive.

63 Article 31 (1) and (2) of the New Procurement Directive.

64 See Recital 49 of the New Procurement Directive.

65 Article 38 of the New Procurement Directive.

66 Article 38 of the New Procurement Directive.

67 See Recital 71 of the New Procurement Directive.

68 Some limited guidance is, however, provided in case on cross-border joint procurement regulated by article 39 of the New procurement Directive. Accordingly, in case several contracting authorities from different Member States jointly award a public contract, they need to conclude an agreement determining the responsibilities of the parties and the internal organization of the procurement procedure. Furthermore, in case several contracting authorities from different member States have set up a joint entity, such as a European Groupings of territorial cooperation or other entities established under the Union Law (for the purpose of conducting a joint cross-border procurement), the participating contracting authorities shall agree on the applicable national procurement rules of one of the following Member States: (i) the national provisions of the Member State where the joint entity has its registered office; (ii) the national provisions of the member State where the joint entity is carrying out its activities.

69 In the Netherlands, for example, The Aanbestedingswet 2012 includes provisions that specifically prohibit the unnecessarily "joining" of procurements, due to the fact that such as approach could prevent the participation of SMEs in these procurement

procedures. The following main aspects should be considered when deciding upon the joining of procurements: the structure of the relevant market and the influence of such joining on the competition and ability of SMEs to participate in these procurements; the organizational implications and risks of such joining for the contracting authorities, as well as for the suppliers; and the coherence of the procurement. Furthermore, according to specific provisions under Aanbestedingswet 2012, in case of joining procurements, the contracting authorities need to motivate, within the procurement documents, the reasons for employing this approach. Additionally, it is deemed that the contracting authorities should first consider dividing the object of the procurement into lots, unless this is not a feasible option, situation in which the contracting authorities need to justify its approach within the tender documentation.

References

Apostol, A. R. (2012) Pre-commercial procurement in support of innovation: Regulatory effectiveness?. In: *Public Procurement Law Review* Issue 6. Thomson Reuters (Professional) UK Ltd. and Contributors.

Bos, L., and Corvers, S. (2006) Pre-commercial Public Procurement. A missing link in the European Innovation Cycle. Public Needs as a driver for innovation. In: *Tijdschrijft Aanbestendingsrecht*. Sdu uitgevers.

Brody, R. J. (1996) Effective partnering: A report to congress on federal technology partnerships. U.S Department of Commerce, Office of Technology Policy. Washington, D.C.

Cave, J., and Frinking, E. (2003) Public procurement and R&D: Short analysis of the potential and practices. Chapter 1. In: J. P. Gavigan (ed.) *Public procurement and R&D: A JRC/IPTS-ESTO fast track working paper*. European Commission Joint Research Centre – Institute for Prospective Technological Studies – European Science and Technology Observatory.

Edquist, C. (2013) Innovation Policy in Sweden. Paper presented at the 14th International Conference on Industrial Technology Innovation, Taipei. Available at: http://itc.tier.org.tw/2013/pres_2_1.pdf.

Edquist, C., and Hommen, L. (2000) Public technology procurement and innovation theory. In: C. Edquist, L. Hommen and L. J. Tsipairi, (eds), *Public Technology Procurement and Innovation*. Boston: Kluwer.

Fukasaku, Y. (1999) Public–private partnerships for developing environmental technology. In: *OECD STI Review* 23: 105–130.

Georgiu, L. (1996) The UK Technology Foresight Programme. In: *Futures*, Vol. 28, No. 4: 359–377.

Goworek, H. (2011) Social and environmental sustainability in the clothing industry: a case study of a fair trade retailer. In: *Social Responsibility Journal*, Vol. 7, No. 2: 74–86.

Hommen, L., and Rolfstan, M. (2006) Classifying Public Procurement of Innovation: A Taxonomy. In: *Tijdschrijft Aanbestendingsrecht*. Sdu uitgevers.

Kautsch, M. (2013) Innovative public procurement of a bio-based product: Poland ppt. Presentation given during the Innovation Procurement for the benefit of industries, SMEs & stronger public services conference in Krakow.

Lundvall, B. (1985) Product innovation and user–producer interaction. In: *Aalborg*: Aalborg University Press. http://vbn.aau.dk/files/7556474/user-producer.pdf.

Meyes-Krahmer (2001) Industrial innovation and sustainability – Conflicts and coherence. In: D. Archibugi and B.-A. Lundvall (eds.), *The globalizing learning economy*. Oxford/New York: Oxford University Press.

Theuws, M., and Van Huijstee, M. (2013) Corporate Responsibility Instruments: A Comparison of the OECD Guidelines, ISO 26000 & the UN Global Compact. SOMO.

Wert, B. (2012) Driving Innovation Through Public Procurement – Future European Support. Paper presented during the European High Level Events on: Supporting Public Procurement of Innovation, Launching Events of the European projects Financed by the Competitiveness and Innovation Programme.

9 Innovation partnership and its predecessors

Marta Andrecka

1 Introduction

At the beginning of 2014, the European Parliament and the Council adopted the new directive on public procurement (Directive 2014/24/EU; hereafter the Directive). Inter alia, the Directive introduces a new procedure called the innovation partnership. The availability of the new provisions maybe valuable particularly from the perspective of complex contracts, which are characterised as mixed contracts.[1] This is because the innovation partnership has a potential to enable a contracting authority to procure complex contracts with more than one type of subject matter regarding development of innovation and its delivery.

On the one hand, the innovation partnership has a potential to overcome the primary challenge and uncertainty regarding the usage of a two-stage procedure divided into pre-commercial and commercial procurement, relating to the unfair competition and the conflict of interest that may occur based on cooperation within the pre-commercial phase. On the other hand, the establishment of an innovation partnership may be seen not only as an answer to existing challenges, but also as a new way of realising the objective of a smart, sustainable and inclusive growth that characterises the Europe 2020 strategy (EC SSIG, 2010). However, at the same time the application of the innovation partnership provisions may pose certain challenges. The aim of this chapter is to identify and discuss these challenges.

To achieve this aim first, the scene for the discussion will be set by a presentation of background information. Second, three methods of procuring innovation will be discussed: first, the pre-commercial procurement; second, delivery of innovation throughout the competitive dialogue procedure; and, finally, the newly introduced innovation partnership. Third, a particular attention will be given to the innovation partnership provision in the Directive. Focus will be given to the proposed procedure and structure of the partnership. Fourth, considered will be what new solutions the new procedure introduce. Finally, the last section will conclude the discussion.

2 Background

The EU, as well as any other region, is faced with important societal challenges such as ensuring high quality and accessible healthcare, the fight against climate change and improvement of energy efficiency. Addressing these challenges often requires new and better solutions (EC PCP, 2007). As research and innovation play a central role in the Europe 2020 strategy for a smart, sustainable and inclusive growth, the procurement of innovation is of high value.

However, delivery of innovation brings specific legal challenges which need to be considered. One of the challenges is how innovation should be understood. Until now there has not been any legal definition of innovation in EU public procurement law, and this could potentially cause uncertainties. Among others it was unclear how to procure a contract including innovation and how to classify such a contract, especially since it is often difficult to specify the subject matter of an innovation contract. With the introduction of an innovation partnership the Directive also introduces a legal definition of an innovation in Article 2(22) stating:

> 'innovation' means the implementation of a new or significantly improved product, service or process, including but not limited to production, building or construction processes, a new marketing method, or a new organisational method in business practices, workplace organisation or external relations inter alia with the purpose of helping to solve societal challenges or to support the Europe 2020 strategy for smart, sustainable and inclusive growth.

There are several downfalls of this definition – in particular, the question how should we understand the concept of 'significantly improved'. In this respect, Recital 47 of the Directive states that innovation should improve efficiency and quality; and that it should contribute to achieving best value for public money as well as wider economic, environmental and societal benefits. Therefore, it seems that the requirement for significant improvement should refer to these elements. The innovation should allow a contracting authority to deliver better public contracts in terms of quality, life-cycle cost, and enable the contracting authority to incorporate better environmental and societal considerations and standards.Also, other elements of the definition can be criticised. First, it is unclear why the legislator would establish a definition which will become outdated, as the definition refers to the Europe 2020 strategy. Second, the definition is too complex. It might be better to refer simply to implementation of a new or significantly improved product, service or process, including but not limited to production, building or construction processes.

There are several ways in which the contracting authority can encourage the introduction of innovation in the procurement procedure. Among others are variants,[2] design contests[3] or a functional description of technical specification which can be used.[4] Nevertheless, these options may increase risks and confusion as how to make sure that the contracting authority is not comparing apples with oranges. Also, when these tools are used in open or restricted procedures they are not traditional innovation processes, as dialogue between contracting authorities and bidders is not allowed.

Until recently the procurement of innovation could also be carried out in the following two ways. First, the procurement of innovation could be carried out in a two-stage process, starting with a pre-commercial procurement where a Research and Development (R&D) service contract is awarded, and followed by a procurement procedure of the already developed innovative solution (construction, services, goods) on a commercial market. Second, the whole process, including the pre-commercial and the commercial procurement, could be combined into one procedure and the subject matter procured – depending on the circumstances of the contract – through the competitive dialogue procedure or, negotiated procedure with a notice (changed and renamed in the Directive to the competitive procedure with negotiation).[5] Currently, the Directive added one more option, where the innovation may be developed and delivered through the newly introduced innovative partnership.[6]

3 Pre-commercial procurement

The aim of a pre-commercial procurement is to award a contract with the objective to develop an invention or an improved product, whereas the subsequent delivery of the already developed innovation is to be procured on the commercial market. The Commission refers to the innovation as a R&D project which covers activities such as, solution exploration and design, prototyping, and development of a limited volume of test series (EC PCP, 2007, p. 2).

With regard to pre-commercial procurement the starting point is that such R&D services will normally be subject to the full procedural obligation of the Directive. However, there is an exclusion of the applicability of the Directive for R&D services in Article 14. On the basis of the exception, the contracting authority is obliged to conduct a public tender only, if it pays for the whole of the service and also kept the results solely for itself. In all other cases – for example, when the contracting authority decides to share the R&D results – it can conclude an innovation contract under an exclusion from the Directive's requirements, which allows for a wide spectrum of flexibility.

3.1 The structure of pre-commercial procurement

According to the Commission's Communication, a pre-commercial procurement can take the form of a single public procurement contract for the R&D managed in three stages (EC PCP, 2007, pp. 2–3; Apostol, 2012, pp. 215–216). The first stage is a solution exploration phase, the second stage evolves around prototyping and the third stage is a test series. The final stage covers the development of a first lot of pre-commercial pre-products. However, nothing prevents the Member States from developing different pre-commercial procurement schemes, as there is no specific procedure under EU law that is required to be used. After the pre-products are tested, the commercial development of the innovation starts – that is, the pre-commercial phase transfers into commercial procurement. The commercial development of innovation will include volume production of the end product, or supply to create commercial validity or to recover the amount invested in R&D (EC PCP, 2007, pp. 2–3; Apostol, 2012 6 pp. 215–216).

3.2 Challenges of pre-commercial procurement

Pre-commercial procurement in different markets has already proven to be extremely successful and has delivered the Internet Protocol technology and the Global Positioning System and more in the US (EURAB, 2014, and Mazzucato, 2013). Nonetheless, in the EU the size of pre-commercial procurement is marginal in comparision with total public procurement (Bos and Corvers, 2006, p. 202). Possibly because innovation delivery in the model of the pre-commercial framework proposed by the Commission is complex and includes certain pitfalls. It is divided into phases, involving many bidders throughout an extended period of time. On the one hand, such an approach stretched over a period of time potentially secures transparency and equality and is ensuring competition between bidders and the creation of multiple options. On the other hand, it bears some challenges and risks. To these may be added: extensive costs and time of handling multiphase procurements, the possibility of many changes of partners during the process, lack of stability and legal certainty, and the challenges of choosing the appropriate procurement procedure. These issues have been acknowledged by the Commission, but until recently there was a strong belief in the Commission that the quality/price ratio and success rate would counteract these challenges (EC PCP, 2007, p. 9).

From the perspective of a bidder, the pre-commercial procurement process suggested by the Commission is very complex. Due to the division into pre-commercial and commercial phase, a bidder has no guarantee that it will be the one who will also deliver the innovation to the contracting authority, and the money most often lies in the commercial part of the innovation development.

There is an argument to be made that it is useful to separate phases of the R&D and commercial procurement, since the risk exists that technological success will not always be the case, or the level of the developed innovation will not be satisfactory for the contracting authority. However, a steady environment for R&D is an important factor which should be taken into consideration as well as the fact that in case of development of an innovation, negotiation, trust and collaboration are crucial elements to achieve the established goals. If the private partner in the innovation project changes during the innovation process, not only an extra amount of time and resources will need to be spent on the contracting process, but such a scenario will also attract certain legal challenges. The latter may include issues regarding intellectual property rights (further: IP rights), problems with the confidentiality of the solution provided by the previous contractual partner and uncertainties regarding how much information the contracting authority can disclose to the new contractual partner, as well as risks of claims for damages.

Dividing a R&D project into slots where on every step in the innovation development there is a potential to change a private partner may involve a type of 'cherry-picking'.[7] That is due to the fact that on every step of the way the contracting authority has a beneficial possibility to choose the best solution provided. Nevertheless, it is debatable, whether the contracting authority in fact would be interested in changing partners all the time due to the financial and legal restrains following such changes of contractual partners. From the perspective of private parties, the opportunity for dividing R&D into slots may be advantageous for Small and Medium Sized Enterprises (SMEs), which often will not have a capacity to deliver a whole innovation development process. This line of argumentation may be supported by the fact that one of the aims of the Directive is to promote SMEs' participation in public procurement.[8] From the opposite perspective the bidders may be hesitant to participate in such a structured pre-commercial procurement, as they fear losing their valuable ideas and confidential 'know-how' without gaining any or enough profit.[9]

3.3 Exclusive development

To ensure that the development of innovation may proceed further, even in a case where the private partner will need to be changed, the contracting authorities will at times opt for exclusive development of the innovation. The exclusive development of the innovation means that the contracting authority reserves all the rights, results and advantages coming from the R&D for itself (EC PCP, 2007, p. 5). In these circumstances, private partners who developed an innovation or innovative solution for a contracting authority are not allowed to reuse it for other potential customers. Consequently, the exclusive development of the innovation will be accompanied by a higher price for the R&D (EC PCP, 2007, p. 5). While in some cases the importance of exclusive development is understandable (defence and national security projects), in a majority of cases it is not indispensable.[10] Often, there is no reason to bear the high costs and risks of exclusive development. If the IP right will be shared as well as the R&D results, the other contractual risks and benefits will also be shared by the contractual partners (EC PCP, 2007, p. 7).

Even though the Directive's requirements will not be applicable to the majority of pre-commercial procurements, if any procedure is required at all,[11] it should reflect good practice. Furthermore, the procedures should be concluded in a fair, transparent and non-discriminatory manner. It could be questioned, whether there is a need for a procedure in the first place, why not just use a regular tender procedure? The answer is that the traditional procurement procedures have many detailed requirements which make them fairly inflexible, costly, and time-consuming. Hence, when the contracting authority wants to follow good practice, it will be keen to apply general EU law principles rather than the Directive's provisions. This gives the contracting authority more flexibility and a bigger scope of discretion in awarding the innovation contract.

3.4 Violation of equal treatment

In case of non-exclusive development of the innovation the contracting authority needs to ensure that the private partner to the pre-commercial procurement agreement will not be given an unfair advantage in the possible subsequent commercial procurement, as such a situation could violate equal treatment principle, distort competition or even – depending from the circumstances of a case – constitute a conflict of interest.[12] To escape these risks the contracting authority may require for the private partner to license IP rights to third parties. This requirement should involve fair and reasonable market conditions.

There is no legal basis in EU law for allowing Member States' legislators to establish a general prohibition for participation in a commercial tender of a private partner who developed the innovation or who was involved in a pre-commercial procurement in a different manner, for example by helping with the establishment of the contract specification. In the *Fabricom* case[13] the European Court of Justice clearly stated that establishing a total prohibition on participation of parties who had been involved in the preparation of the tender is disproportionate. Such a provision goes beyond what is necessary to avoid distortion of competition and to secure transparency and equal treatment in the procurement process.[14] However, the contracting authority may place the burden of proof on the party seeking to participate in the tender to show that there is no unfair competition.[15]

A problem with separating the procurement into pre-commercial and commercial elements is the fact that the private partner who was awarded the contract for the R&D service in the pre-commercial stage needs to compete in multiple procurements – both for R&D and delivery. That party will also be at risk of being excluded from the commercial tender on the basis of having an unfair competitive advantage following involvement in the pre-commercial procurement (EC PCP, 2007, pp. 2–3; Apostol, 2012, p. 220). Thus the contracting authority may try to combine the pre-commercial and commercial process into a one tender procedure.

4 Delivery of an innovation contract in a competitive dialogue procedure[16]

As mentioned, besides procuring innovation in a two-stage process of a pre-commercial and a commercial procurement, the contracting authority may decide to combine all stages of the innovation development into one procurement procedure. For the purpose of such joint innovation procurement, possible procedures under the Directive are, competitive dialogue procedure and competitive procedure with negotiations, which is similar to the previous negotiated procedure with prior notice.

Recital 42 points out that use of the competitive dialogue has significantly increased in terms of contract values over the past years and the procedure is particularly fitted for innovative projects

Potential challenges with competitive dialogue can be seen in an example of a contracting authority seeking to appoint an entity to develop new innovative beds and then deliver them to a hospital (Telles, 2012, p. 231).

The first challenge would be to appropriately classify such a mixed contract for the purpose of procurement law.[17] The question is what will the main purpose of this contract be? For both pre-commercial and commercial stages to be able to be procured in one procedure the delivery of the beds would need to be established as the main purpose of the contract. Furthermore, the delivery of beds could be tendered through the open or restricted procedures. In such an approach the innovation would need to be treated as an 'incidental' element of the contract, according to the concept of mixed contracts (Telles, 2012, p. 231). The problem is that the aim of the described project will not be achieved, if there is no innovation, as it is not just any delivery of beds that the contracting authority is interested in, but it is a delivery of 'the specific beds' (emphasis added) which will be innovative. Therefore, the innovation will need to be developed first and a scope for a dialogue between parties will be required.

Besides the qualification, the contract will also pose challenges from a procedural perspective. In the case of the competitive dialogue procedure it seems that the contract would meet the complexity requirements laid down in Article 26(4) of the Directive. On the one hand, the technical complexity of the project would be satisfied, as the contracting authority's needs are not able to be satisfied by any existing solution; therefore, the contract focuses on developing innovation. On the other hand, the contract will most probably include a complex financial structure which would need to be established and negotiated as it would not be possible to establish the price of the delivery of one bed at the start of the procurement process, since the price will depend on the level of the innovation's success. Also, if the innovation is not delivered, the contracting authority could not be obliged to pay for a delivery of beds of any kind. Also, the legal complexity of the contract would be guaranteed as among others issues of the IP rights would need to be settled and addressed.

When applying the competitive dialogue procedure to the mentioned contract, the problem would be that the element of the contract defined as its main purpose (delivery of beds) would be very briefly elaborated on in the dialogue stage of the procedure, when the main focus would be on the innovation part of the project. Furthermore, in art 30(3) of the Directive states that the contracting authority should open:

> [...] a dialogue the aim of which shall be to identify and define the means best suited to satisfying their needs.

In fact, such a solution would not be achieved in the award procedure, as the innovation would not be developed in the dialogue stage but after award (in the implementation phase). The legal and financial makeup of the process could be developed, but not the innovation in itself.

From the provisions it appears that such a dialogue should be continued until the solution is identified.[18] However, in reality no bidder will be willing to participate in a process which takes extensive time and resources without any guarantee of winning or at least being remunerated for participation.

The new innovation partnership procedure attempts to resolve some of the existing challenges.

5 Innovation partnership[19]

The innovation partnership must aim at the development of an innovative product, service or works and the subsequent purchase of the resulting supplies, services or works.[20] On the one hand, the innovation partnership combines both a pre-commercial and a commercial stage of procurement, as its subject matter is both: an innovation development (pre-commercial stage) and a subsequent purchase of the innovation (commercial stage). The latter is under the condition that the innovation corresponds to the performance levels and maximum costs agreed between the contracting authorities and the bidders.[21] Thus, it could be argued that the major challenge of the above mentioned innovation procurement methods such as risk of the conflict of interest or unequal treatment is overcome. On the other hand, the establishment of the innovation partnership may be seen not only as an answer to existing challenges, but also as a new way of realising the objective of a smart, sustainable and inclusive growth that characterises the Europe 2020 strategy. (EC SSIG, 2010; Melo *et al.*, 2012, p. 106).

According to Recital 49 of the Directive, the innovation partnership may be applied if the authority has a need to procure an innovative product, service or work that does not exist on the market and consequently requires research and a long-term partnership for its development. Unfortunately, the wording of Article 31 regarding the innovation partnership is vague and uncertain posing some challanges. Among others there is a challenge in assessing which projects may be considered sufficiently innovative. Art. 2(22) of the Directive states that the project must result in a 'new or significantly improved' product, service, method etc.[22] – rather vague wording. Nevertheless addition of the legal definition of innovation to the Directive is an improvement on the proposal as to some degree it limits possibilities of abuse of the innovation partnership procedure. In particular, the rules prevent the use of the innovation partnership when innovation is purely incidental. Nevertheless, the risk of the innovation partnership abuse is quite small in practice, because of the detail of regulation of the stages after the conclusion of the procurement agreement and the fact that applicable rules are quite costly, time-consuming and extensive.[23]

5.1 Procedure

There are differences between the original proposal for the Directive[24] and the Directive in itself, particularly in regard to guidance on how the innovation partnership shall be awarded. The proposal for the Directive was limited to stating that: any bidder may submit a request to participate in response to a contract notice with a view to establishing the innovation partnership, to be awarded in accordance with the rules for a competitive procedure with negotiations.[25] In accordance with the latter, only invited bidders could submit offers, and the award of the innovation partnership contract was to be based solely on the most economically advantageous tender.

The Directive elaborates more on the procedure, and includes more details regarding exactly how such a process should be concluded. In the procurement documents, the contracting authority shall identify the need for an innovative product, service or works that cannot be met by purchasing products, services or works already available on the market. It shall indicate which elements of this description define the minimum requirements to be met by all tenders. These minimum requirements are those conditions and characteristics (particularly physical, functional and legal) that any tender should meet or possess in order to allow the contracting authority to award the contract in accordance with the chosen award criteria.[26] The information provided in the procurement documents shall be sufficiently precise to enable bidders to identify the nature and scope of the required solution and decide whether to request to participate in the procedure. It needs to be acknowledged that, unless the needs of the contracting authority are defined broadly enough, there could be a risk of material change to the terms of the contract once entered into, giving rise to a risk of a procurement challenge.[27] Therefore, the first challenge for the contracting authority is to define its needs broadly enough for the procurement process not to be challenged but precisely enough for the potential bidder to make an informed decision on particpation.

Another new addition to the adopted form of the Directive is that the contracting authority may decide to set up the innovation partnership with one partner or with several partners conducting separate research and development activities.[28] Also, in the original proposal, Member States were given the choice of whether to implement the innovation partnership procedure in national law, whereas now it is mandatory. In addition, the wording of the award criteria is changed from 'most economically advantageous tender' to 'the best price–quality ratio'[29] (the terminology used in the 2014 directive for awards that include non-price elements).

The innovation partnership procedure has two stages: the selection of participants and the bidding phase. In selecting bidders, contracting authorities shall pay particular attention to criteria concerning the bidders' capacity in the field of research and development, and developing innovative solutions.[30] Requirements of the selection criteria may potentially pose some challenges, as they need to be read in conjunction with Article 58(c) (4) of the Directive regarding technical and professional ability. As the objective of an innovation partnership is an innovation, it is difficult to prove definitively that the bidder poses 'necessary human and technical recourses and experience.'[31] This can only be proved on the basis of similar projects, and if the innovation is ground-breaking, there is a chance that similar projects were not undertaken in the past. To deal with this issue, the experience of the bidder in different innovation processes should be taken into consideration.

It seems appropriate to state that to a large extent, an innovation partnership will need to be established on the basis of very general criteria. At the same time, it is important to add that besides innovative research and development experience, the bidder should also possess the ability to produce and deliver the developed goods/services/works.

5.2 'Cherry-picking' in the innovation partnership

The introduction of changes to the technical specification and other procurement documentations after a round of negotiation, during the bidding stage of an innovation partnership, signals a possibility of 'cherry-picking' (a possibility first referred to by the Commission in proposing Directive 2004/18/EC introducing the competitive dialogue procedure) (EC Proposal, 2000). 'Cherry-picking' is a practice of selecting all or some of the aspects of various candidades' solutions and including them as the basis for the final tender of other candidates (Arrowsmith and Treumer, 2012. p. 64).

From the contracting authority's perspective, 'cherry-picking' from the proposed solutions could be the most beneficial in developing an innovation. Therefore, the limited confidentiality of the dialogue stage of the competitive dialogue procedure was proposed, by allowing the contracting authority to define its technical specifications for the tender phase, either by including one of the solutions presented by one of the bidders in it, or by combining the presented solutions and asking all the bidders to submit their final tenders on this basis. (Arrowsmith and Treumer, 2012, p. 64). This proposal was met with strong objections from the private market as this threatned protection of confidential information as well as the bidder's competitive advantage in proposing an innovative solution (Rubach-Larsen, 2005, p. 76). Thus Directive 2004/18/EC limited 'cherry-picking' by requiring agreement from participating in tender bidders for such a practice.[32] Nevertheless, since the introduction of the competitive dialogue in 2004 it was identified that in practice this procedure was concluded in different ways, which could be grouped in four models. Authors identified that in some of these models 'cherry-picking' occurs, where the participants share their solutions and try to influence as much as possible on what will be included in the technical specification (Arrowsmith and Treumer, 2012; Telles, 2010; Racca and Casalini, 2010). That is due to the fact that in such a way these bidders will have a larger chance of winning the tender.

How is this issue treated in the new Directive and particularly in the context of innovation partnerships? Article 31 states that during negotiation, the contracting authority may discuss all aspects (with the exception of the minimum requirements) of the innovation partnership contract with the bidders. However, throughout this discussion, the contracting authority is obliged to treat all participants equally and in particular may not provide information in a discriminatory manner.[33] For example, the contracting authority is not allowed to provide information to one bidder and not others, and it is prohibited from informing selected bidders about certain tender requirements ahead of time. As well as this, the contracting authority cannot reveal to the other participants confidential information communicated by a bidder participating in the negotiations without its agreement. Such an agreement shall not take the form of a general waiver, but shall be given with reference to the intended communication of specific information.[34] At first glance it seems that the situation regarding 'cherry-picking' in the innovation partnership looks very similar to before – prohibited unless given approval by the bidder.

However, in the previous Directive 2004/18/EC besides the confidential information it was prohibited to share the proposed solution with others. This rule needed to be read in conjunction with the old Article 29(6) of the Directive 2004/18/EC, which implied that the contracting authority must ask bidders to submit their final tenders on the basis of the solution or solutions that were developed during the dialogue stage (Treumer, 2004).

In the current provisions on the innovation partnership it states that in the case of an innovation partnership with several partners, the contracting authority shall not, in accordance with Article 21, reveal to the other partners solutions proposed or other confidential information communicated by a partner in the 'framework of the partnership' without that partner's agreement. This part of the provision is placed in the second part of Article 31 which regulates the structure of the innovation partnership not the bidding process per se. The question may be posed should that provision be read in the context of the bidding stage or the implementation stage of the innovation partnership. If the latter interpretation is correct, potentially some scope for 'cherry-picking' without agreement of the relevant bidders would be allowed during the bidding stage. This argument is supported by the fact that it is allowed for the contracting authority to change the technical specification as well as other procurement documents after a round of negotiations. In addition, the contracting authority is required to give an adequate amount of time to bidders to allow them to be able to modify and re-submit amended tenders. Also, the provision in Article 31(4) of the Directive prohibits sharing confidential information, but not the solutions proposed in the tender. There is no reference similar to the those in the competitive dialogue procedure[35] requiring bidders to submit their final tenders on the basis of the solutions presented in the dialogue. Therefore, it could be argued that bidders are allowed to submit their final tenders on the basis of the solution identified and developed during the round of negotiations.

Contrary to the above view, it could be argued that the bidder in such a case would try to classify all aspects of his solution as confidential information, sharing of which he does not agree to. Therefore, it could be argued that it is only permitted to use parts of solutions which are not classified as confidential information, or which the bidders agree to share, and on which basis the technical specifications or other procurement documents are changed.

A different interpretation would be that all paragraphs need to be read in conjunction with each other and the prohibition on sharing solutions without agreement of the relevant bidders, which cannot be provided in the form of a general waiver is applicable to the whole process, including bidding (Arrowsmith, 2014, p. 9.138). The way the wording in the Directive was tighten from 2004 to 2014 indicates that this is most probably the case. This may be supported by the fact that both paragraphs four and six of Article 31 refer to the requirement of the confidentiality established in Article 21. Additionaly it is worth noting that contracting authorities will face a difficult task of redesigning the procurement documents and being able to include changes, as they will need to ensure that the confidentiality of specific information is granted and respected.

One way for the contracting authority to share solutions or information could be to include the promise of reimbursement for sharing of the bidders' knowledge in the tender process. This option is clarified in the competitive dialogue procedure[36] where it is possible to specify prices and payments in return for the participants' consent (Arrowsmith and Treumer, 2012; Arrowsmith, 2014, p. 9.124). Also, in the innovation partnership procurement documents the contracting authority must define the arrangements applicable to IP rights where it could be argued the reinbursment could be included.[37] The price should reflect the time invested in the procedure and the fact that a bidder is willing to share his 'know-how' (and all its future consequences) in the competition for a specific contract (Treumer, 2004, p. 182).

Until recently debatable was if alternatively, the contracting authority could simply set a requirement of information sharing in the contract notice (EC CD, 2006, p. 7). The new Directive states expressly in Article 31(4), a prohibition on revealing to the other participants confidential information communicated by a candidate or tenderer without its agreement, which cannot be provided in the form of a general waver – this seems to imply that a waiver cannot be either general, nor automatic, since agreement must be given for each item of information (Arrowsmith, 2014, p. 9.138). Consequently it seems that under the Directive an establishment of a general entry condition of information sharing is most probably not permitted. It is worth considering what alternatives (if any) would be possible under new regime. Would it be possible to set as an entry requirement sharing of a specific information that way to escape the prohibition of general character of a waiver? If so what legal qualification would have such a requirement.

Authors argued that entry condition of sharing information is to be classified as a selection criterion and therefore is not permitted as this type of selection criterion is not contemplated in the Directive (Rubach-Larsen, 2005, p. 76; Sołtysińska, 2004, p. 182). According to Rubach-Larsen, if the acceptance of any type of 'cherry-picking' assumes a different legal character than that of a condition for participation in the tender, it would be difficult to argue its validity and consequently that the contracting authority would have any means to enforce such a condition (Rubach-Larsen, 2005, p. 77).

However, it could be argued that the requirement of specific information sharing is not a selection criterion, but simply a procedural rule for participation akin to rules on, for example, the required formats of bids. (Arrowsmith and Treumer, 2012, p. 66). This line of argumentation may be supported by the ruling in the *Beentjes* case,[38] which strongly suggests that a tender which is non-compliant with the stated requirements may be rejected (Trepte, 2007, p. 301). However, if such an approach is allowed under new tightened regime is unclear. What is more then certain is that requiring information sharing of any kind general or specific might deter bidders from participating (Arrowsmith and Treumer, 2012, pp. 181–182).

5.3 Structure of the innovation partnership

The innovation partnership is a new type of procurement in that it deals not only with the award procedure but also the structure of the innovation partnership and the position after conclusion of the contract.

The innovation partnership must be structured in consecutive stages, following the research process and possibly but not necessarily up to the manufacturing of the supply or the provision of the work or services, involving intermediate targets to be achieved by the partner and providing for payments in appropriate parts.[39] Based on those targets, the contracting authority may after each phase decide to terminate the innovation partnership or, in the case of an innovation partnership with several partners, to reduce the number of partners by terminating individual contracts, provided that the contracting authority has indicated in the procurement documents those possibilities and the conditions for their use in the procurement documents. However, in the Directive there is a lack of definition or guidance on how certain used terms should be understood. First, there is a lack of explanation of what a 'research process' is. As Apostol correctly points out, it is unclear, whether the consecutive stages of the innovation partnerships correspond to the stages of pre-commercial procurement, i.e. solution exploration, prototyping and field testing (Apostol, 2012, p. 219). It seems as if this matter is left open.

The structure of the innovation partnership requires the contracting authority to (a) define the arrangements applicable to intellectual property rights; and (b) have the right to terminate the innovation partnership after each of the agreed stages, provided that the possibility and conditions for such termination have been specified in the procurement documents.[40] In regards to the IP rights it is not specified by the Directive who should own the resulting IP rights.[41] If the supplier should own the IP rights it could be argued that he would be paid twice – first, for development of innovation and second, by keeping the IP rights in the end. Herefore such a situation may triggers state aid issues. However, there are high stakes when considering the option of contracting authority ownership of the IP rights (allowing the authority to appoint another partner to supply the outcome of the innovation), as the authority may not be an expert in development, and may risk being liable for issues about which it knows little. Another option in practice is for the contracting authority and the supplier to have a share ownership of the IP rights that way they could share all the risks and benefits.

Lastly, in regards to the structure of the innovation partnership the Directive requires that the partnership agreement should include information on how long the contract will last, the scope of the financial remuneration for the private partner and a description of how the progress should be documented.[42] It can be noted that already some authors (Apostol, 2012, p. 220; Steinicke, 2012, p. 271) had identified that the wording of the provision in the original proposal for the new Directive was poorly drafted, especially in regard to price and subsequent purchase of the developed goods/works/services. It seems that the adobted version of the Directive did not resolve these issues.

In the Article 31(7) it states:

> The estimated value of supplies, services or works shall not be dispropor-
> tionate in relation to the investment required for their development.

It is not clear why the costs of development should necessarily affect the price of
the purchasing contract. These seem to be incorporated into an earlier stage of
the innovation partnership. Indeed, Art. 31(2) of the Directive states:

> The innovation partnership shall set intermediate targets to be attained by
> the partners and provide for payment of the remuneration in appropriate
> instalments.

If to argue otherwise one would need to acknowledge that bidders may be
unwilling to take part in the innovation partnership, if there is a risk of being
excluded from later stages without being proportionally remunerated for the
incurred costs (Steinicke, 2012, p. 271). However, Arrowsmith argues that the
contracting authority poses a discretion in deciding what and when should be
paid (Arrowsmith, 2014, pp. 9.140–9.141). She suggests to interpret that the
directive does not necessary requires for all the development work to be renumerated directly at full market rates, but that it gives the contracting authority
flexibility to renumerate the supplier for the development through later purchases, if the contracting authority will find it most beneficial (Arrowsmith,
2014, pp. 9.140–9.141). It seems that as long as principles of transparency and
equal treatment are respected it should not matter if the private partner would be
renumerated at the stage of the development or during the purchasing stage.
What is crucial is to not underestimate the costs of the development for big
innovation projects. These may be a lot bigger then the actual supply order from
one single supplier.

The practical challenge for the contracting authority will be to ensure that it
uses the innovation partnership with respect to the competition rules. That is to
ensure that the contracting authority is purchasing commercial quantities of
innovation, which value is not disproportionate to the acquired investment for its
development. Rather then crossing the border in which the contracting authority
keeps purchasing innovation that is at that point already commercialised and
consequently the contracting authority stops acting as a 'first customer' and stops
being motivated to introduce to the market new innovative solutions (Apostol,
2012, p. 220). Such a practise would be a violation of the law as contracting
authorities must not use the innovation partnerships in such a way as to prevent,
restrict or distort competition.[43]

Another challenge in the innovation partnership may arise, when the research
is truly novel and innovative and, during the course of the research the parties
working in a partnership will potentially discover that the successful bidder is
lacking certain expertise to more fully develop or deliver the service that he has
promised. In such a issues may arise concerning the change in the identity of the

winning bidder. Procurement law permits change in consortium members or changes in key sub-contractors but only within strict parameters (Treumer, 2014).[44] To escape this risk it could be argued that it would be beneficial to conclude the innovation partnership with several partners, so that another partner could step in and take over the development of the innovation in this scenario, However, the principle of confidentiality may preclude the contracting authority from providing the 'stepping-in' partner with the information that he needs. Further, it is not in any case clear that procurement law allows this kind of 'stepping-in' when due to a lack of certain expertise of the primary chosen bidder. It could be argued that the scope of the service provision awarded to this partner is extended without opening competition, given that this partner was chosen to deliver a 'different' part of the innovation development. Thus it may be necessary to conduct a new procurement procedure.

6 What is new?[45]

Looking at the innovation partnership provisions it may be noticed that for a first time procurement directive regulates post-procurement, contractual issues relating to a structure of a partnership. However, in regards to procurement procedural rules these are similar to negotiated procedure with prior notice from Directive 2004/18/EC and competitive procedure with negotiations in the Directive. Therefore, the question is if there was a necessity to establish a whole new procedure?

To answer this question it is worth to consider how the procurement of innovation partnership would look like under the previous regime of Directive 2004/18/EC. The procurement rules would often find its applicability. First, in a scenario of exclusive development of innovation where procurement rules need to be respected. Second, if the development would be non-exclusive the classification of the innovation partnership contract would be based on rules applicable to mixed contracts (contract including elements covered and not covered by the Directive 2004/18/EC). Consequently, for the award of the contract applied would need to be one of the available procedures. It seems that available here would be as previously mentioned competitive dialogue – due to contract complexity – and negotiated procedure with prior notice – in case of services, on the overall pricing grounds or the ground that no specification can be set.

As it was pointed out in previous sections appropriateness of the competitive dialogue procedure is doubtful or at least its usage would post some challenges. However, it seems that if available, negotiated procedure with a prior notice would allow enough flexibility and discretion for the contracting authority to establish a successful innovation partnership and facilitate innovation. Therefore, it can be argued that everything that can be done under innovation partnership could be done using the negotiated procedure with a prior notice under the Directive 2004/18/EC. With one issue, the negotiated procedure with prior notice was an exceptional procedure which should be applied only in specific and limited circumstances. It seems crucial to underline that the limitations on usage of the negotiated procedure with prior notice were connected with the fact that it is one of the less transparent procedures. In consequence only a limited amount of innovation partnerships could be procured using it. In this regards establishment of the innovation partnership is helpful, as it includes explicit rules to enhance equal treatment and transparency (provisions regarding structure of the partnership) and consequently it allows procurement of majority of innovative projects under this procedure. Of course it is debatable if it was necessary to introduce a whole new procedure rather than extend availability of negotiated procedure with prior notice and in the form of a guideline introduce included in the innovation partnership measures that could be taken to assist in a securance of the procurement law principles under Directive 2004/08/EC.

7 Conclusion

The introduction of the innovation partnership is an interesting addition to the Directive, as it is the first procedure to regulate both the procurement process and the contractual structure of the agreement.

A substantial downside of the innovation partnership is that it is not suitable for bodies seeking new services in a short timeframe, as the process has many stages and will require investment of time and money. Also the wording of the innovation partnership provision is defective in places, introducing uncertainty and confusion. Finally, it is complex, as the contracting authority carries an extensive 'burden of contractual awareness' (Steinicke, 2012, p. 272). The authority needs to establish intermediate targets and regulate IP rights, and this may be a difficult task especially for small contracting authorities with limited capacity or experience. These extensive contractual requirements and the potential availability of a limited version of 'cherry-picking' may be an obstacle hindering the development of the innovation partnerships. Perhaps a better approach would be to leave the structure of the innovation partnership open, to be decided by the parties, and rather than having three similar procedures (competitive dialogue, innovation partnership and competitive procedure with negotiations) focus on establishing one flexible procedure allowing among others procurement of innovation projects. Such an approach would add more flexibility to the development of innovation, and at the same time safeguard procurement principles. Further guidance from the Commission would be welcomed to ensure an appropriate application, understanding and development of the innovation partnerships.

Notes

1 Joined Cases C-145/08 and C-149/08 *Club Hotel Loutraki* (2010) ECR I-4165; Case C-215/09 *Oulun kaupunki* (2010).
2 Rectical 48 and Article 45 of the Directive.
3 Article 78 of the Directive.
4 Article 42 of the Directive.
5 See: Articles 29 and 30 of the Directive.

6 Article 31 of the Directive.
7 More on 'cherry picking' see section 5.1.1. of this chapter.
8 Recital 2 of the Directive.
9 Also, the same in the context of Article 31 of the Directive.
10 The Wilkinson Report, Report of the Independent Expert Group lead by DTI – conducted for DG RTD, 'Public Procurement for research and innovation: Developing procurement practices favourable to research and innovation' September 2005 p. 5.
11 The desirability to use a tender procedure for a pre-commercial stage of the innovation development is more based on state aid considerations than on procurement law. More on the issue see: L. Bos, and S. Corvers (2006).
12 Article 24 of the Directive.
13 Joined Cases C-21/03 and C-34/03 *Fabricom SA* v. *Belgian State* (2005) ECR I-1559.
14 Joined Cases C-21/03 and C-34/03 *Fabricom SA* v. *Belgian State* (2005) ECR I-1559 at 33–35.
15 See: Article 24 of the Directive.
16 See: S. Arrowsmith and S. Treumer, *Competitive dialogue in EU procurement* (Cambridge University Press 2012).
17 Article 3 of the Directive.
18 Article 30(5) of the Directive.
19 See further: Arrowsmith (2014), Gomes (2012), Burgi (2012), Steinicke (2012), Dimitri (2013).
20 Article 31 of the Directive.
21 Article 31(2) of the Directive.
22 Article 2(22) of the Directive.
23 See more on the potential risk that the innovation partnership may bring to the competition in Graells (2012).
24 Proposal for a Directive of the European Parliament and of the Council on public procurement, COM (2011) 896 final (further: the proposal).
25 Article 29 of the proposal.
26 Recital 45 of the Directive.
27 Article 72 of the Directive.
28 Article 31(1) of the Directive.
29 Article 31(1) of the Directive.
30 Article 30(6) of the Directive.
31 Article 58(c)(4) of the Directive.
32 Article29 (3) of the Directive 2004/18/EC.
33 Article 31(4) of the Directive.
34 Article 31(4) of the Directive.
35 Article 30(6) of the Directive.
36 Article 30 (8) of the Directive.
37 Articles 31 of the Directive.
38 Case C-31/87 *Gebroeders Beentjes BV* (1988) ECR 4635.
39 Article 31 (2) of the Directive.
40 Article 31(2) and (6) of the Directive.
41 More on the issues of IP rights see: Arrowsmith (2014) p. 9.143; Gomes (2014) pp. 211–218; Graells (2011) pp. 362–364; Telles (2012).
42 Article 31(7) of the Directive.
43 Rectical 49 of the Directive.
44 See: Article 72 of the Directive; and Treumer (2014).
45 See: Arrowsmith (2014) pp. 9.126–9.129.

References

Apostol, R. (2012): 'Pre-commercial procurement in support of innovation: regulatory effectiveness?' *P.P.L.R.* 2012 6 pp. 213–216.

Arrowsmith, S. (2014): *The Law of Public and Utilities Procurement* (Sweet and Maxwell, 3rd edn, 2014).

Arrowsmith, S. Treumer, S. (2012): *Competitive dialogue in EU procurement* (Cambridge University Press 2012).

Bos, L., and Corvers, S. (2006): 'Pre-commercial Public Procurement – A missing link in the European Innovation Cycle Public Needs as a driver for innovation' *Tijdschrift Aanbestedingsrecht* 2006 5, 198–218.

Burgi, M. (2012): 'Can secondary considerations in procurement contracts be a tool for increasing innovative solutions?', in Grith Skovgaard Ølykke, Carina Risvig Hansen and Christina D. Tvarnø: *EU-Public Procurement – Modernisation Growth and Innovation Discussions on the 2011 proposals for Procurement Directives* (Djøf Publishing 2012).

Dimitri, N. (2013): 'Some law and economics considerations on the EU pre-commercial procurement of innovation', Ch. 4 in G. Piga and S. Treumer (eds), *The Applied Law and Economics of Public Procurement* (Routledge, 2013).

EC CD (2006): Commissions' explanatory note on competitive dialogue in the classic sector, January 2006, p. 7. http://ec.europa.eu/internal_market/publicprocurement/docs/explan-notes/classic-dir-dialogue_en.pdf.

EC SSIG (2010): Commission's Communication Europe 2020 on a strategy for smart, sustainable and inclusive growth, Brussels COM (2010) 2020 final.

EC PCP (2007): Commission's Communication on Pre-commercial procurement: Driving innovation to ensure sustainable high quality public services in Europe, Brussels COM (2007) 799 final.

EC Proposal (2000): Commission's Proposal for a Directive of the European parliament and of the council on the coordination of procedures for the award of public supply contracts, public service contracts and public works contracts, COM (2000) 275 final.

EURAB (2004): EURAB Report: 'US defence R&D spending: an analysis of the impact', PREST, 2004.

Gomes, C. (2014): 'The innovative Innovation Partnerships under the new EU directive for the public sector', *P.P.L.R.* 2014 4, pp. 211–218.

Graells, A. (2012):, 'Public procurement and state aid: reopening the debate?' *P.P.L.R* 2012 6.

Mazzucato, M. (2013), *The Entrepreneurial State: Debunking Public vs Private Sector Myths* Anthem Press, 266 pages.

Melo, P., de Campos, D. D. and Machado, C. (2012). New Public Procurement Directives and the PPC: Practical Implications of EU Law on the Portuguese Public Procurement Code, *The. Eur. Procurement & Pub. Private Partnership L. Rev.*, 105.

Racca, G. M., and Casalini, D. (2010) 'Implementation and application of competitive dialogue: experience in Italy', paper presented at the Global Revolution V conference in Copenhagen 2010.

Rubach-Larsen, A. (2005): 'Competitive Dialogue' in R. Nelsen and S. Treumer, *The New EU Public Procurement Directives* (DJØF Publishing 2005).

Sołtysińska, A. (2004): Europejskie Prawo Zamówień Publicznych. Komantarz (Warszawa, Lex Wolters Kluwer, 2nd edn, 2012) p. 202; S. Treumer, 'Competitive dialogue' *P.P.L.R.* 2004 4.

Steinicke, M. (2012): 'The Public Procurement Rules and Innovation' in Grith Skovgaard Ølykke, Carina Risvig Hansen and Christina D. Tvarnø: *EU-Public Procurement – Modernisation Growth and Innovation Discussions on the 2011 proposals for Procurement Directives* (Djøf Publishing 2012).

Telles, P. (2010): Competitive Dialogue's in Portugal and Spain, PhD thesis 2010 Nottingham University, pp. 260–264.

Telles, P. (2012): 'Competitive Dialogue: Should Rules be Fine-tuned to Facilitate Innovation?' in Grith Skovgaard Ølykke, Carina Risvig Hansen and Christina D. Tvarnø: *EU-Public Procurement – Modernisation Growth and Innovation Discussions on the 2011 proposals for Procurement Directives* (Djøf Publishing 2012).

Treumer, S. (2004): 'Competitive dialogue' *P.P.L.R.* 2004 4 pp. 181–182.

Treumer, S. (2014), 'Contract Changes and the Duty to Retender Under the New EU Public Procurement Directive' *P.P.L.R.* 2014 3 pp. 148–155.

Trepte, P. (2007): *Public Procurement in the EC A Practitioner's Guide*, (Oxford 2nd edn, 2007) p. 301.

Part IV
Green public procurement

10 Colloquium

Carine Staropoli
Marc Steiner

1 Carine Staropoli – Green public procurement: myths and realities – where do we stand?

The Europe 2020 strategy sees public procurement as one of the market-based instruments that should be used to achieve the objectives of smart, sustainable and inclusive growth. The idea of using the purchasing power of the public sector (public spending reach some €2 trillion each year, equivalent to 19 percent of the EU's GDP) to achieve policy goals is not a new phenomenon. In the new procurement rules adopted in 2014 (Directives 2014/23/EU, 2014/24/ EU and 2014/25/EU), public procurement is explicitly considered as a policy strategy instrument: public procurement procedures should help public buyers to implement environmental policies, as well as those governing social integration and innovation. As far as environmental, climate and energy goals are concerned, it is known as Green Public Procurement (GPP). The European Commission (2008) states that GPP is "…a process whereby public authorities seek to procure goods, services and works with a reduced environmental impact throughout their life cycle when compared to good, services and works with the same primary function that would otherwise be procured (p. 4)". Taken in a broad sense, GPP concerns all types of public spending modes which may potentially be greened such as traditional public procurement (Directive 2014/24/EU and 2014/25/EU on public procurement), concession contracts (Directive 2014/23/EU) as well as other public–private partnerships[1] In practice, it implies introducing environmental considerations in procurement procedures through either qualification criteria and award criteria addressing the bidder and/or the subject matter, and/or bid preference program. The new EU procurement rules include a horizontal clause relating inter alia to environmental requirements, provisions on the use of environmental labels and the option to take account of environmental factors in the whole production process and a life-cycle costing approach.[2] In addition to guidance and help for developing action plans, the GPP toolkit prepared by the European Commission also contains ready sets of criteria[3] which can be included in technical documentation of the tender document. What is behind the continuous strengthening of the legislation on GPP? Does it contribute to the myth of a

Green Economy, in the sense that it has no real impact, or does it help to finally translate the idea into a reality?

At this stage, where do we stand in terms of GPP as environmental policy instrument? How to judge GPP as an environmental policy instrument? Is it really efficient in terms of greenhouse gas emission reduction and energy efficiency targets? Does GPP work as a cost-effective environmental policy instrument in terms of leading to reducing greenhouse gas emissions and/or increasing energy efficiency at least cost to society? How to prevent "green washing" in GPP? What are the factors influencing the uptake of GPP practices? What is the most appropriate contractual form to promote GPP given the circumstances?

Academic papers have not been so numerous to address all these issues and GPP is a relatively new area of research for economists. This might be due to the fact that systematic data are still lacking or they only allow studies focusing on the sole obligation of means. Focusing on the degree and frequency of GPP implementation, this type of study provides a rather mitigate picture. Typically, one of the latest study published by the Center for European Policy Studies (CEPS 2012) based on a survey over 850 public authorities from 26 Member States (more than 230,000 contracts signed by public authorities in 2009–2010, for a value of approx. €117.5 billion), shows that only 26 percent of the last contracts signed in the 2009–2010 period by public authorities in the EU included all surveyed EU core GPP criteria. Among these contracts, 55 percent included at least one EU core GPP criterion, showing that some form of green procurement is being done at a large scale. The up side – if any – is that, in the period 2009–2010, the last contracts as regards the inclusion of at least one core criterion are significantly higher (55 percent) than those for the whole period 2009–2010. In addition, the greenness of contracts seems to be higher when looking at the value of contracts compared to the number of contracts: 38 percent of the total value of the contracts included green criteria. However, the gap between the good and the bad performers is high: in the four "top performing" countries (Belgium, Denmark, Netherlands and Sweden), all EU core GPP criteria were applied in 40–60 percent of the cases. Isn't it the tree that hides the forest? As a matter of fact, there are as many as 12 countries where this occurred in less than 20 percent of the last contracts. This is not surprising given the timing of adoption of GPP as environmental policy instruments in the different countries. While the Nordic countries have initiated in the late nineties, the Member States, following the EC recommendations of the Handbook "Buying Green!" (EC 2004) have progressively come up with publicly available National Action Plans (NAPs) on Sustainable Public Procurement for greening public spending. Although NAPs are not legally binding, they provide political impetus to the process of implementing and raising awareness of greener public procurement. Finally, as of May 2014, 22 countries out of 28 have adopted NAP on GPP. Thus, in terms of obligation of means, things should be improving. But to go further, it is necessary to address GPP from an obligation to produce results point of view.

From this perspective, results are not conclusive either. Some early studies have evaluated the potential benefits of GPP in different sectors and countries.

At this stage these results are hardly generalized since they are strongly context-dependent. Above all, these studies address the effectiveness of GPP through the potential gains in absolute terms.

Following the seminal papers by Marron (1997, 2003), Lundberg and Marklund (2011, 2012) are the first ones adopting a welfare point of view, comparing GPP to other environmental policy instruments given a benchmark such as an efficiency perspective. They show that public procurement is not necessarily contributing to achievement of environmental targets at least cost to society. Lundberg and Marklund (2012) highlight the fact that introducing green criteria in the award procedure (through the scoring rule) increases complexity and reduces transparency. As a consequence, the environmental gains achieved by GPP may be at the expense of a reduction of the gains achieved by the procurement auction per se, such as upholding competition. In doing so they theoretically prove that GPP is not a cost-effective environmental policy instrument unless firms are homogeneous (which is unrealistic) or public buyers are able to formulate call for tenders and scoring rule that are "technique neutral" in the sense that they function as a tax and do not regulated input and process choices of the firm. They also confirm Marron's (2003) conclusion that a per-unit tax on emissions à la Baumol and Oates (1971, 1988) leads instead to cost-effective reduction.

Another way to implement GPP is through the use of environmental performance clauses in the contracts. This is notably the case for PPPs and more particularly for the Private Finance Initiatives (PFI) contracts for which the payment is based on making the infrastructure available and is usually affected by the capabilities of the operator to meet performance targets. Merck *et al.* (2012) analyzed how cities use PPPs to achieve their green infrastructure objectives covering a wide diversity of sectors (public transport, energy, water, buildings, waste, urban development) and contractual forms. In brownfield projects, the private sector participates (as investors and operators) in work on or refurbishment of existing infrastructure facilities; greenfield projects develop new infrastructure, such as a new wastewater treatment facility, a stadium or a bicycle sharing system. While both greenfield and brownfield PPPs can have environmentally friendly characteristics, it is easier to make greenfield PPPs truly green through the inclusion of environmental criteria in the tendering procedure.

One of the most innovative green PPPs is Energy Performance Contracting (EPC).[4] The objective of EPC is not the execution of works (supply of goods or services), but the improvement of energy efficiency (i.e. reduction of energy consumption). This is an innovative approach to contract design and thus raises specific issues related to performance measures and verifiability under the context of legal and technological uncertainty. The use of a performance-oriented contract is only possible when energy efficiency is perfectly measurable, with observable and verifiable indicators. Depending on the sector and the objectives of a given project, such a measure may be difficult to establish and contest. The more difficult the control, the more likely ex post conflicts concerning efficiency targets, observed performances and responsibilities will occur. These conflicts are costly and affect the efficiency of PFI.

Indeed, PFI do not fit with all green projects as well as other contractual forms. Urban green PPPs might face challenges if their objectives result in decreased consumption. Such objectives appear incompatible with concession contracts, in which the gains of the private operator is positively linked to the level of consumption. The greening of public services through concession-type contracts is thus problematic. The frequent use of concession-type contracts for water utility contracts in France illustrates this problem: when private operators' payment is based on the amount of water consumed, conserving natural resources (i.e. reducing the quantity of distributed water) conflicts with increasing earnings. Mixed payments provide another alternative: consumers pay for water services, while citizens' taxes cover costs of other services that benefit the whole society (e.g. resource protection, leakage reduction). Thus, a continuum of PPPs is possible, with a mix of features of concessions and PFIs. Given the strength and pitfalls of PPP contracts identified in Merk *et al.* (2012), it is clear that green PPP is not an optimal solution. Its efficiency depends on the circumstances in terms of projects' complexity, public buyers' expertise and private operators' characteristics.

Green Public Procurement is not only a myth, it is now translated in the reality even if its effectiveness is not clear, the EU public buyers cannot stop in the midstream and should go forward.

2 Marc Steiner – Green public procurement from a legal perspective

2.1 Introduction

The concept of Green Public Procurement has undergone a long way to become more or less mainstream, as it is considered to be nowadays in the European Union, after the adoption of the new public procurement directives, especially the new classical directive 2014/24/EU. When asked about the ongoing negotiations on the reform of the public procurement directives a senior official of the Commission said in May 2013 that – unlike when drafting the directives 2004/17/EC and 2004/18/EC – Green Public Procurement was not that much of an issue any more, whereas the consideration of social aspects in public procurement had proved to be a very hot topic. Making "strategic use of public procurement" gives this concept another taste than "pursuing secondary policy goals", as it used to be described in the past. Interestingly enough Green Public Procurement is not – or at least not only – a topic for NGO-romantics any more, but considered to be part of the EU industrial policy. The purpose of the EU in this context is to unlock the full potential of Europe's eco-industries, thereby generating benefits for green jobs and growth. No one is astonished to read this in the General Union Environment Action Programme to 2020. But a very comparable wording is used in the Single Market Act I and in the Directive 2014/24/EU itself. The Single Market Act I aims to pursue "a balanced policy which fosters demand for environmentally sustainable, socially responsible and innovative goods, services and works". The Europe 2020 Strategy includes the promotion of "a more resource efficient, greener and more competitive economy". The first sentences of Recital 95 of the Directive 2014/24/EU read as follows:

> It is of utmost importance to fully exploit the potential of public procurement to achieve the objectives of the Europe 2020 strategy for smart, sustainable and inclusive growth. In this context, it should be recalled that public procurement is crucial to driving innovation, which is of great importance for future growth in Europe.

Interestingly enough the bidders being able to offer products and services with a better environmental impact are now for obvious reasons more and more in favour of Green Public Procurement shaping the public demand towards products and services of a higher standards (Schäfer, 2013, p. 660). It is not exaggerated to describe what has happened during the last 15 years as a paradigm change. Who would have guessed 2001 that the Commission would become almost as "green" as the European Parliament and the European Court of Justice in our context?

2.2 The concept of the best price–quality ratio as a precondition for Green Public Procurement

As it is said in the Green Paper of the Commission on the modernisation of EU public procurement policy the first objective of public procurement is to increase the efficiency of public spending, normally called "best value for money". But there is already a first important step to make in this context when thinking of what public procurement is really about. "Best value for money" is the relation or the balance between quality and price and does not mean to ask for the "lowest price only". So in Switzerland we say – unlike the wording of Art. 53 of the directive 2004/18/EC or Art. XIII (4)(b) GPA – that to ask for the "economically most advantageous offer" is the rule and the award based solely on the basis of the lowest price is the exception which only applies for largely standardised products (Art. 21 FAPP). The more complex the demand of the public authority is – for instance when dealing with services –, the more obvious it is that you won't get the best solution if the price is the only relevant aspect. These days there has been a telling post on the internet saying that the bitterness of poor quality remains long after the sweetness of low price is forgotten. In my view it is obvious that – as far as a public authority can afford it – a clear commitment to reach a quality-oriented purchasing culture is a precondition of every Green Public Procurement concept. A very similar view was adopted by the European Parliament in its resolution of 25 October 2011 on the modernisation of public procurement saying

> that, in order to develop the full potential of public procurement, the criterion of lowest price should no longer be the determining one for the award

> of contracts, and that it should, in general, be replaced by the criterion of most economically advantageous tender, in terms of economic, social and environmental benefits – taking into account the entire life-cycle costs of the relevant goods, services or works

and stressed "that this would not exclude the lowest price as a decisive criterion in the case of highly standardized goods or services".

According to the draft version of the article on award criteria (Art. 67 of the adopted Directive 2014/24/EU) proposed by the Commission there was foreseen a choice between the most economically advantageous tender and the lowest cost. The proposal was in so far inspired by Art. 53 of the directive 2004/18/EC and Art. XIII(4)(b) GPA. The text of the proposal is nevertheless very interesting because the classical wording "the lowest price" is replaced by "the lowest cost", which is more than just the price paid to the supplier. According to the proposal the lowest cost would certainly allow, but not urge public authorities to include the energy consumption costs with the possibility to outweigh them against the price of a product, which leads for instance to a preference for more energy-efficient products.

After having seen that even the approach of the Commission means compared to the current regulation a shift towards a more quality-oriented public purchasing, the question has to be answered how far the approach of the Parliament has been decisive when shaping Article 67 of the Directive 2014/24/EU. Considering that the agreed text is the result of a compromise, which is easily recognisable as such, the question how the two paragraphs should be interpreted is not an easy one. One important statement is contained in Recital 92, which reads as follows:

> When assessing the best price–quality ratio contracting authorities should determine the economic and qualitative criteria linked to the subject matter of the contract that they will use for that purpose. [...] Contracting authorities should be encouraged to choose award criteria that allow them to obtain high-quality works, supplies and services that are optimally suited to their needs.

It is interesting that the proposal of the Commission on Recital 92 didn't contain this last sentence. So the described approach probably implies policy choice far beyond the revised GPA (especially Art. X(9) revGPA) and also beyond the current classical directive. This view is supported by the provision of Article 67(2), where it is stated that member states may provide that contracting authorities may not use price only or cost only as the sole award criterion or restrict their use to certain categories of contracting authorities or certain types of contracts. At the same time the best price–quality ratio should always include a price or cost element (Recital 90 of the Directive 2014/24/EU). This example shows that already the definition of the most economically advantageous tender can be seen as a try to strike a balance between the classical internal market rationale and the strategic use of public procurement, as far as this can be done in the context of the award criteria.

2.3 Green Public Procurement as an example for striving towards consistency

Taking into account the principle of sustainable development Article 3 TEU provides, inter alia, that the Union shall "establish an internal market" striving at the same time for "a high level of protection and improvement of the quality of the environment". Art. 3 TEU has not to be interpreted in way to assume that this provision contains a discernable statement on the hierarchy of the different purposes enshrined in this article. Nevertheless there must be a method to deal with possibly conflicting Treaty goals. Very comparable to a situation where two fundamental guarantees or constitutional purposes are in conflict, according to German legal thinking a balancing of the interests in practical concordance is needed to solve the problem. Following the same logic there are legitimate reasons to restrict in a proportionate way one of the fundamental freedoms such as Article 34 TFEU concerning the free movement of goods respectively restrictions on imports. This can be assessed as especially consistent if the justification for the restriction at stake is itself equally based on EU primary law, which is definitely the case for the protection of the environment (Art. 191 ss. TFEU) and the energy policy goals "with regard for the need to preserve and improve the environment" (Art. 194(1) TFEU) inluding the promotion of "energy efficiency and energy saving and the development of new and renewable forms of energy" (Art. 194(1)(c) TFEU). In Recital 59 of the new classical directive 2014/24/EU it is stated that nothing in this directive should prevent the "[...] enforcement of measures necessary to protect [...] human and animal life, the preservation of plant life or other environmental measures, in particular with a view to sustainable development, provided that these measures are in conformity with the Treaty." Especially noteworthy in this context is Art. 11 TFEU providing a cross-sectional approach when discussing the environment. According to this provision environmental protection requirements must be integrated into the definition and implementation of the Union's policies and activities, in particular with a view to promoting sustainable development. The strategy "Europe 2020" itself can partly be seen as an implementation of Art. 11 TFEU. Unfortunately, sustainable public procurement is rarely mentioned in the literature dealing with EU primary law as a perfect example, whereas state aids are sometimes addressed to explain the effects of Art. 11 TFEU on economic administrative law. This is even more astonishing considering that the ECJ has explicitely referred to Art. 6 TEC, the predecessor of Art. 11 TFEU, when decising the famous Helsinki Bus-Case. Art. 11 TFEU provides for a method of interpreting economic administrative law. If the environmental protection requirements have to be integrated into the definition and implementation of "Community policies and activities", it must – as stated by the Court – be concluded that the rules governing award criteria in the procurement directives must be interpreted in such a way so as not to exclude the possibility for the contracting authority to consider criteria relating to the preservation of the environment when assessing the economically most advantageous tender. Nothing else is said in Recital 91 of the new classical directive explicitly referring to Article 11 TFEU, according to which the directive clarifies how the contracting authorities may contribute to the protection of the environment "[…] whilst ensuring that they can obtain the best value for money for their contracts." An approach on public procurement integrating environmental aspects without impairing the traditional public procurement rationale, as initiated by the ECJ, is at the same time an inspiring concept when discussing Art. 7 TFEU providing that the Union shall ensure consistency (French version "cohérence", German version "Kohärenz") between its policies and activities, taking all of its objectives into account. The pursuit of an at least to a certain degree coherent legal order as a thougt to use when interpreting legal provisions is not only relevant as a governance factor from a political science perspective, but is also part of European legal thinking and due to Art. 7 TFEU of a quasi-constitutional character.

3 Carine Staropoli – Response to Paper 2

In his paper, Marc Steiner proposes a legal perspective on GPP. His view is clearly in line with the first part of my own first paper which aims at addressing the main economic issues at stake with GPP in terms of implementation and efficiency conditions. While I am starting with the statement that GPP is now considered as a policy strategy instrument in the new procurement rules (Directives 2014/23/EU, 2014/24/EU, 2014/25/EU), he outlines in great detail the evolution of the European institutional context of GPP, notably the progressive "greening" of all European decision-making bodies (Commission, European Parliament as well as the European Court of Justice) and its consequences in terms of the politicization of procurement policy and the increasing consistency of European legislation. In doing so, he emphasizes the importance of institutional environment to give impetus to the GPP policy especially in the European context where opposed forces are strong and may jeopardize the capacity to adopt such policy. Indeed, as analyzed by Marc Steiner, the lack of coherent legal order may lead to inconsistency in particular as regards sustainable development. Establishing an internal market and striving at the same time for "a high level of protection and improvement of the quality of environment" as in Art. 3 of the EU Treaty is quite a challenge. There are conflicting goals in the Treaty because there is no clear hierarchy of the purposes enshrined in the different articles and even within an article as illustrated by Marc Steiner in the Article 3 TEU. This situation is not irretrievable and can be compared to a situation where two fundamental guarantees or constitutional purposes are in conflict. This supposes to make compromises as when restricting the free movement of goods (internal market rationale) in order to preserve and improve environment. Unfortunately, from a legal perspective Marc Steiner doesn't give any indication on the method that would help to deal with these conflicting Treaty goals. As an economist, one could think of a cost–benefit analysis which should lead to conclusions not far from the logic of the economically most advantageous tender. As a matter of fact, Marc Steiner highlights the fundamental role of the best price–quality ratio to "convert the try" of GPP. Price cannot be the only relevant aspect especially for complex projects (like services) and in the perspective to change the purchasing culture toward quality-oriented public purchasing, as observed by Marc Steiner. The criterion of most economically advantageous tender is now the norm event if "this would not exclude the lowest price as a decisive criterion in the case of highly standardized goods or services" European Parliament resolution of 25 October 2011). The fact that the European Parliament and the Commission are finally on the same page regarding the fact that the concept of the best price–quality ratio is a precondition for GPP confirm the change of paradigm. Notwithstanding the above, the main issues raised in my first paper remain.

What is behind the continuous strengthening of the legislation on GPP? Does it contribute to the myth of a Green Economy, in the sense that it has no real impact, or does it help to finally translate the idea into a reality? Does GPP work as a cost-effective environmental policy instrument in terms of leading to reducing greenhouse gas emissions and/or increasing energy efficiency at least cost to society? How to prevent "green washing" in GPP? What are the factors influencing the uptake of GPP practices? What is the most appropriate contractual form to promote GPP given the circumstances? To answer these issues, it is necessary to go beyond the statement that the conditions are in place for an implementation of GPP which does not mean that it leads to efficient outcomes. From this perspective, results are not conclusive. Some early studies have evaluated the potential benefits of GPP in different sectors and countries. At this stage these results are hardly generalized since they are strongly context-dependent. Above all, these studies address the effectiveness of GPP through the potential gains in absolute terms. However, Lundberg and Marklund (2012) show that public procurement is not necessarily contributing to achievement of environmental targets at least cost to society. They highlight the fact that introducing green criteria in the award procedure (through the scoring rule) increases complexity and reduces transparency. As a consequence, the environmental gains achieved by GPP may be at the expense of a reduction of the gains achieved by the procurement auction per se, such as upholding competition. In doing so they theoretically prove that GPP is not a cost-effective environmental policy instrument unless firms are homogeneous (which is unrealistic) or public buyers are able to formulate call for tenders and scoring rule that are "technique neutral" in the sense that they function as a tax and do not regulated input and process choices of the firm.

Another way to implement GPP is through the use of environmental performance clauses in the contracts. This is notably the case for PPPs and more particularly for the Private Finance Initiatives (PFI) contracts for which the payment is based on making the infrastructure available and is usually affected by the capabilities of the operator to meet performance targets. One of the most innovative green PPPs is Energy Performance Contracting (EPC) for which it is possible to assess the efficiency. Some studies highlighted that these contracts raise specific issues related to performance measures and verifiability under the context of legal and technological uncertainty. They are not relevant for all types of projects. Indeed, PFI do not fit with all green projects as well as other contractual forms. Urban green PPPs might face challenges if their objectives result in decreased consumption. Such objectives appear incompatible with concession contracts, in which the gains of the private operator are positively linked to the level of consumption. The greening of public services through concession-type contracts is thus problematic.

Thus, a continuum of PPPs is possible, with a mix of features of concessions and PFIs. Given the strength and pitfalls of PPP contracts identified in Merk *et al.* (2012), it is clear that green PPP is not an optimal solution under any circumstances. Its efficiency depends on the projects' complexity, the public buyers' expertise and the private operators' characteristics.

Marc Steiner's paper confirms that GPP is now translated in the reality thanks to the legal evolution which will guarantee its perpetuity. Even if its effectiveness is not clear, the EU public buyers cannot stop in the midstream and should go forward.

4 Marc Steiner – Response to Paper 1

4.1 Market-based instrument/consumer choice

From an economic as well as from a legal perspective it is important to discern, whether an instrument to change production methods and consumption behaviour is "market-based". A second distinction may be made on whether the instrument serves the purpose to steer private consumption or supply chain management behaviour of the industry or whether the instrument consists in defining the logics of the public consumer choice itself. Public procurement regulation is basically defining the framework of the public consumer choice. The legal argument in this context would be that the internal market rationale (EU) or international trade rationale (WTO) set on the one hand serious limits when regulating private supply chain management or private consumption (keyword: process and production method/PPM). On the other hand public authorities enjoy a broader margin when defining her own consumer choice (including PPMs) without impairing the private consumer choice (Arrowsmith and Kunzlik, 2009, p. 21). From a WTO-perspective Art. VI GPA on technical specifications can be considered as a lex specialis when comparing it to the WTO standard argumentation (and debate) on PPMs.

4.2 Greening economic administrative law

As Carine Staropoli consistently argues Green Public Procurement concerns all types of public spending modes which may potentially be greened such as traditional public procurement, concessions contracts and public private partnerships. From a legal perspective one might take this argument even a step further saying that the question arises whether economic administrative law is greening as a whole. When discussing state aids, competition law and public procurement regulation more or less comparable problems arise. Especially noteworthy in this context is the recent ECJ-decision C-573/12 (1 July 2014) on article 34 TFEU dealing with the refusal to award green certificates for electricity production installations located outside the Member State in question. According to the EJC "it does not appear that, merely by reserving a support scheme using green certificates [...] exclusively to green electricity produced in the national territory, the Kingdom of Sweden has acted in breach of the principle of proportionality". This seems to confirm the idea expressed in the first paper, that a balance can be struck preserving the internal market rationale, i.e. in the case at hand the free movement of goods between Member States, and at the same time allowing justifications for proportional "green" barriers to trade.

4.3 Data, reporting and monitoring

Carine Staropoli stresses the fact that systematic data are still lacking. This was also the finding of the expert group on statistics and monitoring of the German Alliance Sustainable Procurement (Report of FMEAE, 2012. p. 118). This is particularly delicate bearing in mind the legal obligations on statistics and monitoring in general (regardless whether there should be a focus on sustainability topics or not) imposed by the WTO Government Procurement Agreement and the new EU public procurement directives. But meanwhile the situation starts changing. The German Ministry for Economic Affairs announced plans to implement a robust electronic statistics tool in order to comply with the new EU rules. In this context the Alliance Sustainable Procurement managed to integrate in the project also the target to establish statistics on sustainable public procurement (Report of FMEAE, p. 54). A comparable project (including monitoring) can be seen in Switzerland on federal level. Specific monitoring on sustainable public procurement is foreseen (Steiner, 2013, p. 77).

When entering a store of a major Swiss retailer ("MIGROS") to buy (for instance) food using a personal card the customer gets a statistic on how many percent of his consumption is green ("Green Cumulus"). This tool is meant to raise awareness on what to buy. If something comparable can be done assessing the purchasing behaviour of public entities the different Swiss ministries on federal level will find themselves in a benchmark situation. The Swiss Federal Department of Defence for instance has chosen to set some sustainability standards when buying textiles (i.e. for instance uniforms) and recently food. This is not because this ministry is "greener" than the Federal Office for the Environment, but this is a strategy to avoid reputational risks being politically exposed anyway. So sooner or later the other ministries will be asked how their uniforms are procured. To conclude it may be said that – if implemented effectively – statistics and monitoring schemes can to a certain degree replace mandatory provisions on what to buy. The new EU public procurement directives do deliberately not contain any "what to buy" obligation; they are a regulation on "how to buy".

4.4 GPP as a cost-effective instrument?

During the nineties there was a broadly supported economic argument that secondary or horizontal policy goals (like Green Public Procurement) should be pursued outside public procurement regulation and practice and that it is at the same time more efficient to do so. Even if the same economists might still ask whether the integration of long term unemployed has to be a purpose of a public procurement regulation, there can be discerned a mindset change as far as product properties are concerned. If a public entity wants to promote the consumption of renewable energy procuring renewable energy is obviously a measure suited to achieve that goal. Purchasing a different product makes the difference! At the same time it is true that sustainable public procurement can increase complexity and reduce transparency. Therefore there is an interplay between governance standards and sustainable public procurement. The more complex the targets in terms of sustainability are, the more governance and legal compliance standards are needed in order to avoid negative effects (UNEP SPP, p. 20). On the other hand there can be defined, simple but ambitious goals. Finally from a legal and from a political science perspective public procuring entities must act as a model and benchmark if the EU wants at the same time to influence the supply chain management of private enterprises (Corporate Social Responsibility). This is a matter of policy coherence. So the efficiency is not the only argument to be taken into account when discussing the desirable procuring behavior of public entities. But there are certainly more and less efficient ways to pursue Green Public Procurement goals.

5 Carine Staropoli – Conclusions

In his second paper Marc Steiner discusses two of the issues I have raised in my paper and takes an optimistic look on problem of access to data and reporting and the more fundamental issue of the cost effectiveness of GPP as a policy instrument. He reminds that the legal obligations imposed by the WTO Government Procurement Agreement and the new EU public procurement directives should systematize the production of data and reporting through innovative mechanisms. He also considers the positive impact of such monitoring on sustainable public procurement arguing that reputational motivation may also force any public buyers to follow the best practices. Statistics and monitoring schemes can to a certain degree replace mandatory provisions on what to buy. This goes beyond what is currently in the new Public procurement directives which deal with the "how to buy". Altogether the monitoring of GPP practices should generate positive externalities. Regarding the still unknown cost-effectiveness of GPP, he also adopts an optimistic view considering that efficiency is not the only argument to be taken into account. Public bodies must be forerunner in the pursuit of green procurement so as to be imitated by private actors thereby generating positive externalities through the Corporate Social Responsibility. As he noted this doesn't prevent to be as efficient as possible. I would add that, up to now, this exemplary role of public bodies has not proven to be efficient.

6 Marc Steiner – Conclusions/interface between economics, law and political science

Economic and legal mindsets have undergone a remarkable change in recent years. Green Public Procurement is a perfect example to describe the paradigm change we are facing. Economy and law are comparable with theology when it comes to their history of dogmas. The nineties of the last century were the time of predominance of international trade, market access and internal market rationale as (the) purpose of the legal order. Other policy goals like the protection of the environment or combating climate change were perceived as extraneous to the logics of economic administrative law. The Court of Justice of the European Union was responsible for replacing this idea when arguing that the coherence of the legal order is more important than the internal market rationale (Helsinki Bus Case C-513/99). A balance must be struck between the different goals to achieve the internal market rationale and environmental protection. Meanwhile "encouraging the wider use of green public procurement" is part of the flagship initiative "Resource efficient Europe" and described as a market-based instrument being part of the "Europe 2020 Strategy" (as emissions trading, revision of energy taxation and state aid framework). The concept of Green Public Procurement has become more or less mainstream, being described as innovation and industrial policy. So it's not (or at least not only) about a more sustainable better world, but about a first mover advantage of the economy through innovation leading to better products and services gaining market shares in the future. This view is combined with the idea that the public entities should contribute to this development by abandoning the procurement culture focusing on lowest price only but fostering the quality of the products to be purchased (price–quality ratio). The new directives 2014/24/EU and 2014/25/EU are a firm commitment of the legislator and a clear message that Green Public Procurement is as widely accepted as it has never been before. This is not only interesting for lawyers and economists, but also from a political science perspective. The approach of the nineties led to a rather inconsistent system of values and included obvious contradictions. The new approach aims to avoid a total inconsistency between internal market rationale and environmental policy goals. At the same time Green Public Procurement is not so much exposed to the criticism of regulating instead of providing incentives because the public consumption behaviour is not the same as steering private consumption behaviour. The interface between law and economics is also touched when it comes to life-cycle costing. Whereas according to the directive 2004/18/EC life-cycle costing included the total costs of ownership, Art. 68 of the directive 2014/24/EU allows to include environmental (but not social) externalities, provided there monetary value can be determined and verified. As an example the cost of emissions of greenhouse gases is mentioned. From a legal perspective it doesn't matter that much whether less greenhouse gas emissions are rewarded when assessing the quality of the product or whether the emissions are considered when calculating the "real" price of the product. But from an economic and political science perspective there is again a strong signal that the concept of "best value for money" means something new.

Notes

1 PPPs are broadly defined as long-term contractual agreements between a private operator/company (or a consortium) and a public entity, under which a service is provided, generally with related investments. Unlike traditional public sector procurement, where the private contractor simply designs and/or builds what the public sector orders, PPPs involve a process in which private operators bid for a contract to design, finance and manage the risks involved in delivering public services or assets. In return, the private contractor receives fees from the public body (as in the Private Finance Initiative type of PPP) and/or user tolls for the long-term operation and maintenance of the assets (as in a concession contract).
2 The Life-Cycle Cost approach means "considering all the costs that will be incurred during the lifetime of a product, a work or a service (EC, 2011, p. 42). This may also include the societal cost of negative externalities such as greenhouse gas emission. In that case, it is referred as Whole-Life Costing (EC, 2011).
3 The GPP criteria are divided into two sets – "core" and "comprehensive". The "core" set is group of basic criteria which focus on the main environmental factors of the product or service. The "comprehensive" set consists of more ambitious criteria and takes into account other environmental factors. Those criteria sets are accessible from the European Commission website:http://ec.europa.eu/environment/gpp/toolkit_en.htm.
4 The EU Directive 2006/32/EC, which lays the legal foundation for such contracts in the EU, defines EPC as —a contractual arrangement between the beneficiary and the provider (usually an Energy Service Company – ESCO) of an energy efficiency improvement measure, where investments in that measure are paid for in relation to a contractually agreed level of energy efficiency improvement. For an analysis of the efficiency conditions of this type of contract, see Chong, E., Le Lannier, A. and Staropoli, C. (2012) "Les conditions d'efficacité des contrats de performance énergétique en France", www.wec-france.org/DocumentsPDF/RECHERCHE/62synthese.pdf.

References

Arrowsmith, S., and Kunzlik, P. (2009): Social and Environmental Policies in EC Public Procurement Law, *New Directives and New Directions*. Cambridge University Press, Cambridge.

Baumol, W. J., and Oates, W. E. (1971): The Use of Standards and Prices for Protection of the Environment. *Swedish Journal of Economics* 73(1): 42–54.

Baumol, W. J., and Oates, W. E. (1988): *The Theory of Environmental Policy*. Cambridge University Press, Cambridge.

Caranta, R., and Trybus, M. (2010): *The Law of Green and Social Procurement in Europe*. Djøf Publishing, Copenhagen, 330 pp.

CEPS (2012): "The uptake of Green Public Procurement in the EU27", Brussels, 29/02. http://ec.europa.eu/environment/gpp/pdf/CEPS-CoE-GPP%20MAIN%20REPORT. pdf.

European Public Procurement and Public Private Partnership Review EPPPL 2013/1, Special Issue: Sustainable Procurement.

European Commission (2008): "Public Procurement for a Better Environment", Communication form the Commission, COM 2008/0400 Final. http://eur-lex.europa.eu/legal-content/EN/TXT/?uri=CELEX:52008DC0400.

Lundberg, S., and Marklund, P.-O. (2011): "The Pivotal Nature of Award Method in Green Public Procurement", *Environmental Economics*, 2(3): 61–70.

Lundberg, S., and Marklund, P.-O. (2012): "Green Public Procurement as an Environmental Policy Instrument: Cost Effectiveness", WP. Umea University.

Marron, D. B. (1997): Buying Green: Government Procurement as an Instrument of Environmental Policy. *Public Finance Review* 25(3): 285–305.

Marron, D. B. (2003): Greener Public Purchasing as an Environmental Policy Instrument, in *The Environmental Performance of Public Procurement: Issues of Policy Coherence*, OECD, 2003.

Merk, O., Saussier, S., Staropoli, C., Slack, E. and Kim, J.-H. (2012): Financing Green Urban Infrastructure, OECD Regional Development Working Papers 2012/10, OECD Publishing; http://dc.doi.org/10.1787/5k92p0c6j6r0-en.

Report of FMEAE (2012): Report of the Federal Ministry for Economic Affairs and Energy "Allianz für eine nachhaltige Beschaffung", 22 October 2012.

Report of FMEAE (2013): Report of the Federal Ministry for Economic Affairs and Energy "Allianz für eine nachhaltige Beschaffung", 14 October 2013.

Schäfer, P. (2013): Green Public Procurement im Rahmen der EU-Umwelt- und Nachhaltigkeitspolitik, in: *Festschrift Fridhelm Marx*, Munich 2013.

Steiner, M. (2013): Is there a Swiss Approach towards Sustainable Public Procurement?, EPPPL 1/2013.

UNEP SPP (2012): UNEP Sustainable Public Procurement Implementation Guidelines, Paris 2012.

11 Procurement for sustainable development

A view from multilateral development banks

Veljko Sikirica

1 Introduction

"Global Footprint Network", in preparation for "Earth Overshoot Day 2014", has recently reported that:

> In mid-August (2014), we will hit the date when humanity has exhausted nature's budget for the year. For the rest of the year, we will maintain our ecological deficit by drawing down local resource stocks and accumulating carbon dioxide in the atmosphere. We will be operating in overshoot.

Global Footprint Network, as indicated on their web page, was established just about ten years ago, as a 501c (3) nonprofit organization, to enable a sustainable future where all people have the opportunity to live satisfying lives within the means of one planet.[1]

Rightly so, MDBs have subscribed to the concept that Sustainable Development has been conceived as an objective in the goal of long-term survival of humanity (human civilization). This objective derives from the very reality that the Earth's resources, save for solar energy, are finite and that proper management of resources in the course of production and consumption activities is a sine qua non condition for the preservation of a stable ecosystem capable of supporting human life for a long period of time.

It is true that economic growth in developed countries has generated wealth that has contributed to improve the standard of living. However, economic growth was accompanied by ecosystem degradation, wealth inequalities and the threat of climate change. Measures of economic growth consequently gave only partial signals and indications of societal progress. However, the total costs of production and consumption activities were not fully taken into account in the standard measures of economic development.

The emerging consensus is that sustainable development should be the goal adopted by individuals, governments and countries in order to preserve the earth's ability to support humanity. The basic economic principle of sustainable development is to maximize returns from natural and human built resources. The concept of sustainable development has received support from individuals, local authorities and citizen groups in many countries and from national governments and international organizations.

The International Union for the Conservation of Nature in its report "World Conservation Strategy" published in 1980, was one among the first to give global exposure to the term "sustainable development". In 1987, the United Nations World Commission on Environment and Development defined sustainable development as: "development that meets the needs of the present generation without compromising the ability of future generations to meet their own needs". The United Nations Conference on the Environment and Development (Rio de Janeiro, Brasil 1992) and the World Summit on Sustainable Development (Johannesburg, South Africa, 2002) outlined actions through which sustainable development could be realized.

Sustainable development is multidimensional and implies that economic and social progress will be measured not only by expansion of the scope and scale of the market economy but also by improvements in the well-being of the population. It also addresses the issue of intergenerational transfer of assets.

Different policy instruments have been used to advance the process of sustainable development. Among them are legislation, tax incentives, technical means such as setting standards and creation of preferred list of products and environmental policies and public procurement.

Public procurement has been promoted as a key avenue to sustainable development because government procurement accounts for up to 30 per cent of GDP in both developed and emerging economies. Further, governments could exercise strong influence on private sector through its public procurement policies, procedures and practices.

Procurement for sustainable development covers the environmental, economic, social, technical and legal aspects of the procurement of works, goods or services. It could be described as endogenous to the economic system when it arises logically from national economic development policies based on sustainability. It may be said to be exogenous when the impetus for adherence to it comes from external sources and it is not embedded in explicit national policies.

The MDBs, each one on its own initiative, began the process of giving central importance to sustainable development within the Strategies for sustainable economic growth (IDB, July, 2003) and Poverty reduction and promotion of social equity. The MDBs have also emphasized the critical role of public procurement for the promotion of sustainable development.

Consequently, the MDBs engaged in the review of harmonized procurement policies, guidelines and practices to make them more suited to the pursuit of the goal of sustainable development. The main objective of the proposed changes was to give procurement a more substantive role as an instrument of the MDS's development agenda. Procurement would be transformed into an integral part of the MDB's institutional development initiatives and not function merely as a support or process activity. Procurement for sustainable development would encompass and extend beyond conventional procurement, green procurement and sustainable procurement.

Specifically, in the area of public procurement, multilateral development banks (MDBs), including the EBRD, adopted a new version of the MDB Harmonised Edition of the International Federation of Consulting Engineers (FIDIC) General Conditions of Contract for Construction in June 2010. The Conditions include expanded provisions on labour standards and health and safety and thus present an important step in promoting good labour practices in large construction projects worldwide. The EBRD's own Standard Tender Documents for the Procurement of Works and User Guide was issued in 2010. This updated version is in line with the current MDB Harmonised General Conditions, and it includs additional provisions and guidance to promote the effective implementation of the labour and health and safety standards in the EBRD's PR 2.

2 What is sustainable development?

Sustainable Development has been conceived as an objective in the goal of long-term survival of humanity (human civilization). This objective derives from the very reality that the Earth's resources, save for solar energy, are finite and that proper management of resources in the course of production and consumption activities is a sine qua non condition for the preservation of a stable ecosystem capable of supporting human life for a long period of time.

There is now a growing body of economic thought that sees the main economic challenge of the modern era is to satisfy the needs of the world population with the least cost to the natural environment. With population growth, the impact of human economic activities on the planet, the "ecological foot print", has increased significantly to the point where serious questions about the earth's capacity to serve humanity are vigorously debated with urgency as industrial economies deplete reserves of forests, groundwater, the atmosphere and other natural resources.

The new emerging consensus is that the conventional economic model built on the assumption that economic activity is independent of nature with production dependent on fossil fuels and characterized by use and dispose practices for materials, is no longer relevant. The evolving sustainable economy seeks to operate within environmental boundaries. Natural resources are no longer considered to be inexhaustible even with technological advances.

There is gradual acceptance of the view that the economy is hosted within the ecosystem from which raw materials for humanity such as food, fuel and minerals, are obtained. In addition, the ecosystem provides invaluable services such as air and water purification, mitigation of droughts and floods, soil generation and soil fertility renewal, waste detoxification and breakdown, pollination, seed dispersal, nutrient cycling and movement, pest control, bio-diversity maintenance shoreline erosion protection, protection from solar ultra-violet rays, partial climate stabilization and moderation of weather extremes. Economic activity should take into consideration and account for the contribution of environmental/ecological services and should preserve and enhance and not deplete these services.

Economic growth in developed countries has generated wealth that has contributed to improve the standard of living. However, economic growth was accompanied by ecosystem degradation, wealth inequalities and the threat of climate change. Measures of economic growth consequently gave only partial signals and indications of societal progress. However, the total costs of production and consumption activities were not fully taken into account in the standard measures of economic development. Further, the environmental impact of economic growth is no longer confined to isolated localities but is now global in scope.

In response to climate change, resource depletion, economic equalities and the disproportionate exposure of disadvantaged groups to these changes, a generally accepted view is emerging that governments and civil society should cooperate in the management of economic activities where human needs can be satisfied and a higher quality of life secured with less consumption of natural resources. The emerging consensus is that sustainable development should be the standard adopted by individuals, governments and countries in order to preserve the earth's ability to support humanity. The basic economic principle of sustainable development is to maximize returns from natural and human built resources.

The International Union for the Conservation of Nature in its report "World Conservation Strategy" published in 1980 gave global exposure to the term "sustainable development".

In 1987, the World Commission on Environment and Development, created by the United Nations General Assembly and popularly known as the "Brundtland Commission", gave the concept of sustainable development a widely quoted definition as "development that meets the needs of the present generation without compromising the ability of future generations to meet their own needs". Sustainable development implies that economic and social progress will be measured not only by expansion of the scope and scale of the market economy but also by improvements in the well-being of the population. It also addresses the issue of intergenerational transfer of assets.

Several attempts have been made to define specific goals, objectives, standards and indicators of sustainable development. Most definitions suggest that sustainable development is a long-term process with broader macro-economic objectives of: (i) genuine human progress, (ii) renewable energy (iii) social equity (iv) protection and restoration of natural capital, (v) preservation of cultural capital and (v) local community development.

The United Nations World Summit on Sustainable Development, (Johannesburg Summit, 2002) specified priority areas for action in which the principles of sustainable development should be applied. Priority areas listed were: sanitation, chemicals, agriculture, biodiversity, energy, health, ecosystem management, finance, trade, globalization, production and consumption.

The international effort to develop indicators of sustainable development receive impetus from Chapter 40 of Agenda 21, the Action Plan adopted at the United Nations Conference on Environment and Development held in Rio de

Janeiro, Brasil in 1992. The Action Plan called on countries, international institutions and non-governmental organizations to develop indicators of sustainable development that can provide a solid basis for decision-making at all levels. Agenda 21 also called for cooperation and harmonization in work to develop the indicators.

Through a collaboration of experts and public and private organizations a set of indicators was published in 1996 under the auspices of the United Nations Commission on Sustainable Development (CSD). After national tests, appraisal, research and revisions, a new core set of 50 indicators that are part of a larger set of 96 indicators was finalized in October 2007.

Core indicators and other indicators of sustainable development were organized according to themes, each with sub-themes. The themes were: poverty; governance; health; education; demographics; natural hazards; atmosphere; land; oceans, seas, coasts; freshwater; biodiversity; economic development; global economic partnership; consumption and production patterns. It is claimed that the theme/sub-theme framework is consistent with the practice of most countries in applying national sustainable indicator sets and is also directly relevant to the monitoring of national sustainable development strategies.

According to the CSD, core indicators were designed to cover issues that are relevant for sustainable development in most countries; provide information that are not available from other core indicators and can be calculated by most countries from data that are readily available or could be made available within reasonable time and costs.

The core indicators are not divided explicitly along the five baseline areas of economic, social, environmental, technical and legal matters. The emphasis is in integrating all aspects of sustainable development in order to demonstrate its multidimensional nature.

Countries have been using the indicators as a basis for building their own framework of national sustainable development indicators and capacity for monitoring their application. Other indicator frameworks available to countries during the capacity building exercise, in the last decade, have been: (i) Millenium Development Goals; (ii) Biodiversity Indicators Partnership; (iii) Hyogo Framework for Action on Disaster Reduction; (iv) The Global Forest Resource Assessment; and (v) Sustainable Tourism Indicators.

Sustainable development, for which there is some consensus on indicators, has been defined also as a socio-ecological process in which human needs are fulfilled while the quality of the environment is maintained indefinitely. Implicit in either formulation is an admission that unregulated economic activities could supply present needs while inflicting severe damage on the environment and that such an approach is not sustainable.

Some definitions of sustainable development include also a cultural diversity as a fourth element of sustainable development on the basis that cultural diversity is as necessary for the attainment of a satisfying human existence as biodiversity is for the world of nature. Sustainable development incorporates and constantly takes into explicit account linkages, impacts and feedbacks among economic and social development and the environment.

Sustainable development is broader in scope than "green development" which emphasizes environmental sustainability over economic, social and cultural factors. Green development initially focused on climate change and natural resource protection.

The emergence of the sustainable economy as a desirable goal has shifted emphasis from growth to development even when rapidly expanding population made growth the primary objective. Development was seen as incorporating a "well-being" or "sustainability element". "Well-being" is usually defined as meeting the fundamental human needs for food, shelter, security, health and opportunity to achieve individual potential.

Sustainable development is multidimensional. At different times certain aspects are isolated for special attention. For example, "education for sustainable development", "sustainable production and consumption", "sustainable tourism" and "sustainable procurement" is each occasionally considered as separate programmes outside the ambit of a national sustainable development policy. Though efforts in each area may be commendable it does obviate the real possibility of contradictory actions at the national level.

The prevailing concept of sustainable development seeks to integrate and harmonize the three main spheres of national development: social progress, economic improvement and environmental balance. The social aspect deals with human development, education, poverty elimination, reduction of inequality, security and social inclusion. The economic element covers economic growth, employment, income generation and the integration of social and environmental costs in economic appraisals of procurement decisions. The environmental dimension relates to the preservation of natural resources, ecosystems and biodiversity and the rationalization of international consumption of natural and renewable resources.

Since the negative externalities of production and consumption are hardly confined within national boundaries, sustainable development has attracted international attention.

Several international organizations have adopted and are promoting the concept of sustainable development giving it the status of an international best practice benchmark. Commitment to the idea is evidenced in the many international treaties and conventions to which many developed and developing nations alike are signatories. In addition, many countries have engaged in preparing national sustainable development strategies for which the indicators could be useful in assessments, monitoring and evaluation.

The primary benefit of sustainable development, in its broadest definition, is that it provides the best available means for the long-term survival of humanity within a relatively stable and nurturing environment. Sustainability therefore assumes the position of the fundamental principle in planning social and economic development. All public policy decisions and choice of policy instruments should be informed by the principle of sustainable development.

In practical terms, sustainable development therefore comprises economic sustainability, financial sustainability, environmental sustainability, social sustainability and political sustainability. In previous practice, the tendency was a concentration on mitigation of damage to the environment caused by large-scale projects. Today the scope is wider and it includes living conditions and health of the national and global population.

Among others, more direct benefits are, as follows: (i) Reduction of emissions and waste generation; (ii) Improved air and water quality; (iii) More efficient use of natural resources; (iv) Modernization of industry through research and innovation; (v) Improvements to labour standards, health and safety; (vi) Inclusion of disadvantaged groups in the economic system; (vii) Global environmental alleviation; (viii) Modernization and global competitiveness of local industry; and (ix) Improved efficiency of the public sector.

3 MDBs and sustainable development

MDBs' commitment to sustainable development has been expressed in various strategy documents and directives for action as well as through results of implemented projects. The objective of the sustainable economic growth strategy was to contribute in increased growth rates of per capita GDP and income under conditions that lead to improving the quality of life of the population, alleviating poverty and preserving or improving the natural resource base. The strategy was multidimensional in focus and established the bases for action in various areas of priority that would ensure that actions taken would contribute to the promotion of economic growth in a sustainable manner. A few highlights identified are, as follows:

1 Improvements of the economic and institutional arrangements (environments) in order to promote the sustainable development of productive economic activities and to increase productivity. Crucially, the strategy asserted that progress in productivity was sustainable only if it also contributed to environmental improvements and conservation.

2 The sustainable development requires a democratic modern and efficient state that promotes economic growth within a regulatory framework which is conducive to the functioning of markets.

3 The Social development strategy was put forward to reduce poverty and inequality especially inequities based on gender, ethnicity, race and disability. Actions identified consisted of: reforms in education, health and housing; development of human capital through the life cycle approach; development of social capital; promotion of development in local areas; environmental and social development.

4 MDB Environmental policy stresses the importance of environmental and social sustainability for MDBs' financed operations.

The strategies were results oriented with monitoring and evaluation system to monitor and evaluate outcomes of the MDBs' actions. The monitoring and evaluation function was supported by lessons learnt in order to improve the measurement of development effectiveness.

Based on the strategies as outlined above, it is clear that the MDBs have been moving in the direction of identifying sustainable development as a goal and point of departure for it operations in borrowing countries.

4 The procurement process in sustainable development

Procurement entails the acquisition of property, goods and/or contracting of works or services. The procurement process includes the management of the acquisition activity which may encompass specifications development, value analysis, supplier market research, tendering, negotiations, contracting and contract administration, receiving and storage.

Conventional procurement was geared to deliver the right quantity and quality at the appropriate time at the best price with the aim of maximizing net benefits for the organization, firm, entity or individual. Procurement for sustainable development broadens the traditional process to include the effects of procurement decisions on third parties. This is achieved by incorporating environmental, social and economic considerations in procurement appraisal or value analysis. Specifically, total life-cycle cost of procurement decisions should be factored into the analysis. The aim is to maximize net benefits to society.

Procurement for sustainable development implies that there is a planned, comprehensive, known and accepted national policy and appropriate strategies to realize the specific outcome of sustainable development. In this context, individual procurement decisions are made within the framework of the national policy and must positively contribute to its realization. The policy may be activated through a system of technical and procedural standards with incentives for compliance and penalties applicable for non-compliance. The perspective is one of sustainable development criteria driving procurement.

The terms "sustainable procurement" and "procurement for sustainable development" are occasionally used interchangeably. Sustainable procurement was predominantly used as a tool to promote socially responsible policies and is frequently referred to as "social procurement". However, sustainable procurement has emphasized environmental sustainability through application of resource saving technologies.

Sustainable procurement was responsible for the significant changes in labour relations with the passage of the Fair Wages Resolution in the United Kingdom and the Davis-Bacon Act in the United States of America. Sustainable procurement concerns have also encouraged the development of Corporate Social Responsibility. Two examples of sustainable procurement in effect are the World Bank's collaboration with the International Labour Organisation (ILO) for sustainable procurement for construction projects and the launch in 2006 of the Marrakech Task Force on Sustainable Procurement led by Sweden. These activities combined social progress and environmental sustainability.

Green procurement advocates that production and consumption should be conducted in a manner that reduces or eliminates the emission of harmful gases in the atmosphere in order to avoid global warming and probable disastrous ecological changes. Green procurement is now generally identified with the issue of emissions of green house gases and their contribution to climate change.

The issues of climate change and natural resource protection receive priority attention from the "green procurement" and "sustainable procurement" movements. Essentially, the focus is on immediate action to save the planet from damage caused by the inappropriate exploitation of natural resources. Developing countries may see the movements as originating in developed countries and their activities adverse to the economic development agenda of their own developing countries. Both green procurement and sustainable procurement are subsumed under the rubric of procurement for sustainable development.

Public and private procurement have direct economic, social and environmental impact. Some consumers, especially those in developed countries, are increasingly expressing preferences for production and consumption practices that preserve natural resources and protect consumers' health. Such concerns are informing purchasing decisions for food, transportation, household appliances and packaging materials. Health concerns are also influencing waste disposal. Purchasing decisions made by these consumers appear to take into account the interest of future generations.

As consumers express their preferences and demand for ecosystem friendly goods, environmentally conscious commercial enterprises have adjusted production and created new goods to meet the demand. Some businesses are also aware that reacting positively to sustainable development objectives through the creation of new goods and services could boost profitability and create and enhance corporate image. Some are motivated by the knowledge that environmental degradation limits economic opportunities.

Market place selection of goods and services conducive to sustainable development is a growing practice with potentially measureable long-term benefits to society. Even though the momentum of free market choices is increasing, it is considered by experts that reliance on market forces alone will not achieve the desired outcome. Public sector involvement would be necessary to impart greater impetus to the movement for sustainable development. Therefore, public sector authorities, through legislation and regulation, may set and enforce relevant standards for the manufacturing and commercial sectors and for the employment of certain types of services such as labour.

The share of private sector procurement is, on the average, very significant. Without a national procurement strategy and policy, it is possible that private procurement may not observe all the sustainability goals and regulations which apply to public procurement. Where such a situation is present, private procurement may operate at cross-purposes to public procurement standards and overall national development policy. Foreign direct investments may be accompanied by technology choices and labour practices which contradict national policies and hinder the attainment of progress towards sustainable development.

Private procurement process should, ideally, be integrated in the overall set of strategies developed under a national policy to attain sustainable development with specific guidelines to ensure compliance with the sustainable development objective. Alternatively, the public sector may adhere to policies and practices supportive of the objective of sustainability and depend on the demonstration effect to influence private use of technology and resources in production and consumption.

Governments have deployed many different policy instruments in efforts to achieve sustainable development. Among these are legislation, education, political and administrative reforms, administration of justice, fiscal and financial incentives, infrastructure development, healthcare expansion, urban renewal and other public works. Public procurement is one of the instruments available to implement a policy of sustainable development. It is an essential link between planning phase and actual delivery and performs a critical role in the implementation of plans and projects.

Public procurement should therefore be consistent with and supplement other policy instruments.

The administration of public sector procurement is usually identified as an indicator of government's commitment to sustainable development objectives. Public sector procurement of works, goods and services accounts for, approximately, not less than 10 per cent and up to 30 per cent of GDP in both developed and developing countries. Because of its relatively large volume and actual impact, it has attracted intense scrutiny from international, regional and national entities. Therefore, the economic power of public procurement has placed it in a position to lead initiatives that promote the cause of sustainable development.

Increasingly, national authorities and international organizations have been using public sector procurement to advance economic and social development objectives. There are, more and more, examples from EU to South Africa.

MDBs also have, in operations loan contracts with client – borrowing countries, used public sector procurement as an instrument to attain certain outcomes. Procurement policies, rules and/or guidelines have been structured and administered to ensure competition, economy, efficiency, fairness, transparency while discouraging prohibited practices (corruption, collusion...).

The apparent differences reflect different priorities and strategies and tactics, origins and funding. The objectives are generally shared. Effective promotion of sustainable development could benefit from coordination of action, and/or joined campaigns.

Procurement, as suggested above, could be a major mechanism for implementing sustainable development policies. Procurement for sustainable development probably has better chances of success when entrenched within the objective of sustainable development. Ultimate success in this regard depends on public awareness and education, acceptance commitment and organized community support. Public market demand for goods and services viewed as conducive to sustainable development could be a principal driver of the sustainability process.

However, public procurement as a single largest player on the market, which involves governments conducting business with national and international firms, could have stronger impact in promoting and increasing the level of commitment to the sustainable development process. This influence could be reinforced with regulations governing certain technical processes and specifications, and standards for emissions and effluents that could influence procurement decisions.

Many organizations and countries have imposed measures to certify that goods are produced observing high standards of: protection against the use of child labour; exposure to harmful chemicals in production; gender equity; safe working conditions and use of recycled materials.

Procurement could effectively assist sustainable development by screening technology before purchase and use. The aim is to put procedures and mechanisms in place to ascertain if economically viable technology, new or otherwise, is likely to cause harmful consequences such as large carbon emissions per unit of economic output. Procurement decisions would thus be informed by carbon footprint analysis.

Procurement procedures and decisions could foster rural community development and poverty reduction that are subsumed under sustainable development. However, the ability of the communities to utilize and spend funds allocated for development may be stymied by their lack of capacity to prepare and implement development projects, as well as the lack of procurement capacity. Project and procurement capacity building in rural area municipalities could allow for a greater flow of resources in those areas and to avoid waste of financial resources in ways that do not contribute to economic, social or environmental sustainability.

In some cases, resources management and procurement that extends product useful life may have the added effects of saving on resource use in comparison to converting new material into new product. Extension of product life may also substitute labour for energy that, under current conditions, may be expensive and is associated with undesired emissions.

A critical economic consideration of procurement for sustainable development is to ensure that resource use reflect their true costs including cost of environmental degradation which can compromise the flow of goods and services. Environmental costs are not usually recognized by markets. However, such costs are real and are usually borne by agents not directly involved in the production or consumption activity. Market prices in this situation send distorted signal about the cost of the economic activity. Procurement evaluations should adjust for the distortions to derive a more accurate cost of resource use. This approach would require the exposure of both production and consumption agents in accepting their share of responsibility, as well as the corresponding cost.

5 MDBs' procurement policies, rules and practices

The MDBs' procurement policies, rules and/or guidelines, principles and practices have, traditionally, promoted economy, efficiency, competition, integrity, accountability, fairness, geared towards obtaining the best economic value. This was largely accomplished through consistent enforcement of a set of rigorous legal, technical, financial and ethical standards for monitoring and supervision of the procurement process.

Some MDBs also recognized that procurement played a critical role not only in project implementation but also in the attainment of broader economic and social objectives. Some MDBs therefore located procurement policy within the context of Strategy for Social Development. The objective of the Social Development Strategy is to promote social inclusion and sustainable economic development. The Strategy concentrates on priority areas such as health, education, housing and empowerment of disadvantaged people.

This strategy inevitably further led to the road of exploring the opportunity for transforming the traditional procurement process to what was coined as "Sustainable Procurement". The main objective of the proposed changes was to give procurement a more substantive role as an instrument of the MDBs' development agenda. Procurement would be transformed into an integral part of MDBs' institutional development initiative and not function merely as a support or process activity.

European Bank for Reconstruction and Development (EBRD) since 2008 set as part of its agenda the objective of achieving Sustainability Outcomes through Procurement, as follows:

> The Bank recognises that, at times, the projects' ability to achieve environmental or social outcomes will be dependent on third party activities, such as contractors and suppliers. The Bank's project procurement function plays a key role in ensuring the environmental and social sustainability standards dependent on third party activities can be achieved. Therefore, the Bank has taken the opportunity to integrate the environmental and social sustainability considerations into its project procurement practice in the revised (draft) EBRD Procurement Policy and Rules. Whilst the project appraisal and legal documents will themselves set out many of the environmental and social performance requirements for the projects, it is through procurement process that these can systematically and effectively be implemented.
>
> The Bank's clients are responsible for implementing the projects, including all aspects of the procurement process, which is governed by the tender documents, be it for goods, works and services to be furnished for the project. Therefore, the Bank is committed to ensuring that environmental and social sustainability and performance requirements are incorporated into tender documents and taken into consideration when designing the procurement process for a specific assignment. The Bank is amending its Procurement Guidance Notes to include advice to its clients on good practice relating to environmentally and socially sustainable procurement. It is also revising the standard Tender Documents and Contracts for Works to include contract compliance conditions related to occupational health and safety, working conditions and ILO core labour standards as well as for managing sub-contractors. The Bank's environmental and social due diligence will identify and determine the appropriate technical and other performance specifications to be included in the Tender Documents and Contracts for Procurement of Goods (and associated services) on a specific project.

Through these improved practices, the Bank's procurement will be an effective tool to translate the Bank's sustainability mandate into practical outcomes.

Procurement is considered to be sustainable when the purchases meet the needs of the buyer while conforming to the economic, social and financial criteria that define sustainable development. In comparison to traditional procurement, sustainable procurement entails provisions that should result in enhanced environmental and natural resource preservation, the use of total life-cycle costs and equitable working conditions throughout the project life.

Sustainable procurement was also perceived as facilitating good governance and the modernization of the state. Under the new approach, sustainable procurement was to consider the impact of procurement throughout the entire life cycle of the project. It therefore implied an expanded role for MDB clients – executing agencies and countries and the concomitant creation of instruments and building capacity in the country, executing agency, as well as within the MDBs.

The approach of another MDB, the Inter-American Development Bank (IDB) was to examine in utmost detail all pertinent issues, as follows: environmental, social, legal, trans-boundary impacts, technical matters were assessed and evaluated. Part A of IDB's Report discussed support for:

the mainstreaming of the environmental considerations across sectors in country programming and strategy formulation; natural resource management; national initiatives for sustainable development and international agreements; tracking environmental sustainability indicators; assessment of environmental risks and opportunities and the promotion of corporate environmental awareness, responsibility, compliance and supervision.

Part B addressed IDB's policies, country laws and regulations, screening and classification, environmental assessment requirements, natural habitat and cultural sites, hazardous materials, pollution prevention and abatement.

The broad approach and the safeguard analysis incorporated into the new sustainable procurement process would apply to all IDB operations including physical infrastructure projects, non-investment lending and flexible lending instruments, multiphase and repeat loans, co-financing operations and in-country systems.

The comprehensive safeguard analysis was intended to reinforce the concept of the cross sectional aspects of environmental policy and the role of procurement in implementation of that policy.

IDB's sustainable procurement work would comprise three distinct but interrelated aspects: "(i) Developmental – the provision of policy advice and improvement in national procurement systems; (ii) Fiduciary; the obligation of IDB to ensure that borrowers/executing agencies observe IDB's procurement policies; (iii) Service; the rendering of technical support and advice to executing agencies".

In the Action Plan, the IDB identified a number of high priority areas for immediate action. Among them were:

i Appropriate administrative and organizational arrangements, including specific performance milestones and monitoring and reporting systems.

ii Continuation of the revamping of the Procurement Information System being carried out by PDP in conjunction with ITS which conforms to best practice in use elsewhere.

iii Further advancement of the work on electronic government procurement (e-GP) which is fundamental to increasing country capacity to administer procurement.

The outcome of the Action Plan was not expected to be a mere change of responsibilities and procedures but rather a new focus on good governance of which sustainable procurement was a critical component. Three requisites for the success of the implementation of the Action Plan were identified:

1 Clear and unequivocal messages from the Board and Senior Management that sustainable procurement was an important item on the institutional change agenda and strong support for its implementation.

2 Clearly assigned responsibility and accountability for the implementation, monitoring and progress report on the project.

3 A well-conceived communications strategy with respect to the purpose, launching and monitoring and disseminating the ongoing progress of the project, including continuous dialogue with the borrowers and the IDB's stakeholders.

Progress during the initial phase of implementation of the above Action Plan would be measured by specific deliverables and deadlines. It was proposed to measure the impact of the new approach on the quality and timeliness of procurement procedures and decisions; on the economy and efficiency of procurement; the degree of stakeholders' confidence in the system and on the creation of capacity in borrowing member countries or executing agencies. These latter measures would be pursued in the long term when performance indicators were developed and data available.

Multilateral Development Banks (MDB) are cognizant of the fact that public procurement constitutes a very large proportion of purchases of goods and services within an economy. The economic and financial power of public sector purchasing gives it the potential power to help to determine production and consumption patterns which contribute to sustainable development.

MDBs saw sustainable procurement as an effective mechanism through which agreed policies could be implemented. The procurement process also afforded an opportunity for MDBs to monitor project after loan approval. Procurement for sustainable development, in order to be effective, should establish minimum agreed standards during every phase of project planning, appraisal and implementation.

The Board of Executive Directors of the IDB approved on July 28, 2006, the document GN-2208-25 entitled "Implementing Guidelines for the Environment and Safeguard Compliance Policy". Policy Directive B.17 states:

> Where agreed with the borrower, suitable safeguard provisions for procurement of goods and services in Bank-financed projects may be incorporated into project-specific loan agreements, operating regulations and bidding documents, as appropriate, to ensure environmentally responsible procurement. The Bank will foster approaches that help provide goods and services procured under Bank-financed operations that are produced in an environmentally and socially responsible manner in terms of resource use, the work environment, and community relations. Bank procurement procedures will include a Bank-approved exclusion list of environmentally harmful products. The Bank should encourage borrowers and executing agencies to procure environmentally responsible works, goods and services, which in the Bank's opinion are consistent with the principles of economy and efficiency. Environmentally responsible procurement experience and practices will be shared with borrowing member countries and other financial institutions, to promote harmonized approaches.

The corresponding actions recommended for implementing this policy directive states:

1   This directive encourages operations to incorporate goods and services that are environmentally and socially responsible.
2   Project Teams and the borrower may agree on adopting specific environmentally responsible procurement measures, conditions or standards for a given operation, in addition to mitigation measures addressed as part of the environmental assessment process. In such cases, suitable provisions will be included in the loan document or Operating Regulations as well as bidding documents consistent with agreements reached.
3   To the extent that those procurement measures are spelled out loan documents, operating regulations and bidding documents, the Bank will ensure that those commitments are complied with during project execution within the existing regular project supervision and procurement process.

Further, the IDB's Environmental Policies as enunciated in GN2208-18 specified three main objectives:

1   to enhance long-term development benefits by integrating environmental sustainability outcomes in all Bank operations and activities strengthening environmental management capacities in its borrowing countries;
2   to ensure that all Bank operations and activities are environmentally sustainable;
3   to foster corporate environmental responsibility within the Bank.

The policy applied to both IDB and the Multilateral Investment Fund (MIF) including financial and non-financial products, public sector and private sector operations, as well as "environmental aspects of the IDB's project procurement practices and management of their own facilities".

To implement the Environmental Policy there were directives or requirements that country-level environmental studies be conducted. The analysis would involve the identification and appraisal of environmental priority issues across sectors including their links to social and economic drivers and poverty reduction objectives. Also required was a screening and classification based on the impact of the project on the environment, social issues, health and other risks factors.

Apart from screening and classification, the Environmental Policy also called for "environmental mainstreaming" where the IDB will engage with countries in addressing the environmental priorities that have the greatest impact on their social and economic development. It was also directed that the Bank would only finance operations that comply with the directives of the policy and that are also consistent with the relevant provisions of other IDB policies.

The policy directives and actions suggested clearly indicate that the IDB had formulated a commitment backed by specific action for the use of the procurement process as way to integrate sustainable procurement into sustainable development. The major task was to devise a strategy aimed at the dissemination and acceptance of the goal of sustainable development in all borrowing countries. A complementary objective was to produce a guide that would assist practitioners, e.g. project teams, executing agencies and planners in incorporating sustainable development principles, including what was referred to as sustainable procurement, into the pursuit of sustainable development.

The origins of sustainable procurement could be traced to the nineteenth century. At first, it was used mainly as a tool to effect socially responsible policies. In the late twentieth century, it became a mechanism for the promotion of environmental enhancement and sustainability, i.e green procurement. In practice sustainable procurement incorporated the traditional procurement concerns such as technical, financial, legal and administrative as well as placing greater emphasis on social, environmental and economic matters.

Simultaneous growth of interest in the green procurement and sustainable development gave further impetus to the search for social and ethical procurement. In recent years, the international community proposed standards for procurement in a number of priority areas such as sanitation, chemicals, agriculture, biodiversity, energy, health, ecosystem management, etc.

In summary, in the case of IDB, by means of its strategies and action plans, this MDB has established a new conceptual framework and redefined the scope and operational parameters for the management of the procurement function from preparation phase to execution and ex-post evaluation. Procurement activities have been placed within the context of sustainable development where social, economic, and environmental issues were given equal prominence over legal and administrative concerns.

6 Management of procurement for sustainable development

Management of the procurement for sustainable development must also take place within a context of national laws, international treaties, contracts between buyer and seller and between borrower and lender and between public and private sectors. At times the matrix of relationships is very complicated with many agents bound by legal contracts.

Nonetheless, management of procurement for sustainable development should be concentrated on its overall objectives of natural resource conservation, preservation of individual health and safety, resource productivity, human dignity and cultural ecology, including corporate culture. Procurement even when it embodies the sustainable development philosophy, is done at the operational level. It depends on the existence of a set of explicit objectives, standards and indicators for operations and evaluations.

The World Bank (WB) has a comprehensive set of policies dealing with procurement. In its July 2014 "Draft Borrowers' Procurement Procedures" which is at present under review, the WB highlights under General Considerations, the Vision, as follows: Procurement in Bank Operations supports borrowers "to achieve value for money with integrity in delivering sustainable development".

Further, WB defines Sustainable procurement, as follows:

> To deliver sustainable results, the strategic procurement approach should be on a whole life basis – which generates benefits to the procuring entity and the economy, but also to society whilst minimizing damage to the environment (reflecting the confines of the borrowers own procurement policy). Sustainability is especially relevant in such areas as construction, maintenance, and power generation, and applies to the use of scarce resources and to environmental and socioeconomic factors. As necessary, these sustainability factors are turned into procurement-related criteria to be applied at appropriate stages of the procurement cycle.

Within Chapter 2, Procurement Strategy and Planning, WB identifies Sustainable Procurement – a Non-Mandatory Requirement, as follows:

> As requested by the Borrower, the economic, environmental and social sustainability aspects of World Bank-financed activities should initially be identified during project appraisal, prioritized, and addressed as appropriate in the project design, in agreement with the borrower. Sustainable procurement is not a mandatory requirement for borrowers as it may have cost implications. Any sustainability issues that are best addressed during the procurement process are included in the procurement strategy for the procurement and may be used as specific criteria in project design, prequalification, specification/terms of reference, bid evaluation, or post-award performance indicators. Sustainable procurement criteria agreed with the

Borrower during project preparation may also be augmented with specific sustainable procurement criteria from any sustainable procurement policy the borrower may have that is in accordance with the World Bank's Procurement Policy and Core Principles.

In Chapter 3, Approach to Market and Approved Procurement Methods, the WB, under Value for Money, indicates, as follows:

> The procurement strategy must lead to an approach to market that achieves value for money, with integrity in delivering sustainable development. Borrowers will need to determine a fit for purpose approach, selecting the optimum procurement method to be included in the Procurement Plan. To that end, the borrower should take into account the most advantageous combination of cost, quality and sustainability to meet development requirements. In this context, cost means consideration of the whole-life or life-cycle cost, as appropriate; quality means meeting a specification that is fit for purpose and sufficient to meet the customer's requirements; and sustainability means economic, social and environmental benefits, considered in the procurement strategy, in support of the project objectives.

The WB dedicates Annex 4 to Sustainable Procurement – a Non-Mandatory Requirement and spells out the key points (see Annex 1).

It is evident, that further harmonization effort among the MDBs will be required which would revolve around essential modifications to the traditional procurement system in order to ensure that expected outcomes are attained. New standards, technical specifications, products and even legal measures may be necessary. The standards should be cross-sectorial and cover economic, environmental, social, technical and legal matters at a minimum since most of the consequences of a single procurement decision reverberate in these subject areas. Development of standards and guidelines should satisfy the criterion of how effectively and efficiently the objectives of sustainable development are met. The standards and guidelines should not only be compatible with the MDBs' mandate and policies and rules, but also should be sensitive to the emerging situation where many countries are subscribing to the basic premises and principles of sustainable development.

The other side of the management of procurement for sustainable development, as far as the MDBs are concerned, is the role of borrowers and executing agencies. The principal issue is how best to build capacity in these areas in order to make procurement for sustainable development more complementary of the MDB's effort.

Initially, the impetus for sustainable procurement came from multilateral institutions or external organizations. Since these external agents were not the main architects of national economic and social policies and local institutions were weak, the avenue readily available to influence use of resources and bring environmental concerns to the fore was procurement, over which some degree of control was maintained by the MDBs, during project implementation. "Sustainable procurement" allowed the MDB to ensure that procurement complied with its environmental and social strategies. However, sustainable procurement, introduced in this manner, was sometimes seen as an imposition or, at least, a condition for access to MDBs' financial resources.

The management of procurement should consider it a major function to encourage borrowing countries to incorporate the objectives of sustainable development in sectorial and national sustainable development strategies (NSDS). Such plans will provide the orientation for procurement and other policy initiatives. NSDS have the potential to provide structure and meaning to all procurement activities. They could integrate economic, social and environmental issues across sectors, specify indicators and highlight outcomes and means of implementation. These aspects improve chances for proper monitoring and evaluation of individual projects including procurement.

A high priority for management of the procurement process is therefore the capacity building of client-borrowing country personnel in formulating sustainable development policies and in policy appraisal and implementation. The current consensus that, globally, economic activities have the potential for irreversible ecological changes and growing consumer demand for green and "humanely produced" goods could create a more receptive disposition for serious consideration of sustainable development as a societal goal.

Dissemination of the concept should be accompanied by training in how the principles of sustainable development could be incorporated in the New Project Cycle – Principles and Guidelines. This task will necessitate cooperation among the different organisation units within the MDBs to ensure a harmonized strategy and consistency in its execution.

The MDBs should also cooperate with governments to explain the benefits of pursuing sustainable development. The probable outcome of this approach is higher degree of complementary voluntary action in the private and public sectors and less reliance on legislation and command and control measures. Management of procurement should also encourage local authorities to enact laws, regulations and rules that would foster innovations in production, distribution and use that are in compliance with sustainability requirements.

Crafting policies and programmes based on the sustainability principle would necessitate the development of methodologies that could assess, in a consistent manner, positive and negative impacts of said policies and programmes in a consistent manner to allow for the best possible decisions to be made. Economic, environmental and social appraisals made for procurement decisions should take into account the legal framework of planned operations and the possibilities and costs involved in changing laws and regulations governing procurement.

Drawing of technical specifications that meet new sustainable development criteria may present a serious challenge to clients of the MDBs. Technical cooperation programmes designed for individual countries may be necessary to allow countries to avoid disruption in their development efforts. Technical cooperation programmes may also deal with building capacity to evaluate technical proposals or assess expert opinions on technical matters.

In Annex II are a few of the economic, environmental, social, technical and legal issues to be investigated in a review of procurement policies.

The study should provide data and analysis for the development of sustainability indicators that would be useful guides in the procurement of goods and services.

6 Conclusions

Environmental issues have evolved from a focus on mitigatory actions to compensate for damage caused by extraction of minerals, construction of production facilities and waste disposal to the point where it is being advanced by a respected body of opinion that economic activity should operate within the boundaries of the environment. The change in thinking has been influenced by global climate change and ecosystem degradation that has accompanied vast expansion of wealth and income in some countries. In addition the persistence of large scale poverty and income inequalities have led to the questioning of the appropriateness of the rate of growth of GDP as an indicator of national progress.

The view that economic activity is not independent of the natural local and global environment and that ecosystem degradation is borne, disproportionately, by the poor and disadvantaged groups in a society has contributed to the rise of the concept of sustainable development. An expression of this view in economics is that life-cycle costs which frequently differ from market prices should be taken as the true cost of resource use and that resource productivity should be given as much prominence as labour productivity in economic calculations.

Given that the MDBs already subscribe to the idea that development should be sustainable economically, environmentally and socially, it is the next logical step to adopt a holistic approach to sustainable development. All its actions should be designed to contribute to this goal.

Procurement policies, rules and practices still offer a lever for the MDBs to convert resolutions and strategies on sustainable development into concerted action because they represent opportunities for translation of words into deeds. However, procurement should be supported by action in other spheres within the MDBs' programmes and policies.

Borrowing member countries of the Bank are signatories of many international treaties and convention requiring observance of fair trade laws, humane employment practices, equality of opportunity, no discrimination in matters of gender, race and ethnicity and greenhouse gas emissions. All these topics and issues are subsumed under "sustainable development". The MDBs should therefore explore ways to facilitate member countries meeting their obligations.

The MDBs should also prepare programmes to assist member countries in revising public sector procurement policies to make them fully compatible with the objectives of sustainability. The MDBs, especially EBRD, should also use their project lending to private sector companies to strengthen corporate responsibility and sustainable development activities.

The Recommendations below are based on these conclusions:

1   The MDBs should continue the general thrust and, in some cases, the specifics of the Sustainable Economic Growth Strategy. MDBs should, however, use their influence and knowledge to encourage client-borrowing member countries to formulate economic and social development strategies that respect the global boundaries and are therefore constrained by the need for ecosystem preservation and enhancement.

2   The MDBs should help to recast the special concern for the environment into the general issue of sustainability of humanity and structure its relationships with member countries from this perspective. In this setting, sustainable development objectives would permeate and guide all Bank operations.

3   In order to assist countries to see the broader picture of long-term sustainability, the MDBs should foster the development of macroeconomic and microeconomic indicators of sustainability in harmony among the different IFIs.

4   In support of the above, each MDB should review its sustainability oversight system to improve compliance in all aspects of IFI operations including procurement. Where necessary, the policy frameworks should be revised in conformity with the new standards and practices. The responsibility for sustainability would be shared with every organization unit within the MDB and not rest entirely on the Procurement Function or Policy Unit.

5   The MDBs should also consider supporting national or regional technology centres that would help countries meet international conventions such as the Basel Convention on trans-boundary movements of hazardous wastes.

6   The MDBs should consider financing research that may result in innovations and technologies that are more productive of resources and which have smaller carbon or ecological footprints. The MDBs should also fund research aimed at developing valid and useful measures of social progress.

7   The MDBs' operations evaluation systems should be modified to enable assessments of operations on subjects such as emissions, climate change, impact on workplace practices and opportunities for advancement, applying the latest internationally recommended criteria and standards.

8   The MDBs should sponsor seminars and training courses with the specific aim of helping member countries adjust their public procurement policies to support sustainable development.

9   The MDBs should encourage all borrowing member countries to establish procurement review agencies to monitor the observance of agreed legal, financial, ethical, technical and environmental practices in procurement.

Annexes

Annex 1

A4.1 Procurement in World Bank financed projects supports clients to achieve value for money with integrity in delivering sustainable development.

A4.2 Where agreed with the borrower, World Bank and borrower staff will identify specific sustainability risks and opportunities for procurements during the research and planning stages of project preparation. However, Sustainable procurement is not a mandatory requirement for borrowers.

A4.3 Issues identified in project preparation will be categorized into actions for:

a   Project design;
b   Pre-qualification criteria;
c   Specification criteria;
d   Bid evaluation criteria; and
e   Ongoing contract management criteria.

A4.4 Actions identified will be agreed with the borrower as part of project approval processes and integrated into the project/procurement process as appropriate.

A4.5 The World Bank would support borrowers to include other sustainable procurement criteria in World Bank financed procurements where there is full consistency with the borrowers own national policy providing it does not contravene the World Bank's Procurement Framework.

A4.6 As agreed with the borrower, sustainability risks and opportunities would then be addressed at the appropriate stage of the procurement process, a combination of any...

Level 1 – Project procurement strategy:

A4.8 As outlined above, the proposed approach provides opportunities to advance and accommodate borrower sustainable procurement policies and approaches, quality evaluation, corporate and social responsibility provisions, etc. as long as they don't conflict with the World Bank's Policies. In addition, the World Bank will discuss the benefits of sustainable procurement to the borrowers at both a systemic policy level, utilizing its diagnostic tools to support institutional strengthening and at a project level identifying key projects with sustainability impacts.

Sustainability risk:

A4.9 Sustainability aspects of World Bank-financed activities will initially be identified during project appraisal. These requirements will be prioritized and addressed as appropriate within the project design and will be agreed with the borrower. The World Bank takes a risk-based approach to its support to sustainable procurement using review of projects to determine risk in accordance with the World Bank's Environmental and Social Framework Policy. The

Bank, through the Environmental and Social Standards unit, undertakes environmental and social screening of each proposed project to determine the appropriate extent and type of environmental assessment.

A4.10 During the assessment, issues are identified that can be addressed as part of the procurement process. These issues are discussed with the borrower and will be included in the activity level procurement strategy.

Level 2 – Activity level procurement strategy:

A4.11 The following procedures are not an exhaustive list of the ways to implement sustainable procurement, but rather focus attention on those key areas that could be addressed. The specifics of the various countries and markets must be considered when applying sustainable procurement, including the laws governing contracting, World Bank policies and procedures, as well as the technical requirements and market conditions.

A4.12 Any sustainability issues that are best addressed during the procurement process will be included within the activity level procurement strategy for the procurement and will form specific criteria for qualification, specifications/ Terms of Reference, bid evaluation criteria or post award performance indicators. Sustainable procurement criteria agreed during project preparation will also be augmented as needed with any specific sustainable procurement criteria from the borrower's own sustainable procurement policy (if present) that is in accordance with the World Bank's Procurement Framework.

Planning and applicability:

A4.13 Contract specific market research is critical and must be undertaken during development of the activity level procurement strategy (see Annex "Procurement Strategy for Development"). The purpose is to identify the opportunities, strengths and weaknesses in the supply market to deliver the objectives of the procurement. Part of the market analysis should also address the maturity of the sustainable products and services that may be required to support the procurement depending on the risks to be managed. The objective for this aspect of the market analysis is to determine the availability of sustainable solutions to address the risks identified in the sustainability risk assessment. The analysis should address such question as:

a   The maturity and sophistication of suppliers available to provide solutions;
b   The type of solutions available to the procurement;
c   The ease with which these solutions can be monitored evaluated and managed;
d   What performance incentives might be included in the contract; and
e   Performance criteria.

Specifying requirements:

A4.14 As specifications and scopes of work are being prepared for the procurement documents, sustainable procurement factors should be incorporated. It is important that these requirements are undertaken using the information from the risk assessment and the market analysis. National and international specification standards can play a role in influencing the design of products and processes. Many standards include sustainable characteristics such as energy use or waste management procedures. References to international technical standards can be included directly in the requirements definition. Technical standards can take a number of forms. These include common technical specifications, international standards, national standards and national technical specifications. Standards are useful as they are clear and usually developed using a process which includes a wide range of stakeholders. This gives a broad acceptability to the technical solutions provided by standards which are adopted in this way.

A4.15 When selecting technical specifications it is important to keep in mind the entire procurement process, and in particular the required award criteria and contractual provisions. As a general rule, sustainability criteria are minimum requirements which should match the market availability of products, works and services. Knowing the availability of these products or services to meet these criteria will help maintain a strong competitive process. The terms of reference, with the technical specifications, is the core of all procurement procedures. In the technical specifications the contracting authority defines its requirements within a technical description and/or requirements for functionality and performance. For procurements using performance specifications the desired outcomes needs to be defined while allowing flexibility to the bidder on how to meet the performance specifications. In either case, the performance to be provided must be described clearly and understandably so that the bidding company is able to compile an offer. Furthermore, in the technical specifications the contracting authority defines which other services may be required as part of the procurement procedure, for example, initial and advanced training and operational support. Only offers that match the requirements and the specifications should be considered according to the award criteria.

Life-cycle costing:

A4.16 Achieving value for money is a key principle of the World Bank's procurement approach, with integrity and sustainable development. In the context of sustainable procurement, the use of life-cycle costing is essential to demonstrate that the procurement process has moved beyond just considering the base purchase price of a good, service or works. The purchase price alone does not always reflect the financial and non-financial gains that are offered by more sustainable offerings as they those benefits can accrue during the operation and use phases of the asset's useful life.

A4.17 Typical life-cycle costing analyses are based on:

a Purchasing costs and all associated costs such as delivery and installation,
b Operating costs, including utility costs such as energy and water use and maintenance costs;

c End-of-life costs such as removal, recycling or refurbishment, decommission-
ing and any disposal costs; and

d Longevity and warranty time frames of the asset.

A4.18 The selection of offers which present the optimum combination of factors
such as appropriate quality, life-cycle costs and other parameters is in the best
interest of the borrower. Environmental and social considerations can be
included among these parameters.

Prequalification of bidders:

A4.19 The objective of the pre-qualification of bidders is to identify suitable
market players for a contract. This is generally achieved using criteria in
order to determine the economic and technical suitability of a potential
bidder. When assessing the capability of bidders, consideration should be
given to specific experience and competencies concerning environmental,
social and economic issues as it relates to the performance of the contract that
do not conflict with World Bank policies. Additional information can be
found in the Procurement Provisions Annex.

A4.20 For example, if the purpose of the project was to clean up a hazardous
chemical site there are a number of ways to includes sustainable procurement
criteria into the prequalification process. These could include:

a Appropriate experience in chemical/waste identification and treatment; and

b Experience in safety management of sites of a similar nature.

A4.21 Technical capability involving the sustainable execution of the contract
can be demonstrated through references, past performance or other means. It
is important to state exactly which types of information are considered relevant, and what written verification should be submitted.

Contract management:

A4.22 Contractual clauses dealing with sustainability help strengthen the ability
to verify and enforce these requirements. Adherence to the contractual terms
and conditions must be monitored during the execution of the contract. Contractual terms and conditions can contain specific obligations that are entered
into within the contractual terms and conditions. Contractual terms and conditions must be stated in advance and clearly in the procurement documents
in order to ensure that companies are aware of all contractual provisions, and
are in a position to include them in their bids. Furthermore they should
demonstrate a connection to the execution of the contract, i.e. they must refer
to tasks that are necessary for the manufacture and provision of the products,
services or construction work. The conditions to be agreed contractually can
be distinguished roughly as follows:

A4.23 Guaranteed performance parameters are values guaranteed. They normally lie between acceptable agreed deviations (i.e. energy consumption). If

during performance the parameters are outside the acceptable deviations, instructions for remedy and resolution are issued within specific deadlines and possibly with contractual penalties. When formulating a contract, particular attention should be paid to long-term guarantees on the provision of performance and function. Sustainability aspects of implementation especially for supply contracts may include for example:

a For suppliers: product take-back (and recycling or re-utilization) of product packaging as a condition.
b Details on eco-friendly packaging (PVC-free, recyclable materials such as cardboard, paper, protective foil).

A4.24 For construction and service contracts these can be supplemented with the following aspects:

a Minimization of waste generated during the execution of the contract, e.g. through the inclusion of specific targets or by defining maximum amounts and corresponding penalty or bonus clauses.
b Good health and safety procedures and practices.

Capacity building:
A4.25 The World Bank's tool kit includes more training material and guidance on sustainable procurement to improve the borrower's ability to address sustainability issues. Procedures, templates and samples are provided as part of the new tool kit. The goal in providing support to borrowers is to develop sustainability procurement capacity to make sustainability an integral part of the procurement process.

Annex II

1 Accountability through certification of products, operations and supply chains;
2 Eco-efficiency; proportion of materials used as inputs that are recycled and resource intensity of selected technology;
3 Longevity of product;
4 Percentage of waste stream from industrial processes which is recycled;
5 Community involvement as indicated by the proportion of spending on goods and services accruing to local businesses;
6 Allowable standard or range for greenhouse gas emissions;
7 Criteria for rating and ranking of firms according to performance in preserving natural and cultural resources;
8 Appropriate administrative and organization arrangements including indicators and framework for monitoring and reporting;
9 Balancing commercial confidentiality norms with the mandate for transparency in public sector contracting;

10   Integration of sustainability concerns in the various stages of the project cycle;
11   Incorporation of production methods in technical specification;
12   Sustainable development procurement issues facing small and vulnerable developing countries;
13   Systems and methodologies for risk assessment in alternative procurement decisions;
14   How best to relate to private sector regional initiatives such as Caribbean Procurement Institute;
15   How to reconcile or resolve international agreements on sustainable development that conflict with national laws and regulations;
16   Maintenance of balance between procurement reform and environmental/social policies;
17   Use of cost/benefit analysis in tender assessment;
18   How to frame procurement agreements so that national obligations under child labour, equality of treatment, equal remuneration for identical work, non-discrimination on gender, ethnicity and race are observed;
19   How to promote corporate social responsibility so that private procurement practices advance sustainable development;
20   Procurement and the expansion of the local skills base;
21   The estimation of income generation and poverty reduction impacts of procurement decision;
22   How to accomplish the priority tasks from among the above with undue expansion of bureaucracy, fostering of administrative inefficiency, creating opportunities for corruption.

Note

1 www.footprintnetwork.org/en/index.php/GFN/page/at_a_glance/.

12 Green technical specifications under the new procurement directives

Eleanor Aspey

1 Introduction

The key priority for the European Union (EU) in recent years has been recovery from the global financial crisis. As part of this recovery process, there has been a striking focus on the issue of sustainability and environmental protection, often set out as a necessary part of economic recovery. One potential policy tool for promoting sustainability is green public procurement (GPP), highlighted as a key instrument for meeting the EU's sustainability goals both in the European Commission's Sustainable Consumption and Production and Sustainable Industrial Policy Action Plan (SAP, 2008), and also in the Europe 2020 Growth Strategy (Europe 2020 Growth Strategy, 2010, p. l.15). GPP has been defined by Kunzlik (2013) as "the practice whereby public bodies, when purchasing works, supplies and/or services, use their purchasing discretion to advance environmental goals" (Kunzlik, 2013, p. 97). This includes not only the purchase of products or services which themselves have a particular environmental function but also any purchase where the procurer aims to avoid or limit environmental harms which might occur during the course of that procurement process (Kunzlik, 2013). This chapter discusses the extent to which green issues can be integrated into procurement and examines the changes, both positive and negative, made to the potential for GPP under the recent reform to the EU procurement regime.

The chapter focuses on the possibility of integrating sustainability issues into procurement when designing the technical specifications of the product or service which is to be procured, i.e. the stage at which the procuring entity sets out the precise requirements of what it wishes to buy. While there is potential for the inclusion of sustainability issues at all stages of the procurement process, the technical specifications stage was found to be the preferred stage for consideration of green issues in the EU's recent review of the use of GPP policies, with 38 per cent of those surveyed including green requirements at that stage in their last contract (GPP in EU27, 2014, p. 47). It is therefore likely that it is at this stage that the reform to the EU procurement directives will have the most impact in practice.

The chapter will begin with a brief overview of the EU procurement regime and the reform process (Section 2). This will be followed by an overview of the importance of sustainability to the EU, with emphasis on the links to GPP, and examining the key policy documents in the area (Section 3), providing a background to the detailed discussion of key GPP changes in Sections 4–6. This discussion will start with an overview of the requirements for technical specifications generally before looking in detail at two key areas of change, setting requirements for the production process of a product or service (Section 5) and requiring a product or service to carry an eco-label (Section 6). Section 7 will conclude, evaluating the potential impact of the reforms in practice.

2 Overview of the EU procurement regime

The primary source of the EU's regulatory regime on procurement is the Treaty on the Functioning of the European Union (TFEU). While the Treaty does not mention procurement explicitly, a number of the provisions may potentially have an impact on public and utilities contracts, with the most significant being the free movement provisions (covering the free movement of goods (Article 34 TFEU), freedom of establishment (Article 49 TFEU) and the freedom to provide services (Article 56 TFEU)). These provisions prohibit the use of any requirements which discriminate, either directly or indirectly, against goods or services from another Member State and, to support this prohibition, also require some specific positive obligations to ensure the transparency of the procurement process, for example a requirement to advertise contracts.[1]

The EU supports and expands upon the free movement provisions with secondary legislation which regulates procurement more directly, setting out detailed rules relating to the conduct of the procurement process including precise rules on award procedures. The law currently in force covers three sectors. The first is the public sector, for which the relevant substantive directive is Directive 2004/18/EC, with a separate directive setting out the remedies for breach of the substantive requirements, Directive 89/665/EC. The second regulated area is the utilities sector, which is covered by Directive 2004/17/EC, with the remedies for breach being set out in Directive 92/13/EEC. Finally, defence procurement is regulated under Directive 2009/81/EC.

In December 2011, the European Commission announced that they had begun the process of reforming the procurement regulatory regime applicable in the EU (EC Growth, 2011). It was noted that public procurement had been set as one of the EU's 12 priority projects with which the Commission aimed to "relaunch the single market for 2012", with improvement of the single market being seen by the EU as one of the most effective means of recovering from the financial crisis (EC 12 projects, 2011). The Commission set out three main aims for the procurement reform process: to simplify the rules and increase flexibility; to encourage access to public procurement for small and medium sized enterprises (SMEs); and to facilitate a "qualitative improvement in the use of public procurement" by ensuring greater consideration of social and green issues in procurement (EC Growth, 2011). This last aim is where the influence of the Europe 2020 strategy and the sustainability goals within it can be seen most clearly and suggested that sustainability would be integrated into the procurement regime to a much greater extent than was previously the case.

Based on the identified three aims, in 2011 the Commission set out three proposals for directives on public procurement: one revising public sector procurement, one revising utilities procurement, and an entirely new directive on concessions procurement. After a lengthy legislative process, the final versions of all three directives were adopted in February 2014 as Directive 2014/23/EU (concessions), Directive 2014/24/EU (public sector – "the new Public Sector Directive") and Directive 2014/25/EU (utilities sector). With a few minor exceptions, the directives are required to be implemented into national law by the Member States by 2016, with the current directives remaining in force until that point. The requirements relating to technical specifications are very similar across the three new directives and, given this, to avoid repetition this chapter will refer solely to the new Public Sector Directive when providing article references.

3 Sustainability and green procurement in the EU

The first EU Sustainable Development Strategy (SDS) was set out in 2001, with this being renewed and extended in 2006 (EU SDS, 2006). This highlights that sustainable development is an "overarching objective" of the EU, impacting on all policies and activities undertaken by the Union (EU SDS, 2006, p. 2). The overall aim of the SDS is "to identify and develop actions to enable the EU to achieve continuous improvement of quality of life both for current and future generations", with four specific objectives set out for environmental protection, social equity and cohesion, economic prosperity, and meeting international responsibilities (EU SDS, 2006, pp. 2–4). Within this, promoting sustainable consumption and production was identified as a key challenge, and, to develop this area, one of the operational objectives set was to achieve an EU average level of GPP equal to that achieved at the time by the best performing Member States (EU SDS, 2006, p. 12). This was to be achieved by the Commission and Member States developing a structured process to share best practice on GPP, the Commission facilitating benchmarking of GPP performance, and the development of a sustainable consumption and production action plan (EU SDS, 2006).

The promised Sustainable Action Plan was delivered in 2008 and aimed to deliver a "dynamic framework to improve the energy and environmental performance of products and foster their uptake by consumers" (SAP, 2008, p. 2). As part of this, the Commission proposed setting up a harmonised system of minimum requirements and environmental benchmarks for products, supported by development of the existing product labelling schemes, which could then be used as a base for public procurement and incentives provided by the EU and individual Member States (EU SDS, 2006. p. 4). This would include setting environmental standards below which public authorities would not be able to accept products when conducting procurement under the EU regime (EU SDS,

2006, p. 6). In addition to this compulsory GPP, voluntary inclusion of green issues was also to be encouraged through the use of guidance and indicative targets for procurement (EU SDS, 2006. p. 7).

The next crucial point in the development of sustainability and GPP in the EU came with the release of the Europe 2020 Growth Strategy (2010) Announced by President Barrosso in 2010, Europe 2020 sets out a new growth strategy for the coming decade intended to help the EU recover from the global financial crisis. The strategy is based around three priorities; "smart" growth (developing innovation); "sustainable" growth (developing a greener and more resource efficient economy) and; "inclusive" growth (improving employment and social cohesion) (EU SDS, 2006, p. 10). Seven flagship initiatives were to be set up by the Commission in order to help progress in these three areas, though the areas would also need support through the wider EU legal regime (EU SDS, 2006, pp. 5–6).

Within the particular priority area of sustainable growth, three key areas for action were identified: (1) improving competitiveness and ensuring the EU maintains its market lead in green technology; (2) combating climate change, particularly through reduction of emissions, and; (3) improving the use and production of clean and efficient energy (EU SDS, 2006, pp. 14–15). Two of the seven flagship initiatives, *Resource efficient Europe* and *An industrial policy for the globalisation era* are targeted at these sustainable growth actions and both contain explicit reference to procurement as a potential policy tool for supporting development (EU SDS, 2006, pp. 15–16; EC Globalisation, 2010, p. 7). GPP was therefore identified as a key economic tool for wider growth in the EU, though neither flagship initiative contained any specific details about the type or form of GPP to be promoted.

It is also worth noting the potential impact for GPP of another of the Europe 2020 flagship initiatives, the *Innovation Union* initiative. Part of this initiative is focused specifically on eco-innovation and to develop this area the Commission produced an Eco-innovation Action Plan in 2011 (EC Innovation, 2011). Eco-innovation was defined as "any form of innovation resulting in or aiming at significant and demonstrable progress towards the goal of sustainable development", with the Action Plan focusing on supporting innovation which reduces pressure on the environment and helping eco-innovative products and services break into the wider market (EC Innovation, 2011, p. 2). Both public and private procurement are identified as ways of impacting market demand for eco-innovation and therefore an area for action (EC Innovation, 2011, p. 5). In particular, it is suggested that GPP could be tested to determine the extent to which it is promoting eco-innovation, networks of procurers set up to drive development in the area and, crucially for this chapter, tender specifications tested in light of eco-innovation and developed for wider use in both the public and private sectors (EC Innovation, 2011, p. 14).

It can therefore be seen from the above discussion that GPP is seen as a key policy tool for achieving the sustainability goals of the EU, and is an important area of development for the economy. Given this and the specific reference made to development of green and social procurement by the Commission when setting the aims of the procurement reform process (discussed above, Section 2), it would be expected that GPP would have been integrated much more clearly into the procurement regime during the reform. The sections below will consider whether or not this integration has occurred, and the impact of the reform changes on GPP in practice.

4 Technical specifications

This section offers an introduction into the inclusion of green issues in technical specifications, setting out the basic legal requirements for technical specifications under the new Public Sector Directive. The definition of technical specifications under the new Public Sector Directive is set out in Point 1 of Annex VII. As was the case under Directive 2004/18, there are separate definitions for technical specifications for works contracts and supply or service contracts, though the differences between the definitions are relatively minor. For supplies and services, a technical specification is "a specification in a document defining the required characteristics of a product or service".[2] For works, the technical specification should similarly define the required characteristics of the relevant material, product or supply, but here, the technical specifications must specifically define the material, product or supply "so that it fulfils the use for which it is intended by the contracting authority".[3] These definitions are essentially unchanged from the equivalent definitions set out in Point 1 of Annex VI of Directive 2004/18, with only a few minor changes to wording for clarity.

The definitions are followed by examples of acceptable characteristics which can be included in technical specifications. Again, these have only very minor changes from the equivalents in Directive 2004/18, though one of those minor changes is potentially relevant for green procurement; in addition to "environmental performance", an acceptable characteristic to consider under Directive 2004/18, the new Public Sector Directive now also explicitly lists "climate performance" as a potential characteristic for both works and supplies or services.[4] This does, however, seem unlikely to lead to any major changes in practice by procuring entities since emission levels and other climate-related criteria were already clearly allowable as environmental performance criteria. Given this, it is not clear that this reform adds anything of use to the previous law.

The technical specifications may be set out by reference to certain standards listed in the new Public Sector Directive, which provides an order of preference for standards ranging from national standards which transpose European standards as the most preferred option to national standards or national technical approvals as the least.[5] As noted by the European Commission, many European standards contain clauses setting out required environmental characteristics of the relevant product or service (EC Buying Green, 2011, p. 18). Reference to these standards can therefore be useful for procuring entities wishing to guarantee certain levels of environmental protection since a tenderer must prove either that they comply with the standard or that they meet an equivalent level of protection.[6]

Either as an alternative to reference to standards or in addition to such, procuring entities may also set out their technical specifications by setting performance or functional requirements.[7] The European Commission suggests that this approach "allows more scope for market creativity" and could be used to boost the development of innovative environmental products and services (EC Buying Green, 2011, p. 17). Given the emphasis on the importance of eco-innovation seen in the EU policy documents discussed above in Section 3, it is perhaps surprising that the use of functional requirements has not been promoted further in the reformed directives. Instead, the requirements here are identical to those in Directive 2004/18 with functional requirements having equal standing to technical standards. There is therefore little incentive provided by the directives for companies which currently rely primarily on the use of technical standards to change their practice and encourage eco-innovation.

5 Production processes

The production process of a particular product may raise environmental concerns which a procuring entity may wish to change or minimise by setting certain production requirements. For example, a procuring entity may wish to ensure that any energy it purchases is produced from renewable sources, that a minimal number of carbon emissions are generated during the construction process of a building, or that a product is produced as far as possible from recycled materials. As can be seen from these examples, being able to set GPP requirements in this area is therefore potentially important for both the second and third priority areas of the sustainable growth target of Europe 2020, those of combating climate change and improving production of green energy (discussed above, Section 3).

On the face of it, there was no restriction on setting such environmental production requirements under Directive 2004/18. The definition of technical specifications in Annex VI included "production processes and methods" in its list of example characteristics, with no apparent restriction on their inclusion. Production processes generally were also mentioned in Directive 2004/18 in Art. 23(8), which stated, somewhat confusingly in light of Annex VI, "technical specifications shall not refer to ... a particular process". However, given that this article also prohibits requirements such as the use of specific trademarks or makes of product, it seemed that this reference was not a general prohibition on process requirements but simply targeted processes unique to one company, requirement of which would limit competition and could potentially be used by a procuring entity as a means of indirect national discrimination. Non-discriminatory production requirements would therefore appear to be allowable, an interpretation which appears to have been confirmed in the new Public Sector Directive, with Art. 42(4) now clarifying that it is only a "particular process which characterises the products or services provided by a specific economic operator" which is prohibited.

Despite this, the European Commission appeared to interpret the law in a very conservative manner, effectively prohibiting the use of such production methods.

Focusing on the definition of works technical specifications in Annex VI Directive 2004/18, which requires that the specifications should allow the product to "fulfil the use for which it is intended", the Commission suggested that production matters could only be considered where they "contribute to" the characteristics of the product, whether visible or invisible (EC Buying Green, 2011, p. 23; EC IEC, 2001, p. 11). The reasoning appears to have been that any production processes which did *not* impact the characteristics of the product would not affect whether or not that product could fulfil its intended use and were therefore not allowable. The guidance also notes that any requirements which do not impact the characteristics of the product are not sufficiently linked to the subject matter of the contract. (EC Buying Green, 2011, p. 23; EC IEC, 2001, p. 11) This very strict interpretation would appear to prevent any green production requirement which will not physically change the product, such as a requirement that electricity be produced from renewable sources. It also potentially prevents any requirements where any physical change would be minimal and not impact the actual use of the product, for example recycled paper.

Kunzlik (2009), however, has argued that the reasoning of the European Commission is flawed. The Commission states within its guidance that a requirement that electricity be sourced from environmentally friendly sources would be acceptable (EC Buying Green, 2011, p. 23; EC IC, 2011, p. 11). This contradicts the Commission's own argument that production requirements must have an impact on product characteristics since green energy is indistinguishable at the point of consumption from energy generated from non-sustainable sources (Kunzlik, 2009, p. 395). In order to successfully bring green electricity into the scope of the definition of technical specifications set out in the guidance, the Commission has to stretch the meaning of "invisible" characteristics to include the "nature and value of the end product" (EC Buying Green 2011, p. 23), characteristics which Kunzlik argues in fact affect only the market position of the product, not its physical characteristics (Kunzlik, 2009, p. 395). Stretching the definition of product characteristics in such a way makes it so unclear as to be useless.

Given these flaws with the Commission's guidance and the apparently clear wording of Directive 2004/18, it is arguable that production requirements are already allowable under the current law (Kunzlik, 2009, pp. 397–398). So long as the technical specifications comply with the general principles of EU law (i.e. are transparent and non-discriminatory) and they accurately define what the contracting authority wishes to buy, which may include a wish to purchase a sustainable product, the procuring entity should be able to set out any technical specifications it chooses (McCrudden, 2007, p. 542).

The reforms set out in the new Public Sector Directive appear specifically designed to clarify the law in light of the Commission's guidance. Article 42(1) of the new Public Sector Directive states that technical specifications:

> may also refer to the specific process or method of production or provision of the requested works, supplies or services or to a specific process for

another stage of its life cycle *even where such factors do not form part of their material substance*, provided that they are linked to the subject matter of the contract and proportionate to its value and its objectives.

(Emphasis added)

The highlighted section of the article was not present in the original Commission proposal, being added later in the legislative process by the Council (EP FCD, 2009).[8] The aim appears to be to make it clear not only that production processes are valid considerations to include in technical specifications, but particularly that such processes do not, contrary to the Commission guidance, have to have any impact on the final characteristics of the product or service in question.

It is not clear, however, whether or not this change to the wording in the directive will have the intended impact. The article states that production processes do not have to impact the "material" substance of a product or service but the Commission already accepted that this was the case when it stated that the changes to characteristics did not necessarily have to be visible. It is still open to the Commission to argue that, while a material or visible change is not necessary, some form of change to the immaterial substance or invisible characteristics of the product is a requirement. This is particularly so given that the aspect of the technical specifications definition from which this argument was drawn, i.e. that the technical specifications ensure that the product "fulfils the use for which it is intended" remains unchanged in Annex VII of the new Public Sector Directive. If this interpretation is taken by the Commission then the change to the wording of the directive may simply lead to procuring entities having to engage in costly litigation to determine the scope of material and immaterial changes to substance, a prospect which is likely to deter them from including production requirements at all.

It could also still potentially be argued that if a production process has no impact on the characteristics of a product at all, it is not "linked to the subject matter of the contract" as required by Art. 42(1) of the new Public Sector Directive and argued previously by the Commission in their guidance (EC Buying Green, 2011, p. 23). The phrase "subject matter of the contract" is not further defined for technical specifications in the new Public Sector Directive, but is defined for award criteria in Art. 67(3), a definition which also applies to contract performance conditions under Art. 70 and which it therefore appears logical to assume applies to technical specifications also. The definition in Art. 67(3) is very broad, with criteria being linked to the subject matter of the contract "where they relate to the works, supplies or services being provided under that contract in any respect and at any stage of their life cycle", and confirms that production processes are valid, repeating here also that changes to "material substance" are not necessary. Just like the reference to production processes in Art. 42(1), this appears targeted directly at the Commission guidance and the definition is broad enough on the face of it to allow any production requirements for the product or service in question, but without a change to the guidance it also is likely to lead simply to litigation over the precise bounds of the requirement.

Nonetheless, the changed wording both in Art. 42 and Art. 67 can be seen as something of a legislative rebuke to the Commission on the topic, placing pressure on the Commission to change the interpretation set out in the guidance. Equally, it may provide useful clarification to those procuring entities which were unsure of the legality of certain production process requirements in light of the Commission's guidance, although the impact of this might be minimal if the guidance is not also amended. It is also possible that the clearer and more explicit reference to production processes in the directive might inspire greater use of such techniques by procuring entities. Overall, however, the impact of the change is likely to be slight; production process requirements were arguably lawful under the previous law and the real problem area, the guidance, has not been amended, a disappointing result for the development and promotion of GPP.

6 Eco-labelling

When setting out its requirements in the technical specifications, a procuring entity may wish to do so by reference to a particular product or service label, either nationally or internationally recognised. Setting labelling requirements means the procuring entity does not have to either work out the precise requirements of the product itself or check that the tenders meet those requirements beyond checking that they have validly acquired the label, saving time and money. In the specific context of GPP, setting a requirement for a label dealing with environmental concerns (an eco-label) also has benefits where the procuring entity lacks the relevant expertise in environmental issues to set particular requirements. Being able to rely on an accepted external standard enables the procuring entity to have greater certainty in the validity of the requirements than if the particular standards were required to be set in-house. Because of these benefits, development of product labelling schemes is also a key part of the Sustainable Action Plan (see above, Section 2), and ensuring the compatibility of such schemes with procurement is therefore of importance to the wider sustainability aims of the EU.

Despite the potential benefits of using eco-labels to define environmental requirements of products when setting technical specifications, the current law is relatively restrictive in this area. The possibility of reference to eco-labels is set out in Art. 23(6) of Directive 2004/18, which notes that if a procuring entity chooses to set its technical specifications in terms of functional requirements (see above, Section 4), they may reference "the detailed specifications, or, if necessary, parts thereof" of any eco-label which meets certain specified requirements. This article was examined by the Court of Justice of the European Union (CJEU) in *Commission* v. *Netherlands* ("*Dutch Coffee*"), in which a Dutch authority required compliance with both an eco-label (the EKO label) and a social label (the Max Havelaar label) for products supplied in a contract for coffee, though it was later clarified that labels setting equivalent criteria would also be acceptable.[9] The CJEU confirmed that the reference in Art. 23(6) allowed procuring entities to reference the detailed specifications of a label only; they were not permitted to require the label itself.[10] This restrictive interpretation was felt to be necessary given the requirement in Art. 23(3)(b) that technical specifications be sufficiently precise so as to allow bidders to determine the subject matter of the contract, a requirement that the court felt could not be met if there was simply a reference to an eco-label rather than a clear statement of the full requirements.[11] An express statement of the full requirements was, according to the CJEU:

> indispensable in order to allow potential tenderers to refer to a single official document, coming from the contracting authority itself and thus without being subject to the uncertainties of searching for information and the possible temporal variations in the criteria applicable to a particular eco-label.[12]

The findings of the court therefore place the whole burden of finding the relevant information for the technical specifications on the procuring entity. This can be contrasted with the approach suggested by Advocate General Kokott in *Dutch Coffee*, who noted that the administrative burden placed on procuring entities should always be proportionate to the objectives of the public procurement regime.[13] She argued that a general reference to the specifications of an eco-label was sufficient for the requirements of the principle of transparency since a reasonably well-informed tenderer of normal diligence should be expected to be familiar with the relevant eco-labels for the market or, if not, to be able to obtain the information needed from the certifying body.[14] Given this, it would be "excessively formalistic" to require the procuring entity to set out the requirements in full in the contract documents.[15] It is suggested that, in light of the need to promote GPP and the development of eco-labelling aims in the Sustainable Action Plan, the approach of the Advocate General was the more convincing. The extra burden on the procuring entity to determine and set out all requirements in full would be likely to deter many from using eco-label requirements at all.

The burden on procuring entities is compounded by the requirements set out in Art. 23(6) of Directive 2004/18 in relation to acceptable means of proof of compliance with an eco-label. This states that, while a procuring entity is free to state that any product or service bearing the label is presumed to comply with the requirements, they must equally accept all appropriate means of proof from a tenderer which show that the substantive label requirements are met. This removes the vast majority of the benefits of referencing an eco-label since the procuring entity can no longer rely on the certifying body to check compliance but must spend the time and money necessary to do so itself, a task it also may not have the necessary expertise for if the label requires consideration of very technical and complex environmental issues. There is therefore little incentive under Directive 2004/18 to include eco-labels in technical specifications.

Following the reform, the situation seems somewhat more positive. The rules relating to eco-labels have been set out in much more depth in the new Public

Sector Directive, and can be found in Art. 43. Crucially, Art. 43(1) now notes that, when procuring entities intend to purchase products or services "with specific environmental, social or other characteristics", they may "require a specific label as means of proof that the works, services or supplies correspond to the required characteristics", so long as the label specified satisfies certain conditions (discussed below). As noted by Kunzlik (discussing the original Commission proposal for the directive), this appears to effectively reverse the decision of the CJEU in *Dutch Coffee* (Kunzlik, 2009, p. 111). The removal of the reference to the use of the "detailed specifications" as set out in Art. 23(6) of Directive 2004/18 seems to make it clear that under the reformed law, it is not necessary to set out the full specifications in the contract documents with a reference to the required label being sufficient. This is also supported by Recital 75 of the new Public Sector Directive, which states that contracting authorities "should be able to refer to particular labels" and makes no reference to a requirement to also include the full specifications.

The decision of the CJEU in *Dutch Coffee* was, however, based significantly on the requirement to be precise. This requirement remains in place for technical specifications under the new Public Sector Directive in Art. 42(3)(b). Given this, it is potentially arguable that the requirement to be precise still requires the full specifications of the chosen eco-label to be set out such that tenderers retain the benefits of referring to a single authoritative document, as discussed above. However, the CJEU's decision was also influenced explicitly by the previous reference to "detailed specifications", which it felt unable to take an extensive interpretation of given the precision requirement.[16] The requirement for precision therefore needs to be re-evaluated given the new context of the reformed law. Given this, it is suggested that the requirement to be precise should be treated as simply an aspect of the general principle of transparency and the approach of Advocate General Kokott (discussed above) should be adopted to determine if the requirements of transparency have been satisfied. A reference to a specific eco-label is therefore sufficient without the need to include the full requirements of the label so long as the label is one that a reasonably well-informed tenderer would be expected to be aware of given the market and/or for which the requirements can be obtained from the relevant certifying body.

Reforms have also been made to the acceptable means of proof of compliance with a label. As noted above, under Directive 2004/18, a procuring entity had to accept all appropriate means of proof and this position was retained under the original Commission proposal for the new Public Sector Directive.[17] However, following amendments put forward by the Parliament and Council, procuring entities are now able to set stricter requirements for proof if they choose to do so. The key provision is the final paragraph of Art. 43(1), which states that procuring entities must accept other appropriate means of proof where "an economic operator had demonstrably no possibility of obtaining the specific label indicated by the contracting authority or an equivalent label within the relevant time limit for reasons which are not attributable to that economic operator". The inclusion of this condition suggests that outside these circumstances a procuring entity is free to refuse alternative means of proof of compliance with the requested label, greatly reducing the administrative burden on the procuring entity. It is also now clearly stated in the final paragraph of Art. 43(1) that in those circumstances under which the procuring entity is required to accept alternative means of proof, the burden of proving equivalence lies on the economic operator, again shifting some of the administrative burden away from the procuring entity in such cases. The combination of these two changes therefore makes using eco-labels in technical specifications a much more attractive prospect for procuring entities.

The one remaining restriction in this area is that procuring entities must accept not only the specific label requested but also "all labels that confirm that the works, supplies or services meet equivalent label requirements".[18] It is not clear from the directive where the burden of proving equivalence lies in these circumstances, but, given the example set in the case of alternative means of proof as discussed above, it seems likely that it would lie on the economic operator in this case also. If this is the interpretation taken by the courts, it is suggested that this provision sets a fair balance between enabling procuring entities to gain the administrative benefits of requiring labels, and thereby encouraging their use, and the general principle of non-discrimination. Requiring equivalent labels to be accepted prevents reference to niche national labels as a means of hidden national discrimination, while the burden of proving equivalence being placed on the economic operator retains the majority of the benefits of label requirement for the procuring entity.

The final key reform for GPP in this area is to the conditions an eco-label must satisfy in order to be lawfully set as a requirement. These can be found in Art. 43(1)(a)-(e) and are generally similar to the previous requirements for eco-labels under Art. 23(6) of Directive 2004/18. One of the conditions, however, has some significant changes and could potentially have a restrictive impact on the use of eco-labels in practice. Art. 43(1)(a) states that a specific label may be required so long as:

> the label requirements only concern criteria which are linked to the subject matter of the contract and are appropriate to define characteristics of the works, supplies or services that are the subject matter of the contract.

The requirement that the label requirements are "appropriate" to define the relevant characteristics is retained from Art. 23(6) Directive 2004/18. The precise meaning of the term "appropriate" under that directive was not clear, with Wilsher (2009) noting that it could simply refer to a requirement that the criteria are linked to the subject matter of the contract, consistent with the rules for award criteria as were set out in Art. 53 of Directive 2004/18, or it could require an extra, undefined, consideration of the appropriateness of the particular specifications. The wording of the requirement in the new Public Sector Directive is little clearer. It does now state explicitly that the requirements must be linked to the subject matter of the contract (the requirements of which were discussed above, Section 5) *and* appropriate to define the relevant characteristics, which suggests that appropriateness is indeed an additional consideration. No further guidance is given as to what is meant by appropriate, however. As Wilsher (2009, p. 427) notes, requiring a procuring entity to investigate each requirement in an eco-label scheme for appropriateness will involve heavy costs and that, combined with the lack of clarity on what precisely is to be investigated, may well deter many procuring entities from including eco-label requirements.

The section now also requires that the eco-label requirements *only* concern criteria which are linked to the subject matter of the contract. This could potentially prevent reference to labels which consider a wide range of potential environmental concerns as there will be requirements within the label which are not relevant to the particular contract awarded. The directive would seem, therefore, to favour the use of labels targeted at particular products rather than more broadly designed labels which apply in a wide variety of situations, potentially requiring procuring entities to be aware of a large number of niche product labels. The requirement also places a heavy administrative burden on procuring entities, given the difficulty in sorting through lengthy and complex environmental requirements to pick out the relevant issues, especially where they are not environmental experts themselves. The impact is potentially mitigated somewhat, however, by the fact that if a label does include requirements which are not linked to the subject matter of the contract, it is not prohibited entirely. Instead, the law reverts to the situation under Directive 2004/18; Art. 43(2) of the new Public Sector Directive states that procuring entities "shall not require the label as such" but may include in their technical specifications those parts of the label requirements which are linked to the subject matter of the contract. This, however, retains all the problems identified with this approach discussed above. If the court takes a restrictive view of what is linked to the subject matter of the contract, this provision could therefore remove much of the impact of the reform in this area and render the changes discussed above irrelevant.

7 Conclusion

GPP was highlighted in in the Sustainable Action Plan and the Europe 2020 strategy as a key policy tool for developing sustainable growth but, despite this, the potential for inclusion of green issues in procurement was somewhat limited. The reform to the procurement regime therefore offered the perfect opportunity for the EU to align its procurement policy much more closely with the green policy objectives set out in those documents. The initial statements of the Commission that securing a qualitative improvement to procurement by including greater consideration of green and social concerns was one of the main aims of the reform process were promising, suggesting that GPP issues were treated seriously and would be considered fully. This chapter has considered if the final reform has lived up to that promise in the area of technical specifications, the key area for the inclusion of green issues in practice.

It can be seen that there have indeed been some positive changes after the reform process. The changes made to the definition of technical specifications can be seen to clarify that procuring entities are in fact free to set requirements relating to production processes, enabling greater consideration of such concerns in the future. Equally, the changes made to the eco-labelling requirements remove many of the problems of the previous law, allowing procuring entities to require a specific label and consider only that label or equivalent labels acceptable means of proof of compliance with the technical specifications in most circumstances, providing cost and time benefits to procuring entities which could ensure a greater use of such eco-labels. Both clarification of the law and reduction of the administrative burden of conducting GPP on procuring entities are beneficial changes.

However, it has also been shown that the practical impact of the reforms is often likely to be small and in many cases the reforms appear to be to the form of the law rather than the substance. While clarification of the law is generally to be welcomed, production processes were in fact almost certainly valid considerations for technical specifications before the reform, making the change unnecessary and a distraction from the real problem, the Commission's guidance on GPP. For eco-labels, the requirement that all the label criteria must be linked to the subject matter of the contract may limit the potential pool of acceptable labels greatly, meaning in practice that the law will remain unchanged, with full specifications being required for the majority of procurement conducted.

Overall, therefore, the reform may be seen as a missed opportunity. Despite the EU's apparent concern and focus on green issues in recent years, GPP is little easier to complete than it was before the changes and future reform will likely be necessary to fully link EU environmental policy with EU procurement policy.

Notes

1 Case C-324/98, *Telaustria Verlags GmbH* v. *Telekom Austria AG* [2000] E.C.R. I-10745.
2 Point 1(b), Annex VII, New Public Sector Directive.
3 Point 1(a), Annex VII, New Public Sector Directive.
4 Points 1(a) and (b), Annex VII, New Public Sector Directive.
5 Art. 42(3)(b) New Public Sector Directive.
6 Art. 42(5) New Public Sector Directive. For the allowable requirements for proof of compliance or equivalence with a standard, see Art. 44.
7 Art. 42(3)(a) New Public Sector Directive.
8 EP FCD (2009) at Art. 40 (this document refers to the provisional article numbers from the original Commission proposal, rather than the finalised numbers in the new Public Sector Directive).
9 Case C-368/10, *European Commission* v. *Kingdom of the Netherlands*, Judgment of 10 May 2012.
10 Ibid., at para. 63.
11 Ibid.
12 Ibid., at para. 67.
13 Opinion of Advocate General Kokott on Case C-368/10, *European Commission* v. *Kingdom of the Netherlands*, delivered on 15 December 2011, at para. 57.
14 Ibid., at para. 56. The standard of a reasonably well-informed tenderer of normal

diligence was set out in Case C-448/01, *EVN AG and Wienstrom GmbH* v. *Republik Österreich*, [2003] ECR I-14527.

15 Ibid., at para. 57.
16 Case C-368/10, *European Commission* v. *Kingdom of the Netherlands*, Judgment of 10 May 2012, at para. 63.
17 See Art. 41, EP FCD (2009) n.45.
18 Art. 43(1), new Public Sector Directive.

References

EC Buying Green (2011): European Commission, (2011), *Buying Green – A Handbook on Green Public Procurement*, (2nd Ed), available at http://ec.europa.eu/environment/gpp/buying_handbook_en.htm [accessed 17 October 2014].

EC Globalisation (2010): European Commission, An Integrated Industrial Policy for the Globalisation Era Putting Competitiveness and Sustainability at Centre Stage, COM(2010) 614, at p. 20, and European Commission, A resource-efficient Europe – Flagship initiative under the Europe 2020 Strategy, COM(2011) 21.

EC Growth (2011): European Commission, Modernising European public procurement to support growth and employment, IP/11/1580.

EC IC (2011): European Commission, Interpretative Communication of the Commission on the Community Law Applicable to Public Procurement and the Possibilities for Integrating Environmental Considerations into Public Procurement, COM (2001) 274.

EC IEC (2001): European Commission, Interpretative Communication of the Commission on the Community Law Applicable to Public Procurement and the Possibilities for Integrating Environmental Considerations into Public Procurement, COM(2001) 274.

EC Innovation (2011): European Commission, Innovation for a sustainable Future – The Eco-innovation Action Plan (Eco-AP), COM(2011) 899.

EC 12 projects (2011): European Commission, (2011), Twelve projects for the 2012 Single Market: together for new growth, IP/11/469.

EP FCD (2009): European Parliament, Four-Column Document – Directive on public procurement, 05 September 2013, available at www.europarl.europa.eu/meetdocs/2009_2014/organes/imco/imco_20130905_1500.htm [accessed 19 October 2014].

Europe 2020 Growth Strategy (2010): European Commission, Europe 2020: A Strategy for Smart, Sustainable and Inclusive Growth, COM(2010) 2020.

EU SDS (2006): Council of the European Union, Review of the EU Sustainable Development Strategy (EU SDS) – Renewed Strategy, 26 June 2006, 10917/06, available at http://ec.europa.eu/environment/eussd/ [accessed 10 October 2014].

GPP in EU27 (2014): Centre for European Policy Studies and College of Europe, The Uptake of Green Public Procurement in the EU27, Report submitted to the European Commission, DG Environment, 29 February 2012, available at http://ec.europa.eu/environment/gpp/pdf/CEPS-CoE-GPP%20MAIN%20REPORT.pdf [accessed 10 October 2014].

Kunzlik, P. (2009) "The Procurement of 'Green' Energy" Ch.9 in S. Arrowsmith and P. Kunzlik (Eds.), *Social and Environmental Policies in EC Procurement Law: New Directives and New Directions*, Cambridge: Cambridge University Press.

Kunzlik, P. (2013): "From Suspect Practice to Market-Based Instrument: Policy Alignment and the Evolution of EU law's approach to 'green' public procurement" (2013) 3 *P.P.L.R.* 97–115, at 97.

McCrudden, C. (2007) *Buying Social Justice: Equality, Government Procurement and Legal Change*, Oxford: Oxford University Press, at p. 542.

SAP (2008): Sustainable Action Plan (2008): European Commission, Communication from the Commission to the European Parliament, the Council, the European Economic and Social Committee and the Committee of the Regions on the Sustainable Consumption and Production and Sustainable Industrial Policy Action Plan, COM(2008) 397.

Wilsher, D. (2009): "Reconciling national autonomy and trade integration in the context of eco-labelling", Ch. 10 in S. Arrowsmith and P. Kunzlik (eds), *Social and Environmental Policies in EC Procurement Law: New Directives and New Directions*, Cambridge: Cambridge University Press, at pp. 426–427.

Index

Page numbers in *italics* denote tables, those in **bold** denote figures.

For Product Safety Concerns and Information please contact our EU
representative GPSR@taylorandfrancis.com
Taylor & Francis Verlag GmbH, Kaufingerstraße 24, 80331 München, Germany

www.ingramcontent.com/pod-product-compliance
Ingram Content Group UK Ltd.
Pitfield, Milton Keynes, MK11 3LW, UK
UKHW021001180425
457613UK00019B/773